REDUCING INTERPERSONAL VIOLENCE

A Psychological Perspective

Clive R. Hollin

 Routledge
Taylor & Francis Group

LONDON AND NEW YORK

First published 2019
by Routledge
2 Park Square, Milton Park, Abingdon, Oxon OX14 4RN

and by Routledge
711 Third Avenue, New York, NY 10017

Routledge is an imprint of the Taylor & Francis Group, an informa business

British Library Cataloguing-in-Publication Data
A catalogue record for this book is available from the British Library

Library of Congress Cataloging-in-Publication Data
Names: Hollin, Clive R., author.
Title: Reducing interpersonal violence : a psychological perspective /
Clive R. Hollin.
Description: Milton Park, Abingdon, Oxon ; New York, NY :
Routledge, [2019] | Includes bibliographical references.
Identifiers: LCCN 2018020270| ISBN 9781138632493 (hardback) |
ISBN 9781138632509 (pbk.) |
ISBN 9781315208220 (ebook)
Subjects: LCSH: Violence--Prevention. | Interpersonal
conflict--Prevention. | Violence--Psychological aspects.
Classification: LCC HM1116 .H66 2018 | DDC 303.6--dc23LC record
available at https://lccn.loc.gov/2018020270

ISBN: 978-1-138-63249-3 (hbk)
ISBN: 978-1-138-63250-9 (pbk)
ISBN: 978-1-315-20822-0 (ebk)

Typeset in Bembo
by Taylor & Francis Books

REDUCING INTERPERSONAL VIOLENCE

There are many types of interpersonal violence that can lead to short- and long-term physical and psychological effects on those involved. *Reducing Interpersonal Violence* reflects on the World Health Organization's stance that interpersonal violence is a public health problem and considers what steps can realistically be taken towards its reduction.

Clive Hollin examines interpersonal violence across a range of settings, from bullying at school and in the workplace, smacking children and partner violence in the home, to sexual and other forms of criminal violence in the community. This book summarises the research on evidence-based strategies to reduce violence and shows that reducing interpersonal violence can have a positive effect on people's wellbeing and may save a great deal of public expenditure.

This book is an invaluable resource for students and researchers in the fields of psychology, criminology, law, and police studies, as well as professionals such as probation staff and forensic psychologists.

Clive R. Hollin is Emeritus Professor at the University of Leicester. He has written and edited over 20 books, and over 300 academic papers and book chapters, relating to psychology and crime. He edited the journal *Psychology, Crime, & Law* from 1992 to 2012. He has worked at three universities, for two governments departments (Home Office and Department of Health), and in prisons, special hospitals, and regional secure units. In 1998 Clive was presented with the British Psychological Society, Division of Criminological and Legal Psychology, Senior Award for Distinguished Contribution to the Field of Legal, Criminological and Forensic Psychology.

Dedication: For Will Davies, admirable applied psychologist, dinner companion and cricket enthusiast

CONTENTS

TABLES

ACKNOWLEDGEMENTS

I do try not to but I know that I can moan just a little bit, well quite a lot actually, when the day's writing is not going as well as I'd like. My partner in life, Flick Schofield, has after many years habituated to my groaning and pacing about and tells me just to get on with it. Sound advice for any writer. I've also noticed that in my not-too-happy phases our latest dog, Toby, relinquishes his chair in my study and heads for the less fraught environment of his bed in the kitchen. At which point I feel really, really guilty and resolve in future to behave in a better fashion. Anyway, I can reveal that everyone is pleased that this book is finally written and peace now reigns in our household.

PREFACE

I think of this book as a companion to my previous book *The Psychology of Interpersonal Violence*. Indeed, this book started life as Chapter 8 of *The Psychology of Interpersonal Violence* before I realised it was expanding exponentially and taking on a life, now realised, of its own. In agreement with others, it is my view that interpersonal violence is one of the great public health issues of our times, bringing about harm and distress on a global scale. I hope that the ideas and research covered in these pages will act as a resource for both students and practitioners.

1

INTERPERSONAL VIOLENCE

A psychological perspective

The *World Report on Violence and Health* published by the World Health Organization (Krug et al., 2002) was unequivocal in "Declaring violence a major and growing health problem across the world" (p. ix). However, despite the seriousness of the matter, there is some debate in the literature regarding a satisfactory definition of violence. Lee (2015) suggests a wide-ranging definition:

> The intentional reduction of life or thriving of life in human being(s) by human being(s), through physical, structural, or other means of force, that either results in or has a high likelihood of resulting in deprivation, mal-development, psychological harm, injury, death, or extinction of the species.
>
> *(p. 202)*

Lee's definition speaks to the widespread nature of violence and its many adverse physical, sometime fatal, and psychological consequences for the victim. The WHO report attempted to manage the diversity of acts that fall under the rubric of violence by forming the three categories of *self-directed violence, interpersonal violence*, and *collective violence*. The term *interpersonal violence* is used here in the same sense as in the *World Report on Violence and Health*. Thus, interpersonal violence covers of acts of principally face-to-face violence, excluding violence in the wider context of war and terrorism, between people either within the same family or wider community. In addition, many forms of interpersonal violence are punishable by law and may therefore be described as *criminal violence*.

Kazdin (2011) makes the point that interpersonal violence can be considered in two ways. The *molecular view*, to use Kazdin's terminology, conceives of interpersonal violence as a set of different types of violent act, categorised by setting, type of perpetrator, the nature of the act and so on. Thus, for example, a meaningful distinction can be drawn between physical child abuse and the sexual assault of an adult. In contrast, Kazdin's *molar view* takes interpersonal violence as a complex phenomenon, with no neat divisions between its many forms, which is embedded in a nest of other social, political, and economic problems such as inequality and poverty.

The sheer complexity of the molar view, Kazdin argues, means there can be no "silver bullet" that will make interpersonal violence disappear. This view resonates with the view of archaeologists such as LeBlanc (2003) who see warfare as an intractable aspect of human existence. There have been wars between nations and within nations since time immemorial, there are wars being fought as you read this sentence, and there will undoubtedly be wars to be fought in the future. Wars may start and wars may end; warfare is for ever. In contrast to the enormity of conflict between nations, some forms of interpersonal violence, such as violence in the context of sport, are generally accepted as commonplace "everyday" violence.

The scale of the problem of violence, alongside its dynamic, shifting and changing, complex nature means that the evidence base will always be incomplete. A World Health Organization Report (WHO, 2014) laments the gaps in the data which act to hinder progress in developing evidence-based violence prevention strategies. The lack of contemporaneous evidence acts to compound the difficulties of knowing which strategies to apply to reduce violence most effectively.

The broad understanding of interpersonal violence used here, which will be used as a springboard for considering strategies to reduce violence, is that interpersonal violence is a *social* act. This is not to discount non-social influences on behaviour (Fox, 2017), rather to say that the actions of those engaged in the violence are to be considered in their social and situational context. The notion of a person–situation interaction is, of course, highly familiar within mainstream psychology (e.g., Bandura, 1977) and has been applied specifically to violent behaviour (e.g., Allen, Anderson, & Bushman, 2018; Anderson & Bushman, 2002; Bandura, 1978; Nietzel, Hasemann, & Lynam, 1999).

A person–situation approach has three component parts. Thus, as applied to interpersonal violence, the first part is the setting in which the violence takes place. The setting has several characteristics, any and all of which may be present in a given incident, which include the type of place (home, public bar, street, etc.), the presence and numbers of other people, the physical temperature, and whether weapons are present (see Hollin, 2016; Krahé, 2013).

The second part lies in qualities of the individual in the given setting; these qualities will be a combination of static and dynamic factors. Static factors include the person's age, gender, and whether they have a history of violence. Dynamic factors relate to the individual's functioning during the incident which may fluctuate and change as events unfold. Thus, dynamic factors include the individual's cognition and emotion as well as their mental health and use of drugs and alcohol. Finally, the third part concerns the nature of the interactions between those involved in the incident.

In many cases an act of interpersonal violence is the product of a series of exchanges between those involved. Luckenbill (1977) called these exchanges a *situated transaction*. In an analysis of incidents which had culminated in murder, although the sequence applies equally well to other types of interpersonal violence, Luckenbill described six stages in the build-up to the final act.

In the first stage the eventual victim makes the first move in the form of spoken words, an act, or a refusal to comply with a request from the other person. At stage two the eventual offender sees a personal insult in the other person's words or actions leading, at stage three, to the offender seeking confirmation of the perceived insult and reacting with an insult of their own. This insult offers a challenge to the victim to continue the exchanges thereby placing the victim, at stage four, in the same position as the offender in stage two: their options are to respond to the challenge, to apologise, or to leave and "lose face". If the victim responds, so accepting the challenge, a "working agreement" is in place such that violence becomes highly likely.

At stage five the physical battle commences with, in some instances, the use of weapons; Luckenbill reports that in just over one-third of cases the offender was carrying a gun or a knife while in other cases the offender either left and returned with a gun or knife or they seized whatever was at hand, such as a broken glass, to use as a weapon. The use of weapons is culturally bound: Luckenbill's analysis was based on cases in California, USA. In about one-half of the incidents the victim was killed quickly with a single shot or stab; in the other cases the fight was two-sided, with both protagonists armed, and it was after an exchange of blows that the victim was killed. In the final stage about one-half of offenders ran from the scene, about one-third voluntarily waited for the police, and the remainder were prevented from leaving by bystanders until the police arrived.

It is implicit in the description of the social exchanges that, for both offender and victim, the perceptions of the other person's actions and intentions are driving the sequence of interactions. However, as Luckenbill notes, these perceptions are not necessarily accurate and, given the context, situational factors may lead to misperceptions. The exchanges may take place in front of other people, both acquaintances and strangers, who may encourage the protagonists' increasingly aggressive behaviour. In addition, as the transaction progresses so emotions are likely to become heightened with one or both of those involved becoming angry, excited, or anxious as violence draws close.

A myriad of factors may influence the outcome of these social exchanges. Individuals will act differently because of variations in their perception and appraisal of the situation and those involved. There will also be variations in each individual's values, morals, social problem-solving skills, and experience of violence. In addition, factors such as the effects of alcohol, the use of weapons, the presence of mental disorder, and high levels of emotionality may influence interpersonal exchanges, making violence more or less likely to occur. As these factors are potentially active across different types of interpersonal violence a brief overview of each is given below.

The effects of alcohol

The association between alcohol and violence is firmly established in the research literature (e.g., Boden, Fergusson, & Horwood, 2013; Parrott & Eckhardt, 2018) and is recognised around the globe (World Health Organization, 2008). The Institute of Alcohol Studies (2010) have summarised some key statistics about the alcohol–crime relationship: (1) approximately one-third of violent offenders have a drink problem, including binge-drinking; (2) alcohol use is prevalent in close to one-half of convicted domestic violence offenders; (3) about 20 per cent of those arrested by the police test positive for alcohol; (4) alcohol is common in many different types of violent crimes against the person, including homicide, wounding, affray, and domestic violence, as well as property crime (Cordilia, 1985); (5) a high proportion of both offenders and victims of violent crime are under the influence at the time the offence occurs.

Of course, the setting in which the violence takes place is also important: violent incidents cluster around the immediate vicinity of bars and clubs, so it is highly likely that all those involved, offender, victim, and bystanders, will have consumed alcohol (Ratcliffe, 2012). It follows that alcohol problems are widespread among convicted violent offenders (MacAskill et al., 2011) and victims of violent crime (Branas et al., 2009). Yet further, the alcohol-crime relationship is found for males and females, adolescents and young adults (Popovici, et al., 2012).

The use of weapons

The presence of a weapon in a potentially violent situation acts to prime hostile thoughts among those involved, in turn making it more likely that the weapon will be used (Bartholow, et al., 2005; Benjamin & Bushman, 2018; Cukier & Eagen, 2018). If a weapon is used, with some weapons more lethal than others, the risk of serious injury and death is substantially increased. Brennan and Moore (2009) note that in both America and the UK weapons are used in about one-quarter of violent incidents. A person may have a weapon for several reasons: (i) the weapon may be for self-protection; (ii) to threaten other people; (iii) deliberately to harm another person; (iv) to act as a status symbol; (v) to bolster self-image.

Mental disorder

Another factor to consider lies in the quality of the violent individual's mental health. The relationship between mental health and violence, mainly criminal violence, has concentrated upon the disorders of psychosis, mainly schizophrenia, and personality disorder.

There is research evidence to indicate that, compared with the general population, men and women with psychosis have an elevated risk of conviction for violent offences (e.g., Bonta, Blais, & Wilson, 2014; Douglas, Guy, & Hart, 2009; Fazel & Yu, 2009; Hodgins, 2008; Witt, van Dorn, & Fazel, 2013). It appears that people with a mental disorder are overly represented among perpetrators of homicide. In a typical study, Meehan et al. (2006) reviewed 1,594 cases of homicide in England and Wales committed between 1996 and 1999. They reported that 85 (5%) of the sample had a formal diagnosis of schizophrenia: this figure stands in contrast to an incidence of schizophrenia of 1 per cent in the general population.

Violence and schizophrenia

Schizophrenia is characterised by delusions, hallucinations, and confused speech which can be of sufficient severity to bring about changes in behaviour which precipitate social or occupational difficulties. Bo et al. (2011)

described two trajectories to explain the association between schizophrenia and violence. In the first trajectory, the primary explanation lies in the presence of psychopathic and antisocial personality disorder with the psychotic symptoms of secondary concern. Those individuals in this trajectory had a history of antisocial behaviour which preceded the onset of schizophrenia. In the second trajectory, the primary explanation is a high occurrence of symptoms – including persecutory delusions, "threat control override" symptoms, and command hallucinations – often without a history of antisocial behaviour. Threat control override symptoms, often implicated in violence (Braham, Trower, & Birchwood, 2004; Bucci et al., 2013), may be experienced as a delusion that other people are trying to cause personal harm or control one's thoughts and actions. These specific aspects of schizophrenia associated with violence should be seen in the larger context of social conditions and other physiological and psychological aspects of the disorder (Steinert & Whittington, 2013).

An individual may have concurrent, or *comorbid*, mental health problems. A large proportion, perhaps half, of people with schizophrenia have a comorbid substance use disorder (Volkow, 2009). Given the association between alcohol and violence, a combination of schizophrenia and alcohol misuse potentially raises the risk of violence (Fazel et al., 2009).

Violence and personality disorder

There are several types of personality disorder (PD) defined by diagnostic systems such as the *Diagnostic and Statistical Manual of Mental Disorders* (DSM-5; American Psychiatric Association, 2013). Yu, Geddes, and Fazel (2012) conducted a systematic review of the evidence and concluded that as compared to the general population PD was associated with a threefold higher risk of violence. The risk of violence associated with PD was similar to the risk levels for those with other mental disorders such as bipolar disorder and schizophrenia. However, if the PD was specifically Antisocial Personality Disorder (APD) the risk of violence rose significantly to levels comparable to the risks associated with drug and alcohol abuse. In addition, APD increased the probability of reoffending to a higher level than other psychiatric conditions. In a British survey using DSM-IV, Coid et al. (2017) found that APD was the personality disorder most strongly associated with violence and was three times more prevalent in men than in women.

DSM-5 specifies four diagnostic criteria for APD (see Table 1.1): (1) a disregard for the rights of other people which is longstanding and may have been evident from childhood; (2) the individual has reached 18 years of age; (3) there is

TABLE 1.1. Summary of DSM-5 Diagnostic Criteria for APD

A. | Disregard for and violation of the rights of other people since 15 years of age as seen by:

    (i)   Breaking the law;

    (ii)   Lying and manipulation for profit or fun;

    (iii) Impulsive behaviour;

    (iv) High levels of aggression evinced by frequent involvement in fights and assaults;

    (v)   Deliberate disregard for own and other people's safety;

    (vi) A pattern of irresponsibility;

    (vii) An absence of remorse.

B.   The individual is at least 18 years of age.

C.   Conduct disorder was present before 15 years of age.

D.   The individual was not diagnosed with schizophrenia or bipolar disorder when the antisocial behaviour occurred.

evidence of Conduct Disorder before the age of 15 years; (4) the antisocial behaviour is evident not only during an episode of schizophrenia or mania.

DSM-5 presents several specific instances by which the first criterion, a callous disregard for the rights of others, may be seen which illustrate the essence of APD. These instances are: (a) failing to follow accepted social norms as seen by a repetition of behaviours that give grounds for criminal arrest; (b) deceit for gain or personal pleasure through consistent lying or cheating; (c) impulsive behaviour; (d) belligerence leading to involvement in numerous fights or assaults; (e) an irresponsible disregard for the safety of self or others; (f) repeatedly losing employment and failure to maintain financial responsibilities; (g) failure to show remorse for victims.

It is evident that APD is strongly associated with criminal behaviour, particularly when it is comorbid with substance use disorders (Roberts & Coid, 2010; Walter et al., 2010). This association applies to offenders in both the criminal justice and mental health care systems. Similarly, psychopathic disorder, which has features in common with personality disorder, is also strongly associated with the likelihood of violent conduct (Lestico et al., 2008).

Emotional arousal

Anger is the emotion most readily associated with interpersonal violence. A person typically becomes angry when cues from their immediate environment, such as the words or actions of other people, provoke physical feelings and thoughts which, influenced by experience, they label as "anger". This emotional state may lead to an expression of anger in the form of verbal or physical violence directed at another person (Novaco & Welsh, 1989). The way in which an individual expresses their anger depends upon factors such as attribution of hostility and perception of provocation (both of which may be inaccurate), experience and memories of similar situations, and ability to cope with the situation and with feelings of anger. When it is under control, anger can have a positive aspect in that it signals to others the effect of their actions and it can prompt the individual into positive action to protect themselves or others. However, a failure to regulate anger effectively can lead to the emotion becoming dysfunctional in nature.

Anger regulation refers to the ability to remain in a calm state when one perceives provocation. The level of anger control of which an individual is capable may be dependent upon factors such as the way in which they label their internal state, from irritation through to rage, and the appraisal of level of emotional control, from keeping control to "losing it".

While most people will occasionally have been roused to anger, for others anger and aggression can become an established behavioural pattern from an early age (Lemerise & Dodge, 2008). When anger is habitual it may become dysfunctional with adverse consequences for the individual and other people they encounter. Dysfunctional anger may take the form of intermittent explosive disorder (Coccaro, 2000) and alongside an increased likelihood of acts of interpersonal violence, chronic levels of anger can precipitate serious psychological and health problems (Miller et al., 1996).

The hostile processing of social information leading to anger may be exacerbated by qualities of the physical environment such as high temperature and over-crowding. In addition, anger arousal can be intensified through interactions with other conditions, such as alcohol use and mental health problems, which serve to heighten the risk of hostile perception and appraisal of other people.

Payoffs from reducing interpersonal violence

Why is it important to reduce interpersonal violence? What payoffs would there be if the levels of interpersonal violence could be reduced?

The first payoff would be a reduction in the human costs of victimisation. The exact effects of violent victimisation vary across several factors such as the victim's age and gender, the nature of the assault in terms of the degree of force used and sexual intent, and the victim's relationship with the perpetrator. Given these variations, victim surveys (e.g., Tan & Haining, 2016) show the fourfold effects of victimisation. First, there is a high probability of physical harm ranging from the effects of slaps, bites, and punches, through severe tissue damage, broken bones, and internal injuries, to life-threatening conditions. These injuries may require medical attention. Second, the psychological sequelae of victimisation include loss of self-confidence, fear and anxiety for self and others, panic attacks, post-traumatic stress disorder, depression, and thoughts of suicide. Third, the victimisation may precipitate behavioural change as seen with alcohol and drug use, smoking, disrupted sleep patterns, reliance on prescription medication, and appetite change. Finally, the social consequences can include withdrawal from social activities resulting in diminished quality of life and loss of friendships, absences from work causing financial problems, and strains on family life threatening the quality and stability of relationships with relatives including partner and children.

While some of these consequences may be short-term, in that cuts and bruises heal, they all have the potential to have long-term effects from physical scarring to financial instability and breakdown of the family home. As Kazdin (2011) comments, while the adverse consequences of interpersonal violence can be categorised as physical, psychological, and so on, it is likely that these will occur concurrently bringing misery and despair potentially over a period of years. A reduction in the levels of victimisation from interpersonal violence has the potential to alleviate these consequences for the benefit of not just the victim but also their family and friends, as well as helping to maintain their wider social and economic contribution to society.

A second payoff lies in the long-term benefits realised by diminishing the perpetuation of violence across generations. Widom described the continuity of violence across generations within a family as a "cycle of violence" (Widom, 1989a, 1989b). If the familial influences which reinforce and perpetuate such cycles can be ameliorated, there is the possibility of a significant reduction in interpersonal violence.

The third payoff of a reduction in interpersonal violence is a reduction in the financial burden caused by the consequences of interpersonal violence. It is not a simple task to estimate the financial costs of crime: first, as not all crimes, perhaps a minority, are reported, estimates based on recorded crime can only be a sample of the true costs; second, estimating costs for all the agencies immediately involved in the crime – police, courts, medical services, probation, and prison – is not straightforward; third, there are more distal costs such as loss of productivity from an injured employee and shortfalls in public service from injuries to, for example, medical personnel; fourth, costs will vary from crime to crime and will fluctuate over time.

While it is impossible to provide precise figures for the financial costs of crime, the available estimations show that the costs are considerable. Thus, for example, McCollister, French, and Fang (2010) state that "In the United States, more than 23 million criminal offenses were committed in 2007, resulting in approximately $15 billion in economic losses to the victims and $179 billion in government expenditures on police protection, judicial and legal activities, and corrections" (p. 98). In the same way, the costs of compensation to victims of violent crime can run into thousands of dollars (Johnston, Shields, & Suziedelyte, in press). While the sums involved are not as high as those in the United States, in the UK a similar situation may be found with crime bringing about high costs to the public purse (e.g., Welsh & Farrington, 2015; Piquero, Jennings, & Farrington, 2013).

One of the advantages of a reliable estimate of the cost of crime is that it allows the monetary benefits of crime reduction programmes to be calculated. These benefits are sometimes expressed as "£x pounds saved for every £1 invested". As may be anticipated, such financial calculations are of interest to policy-makers who fund crime reduction indicatives (Welsh, Farrington, & Raffan Gowar, 2015).

Conclusion

Interpersonal violence is nested within a broader spectrum of many types of violent acts. Even so, there are several ways in which interpersonal violence can become manifest across a variety of settings involving men, women, and children as both perpetrators and victims. There are several factors reliably related to interpersonal violence including the presence of a weapon, mental health problems, personality disorder, and dysfunctional anger. The costs of interpersonal anger, both human and financial, are high and it is evident that there is much to be gained from reducing the harm we inflict upon other people.

2

PRINCIPLES OF REDUCING BEHAVIOUR

Given that violence has been referred to by the WHO as a public health problem it is a natural step to look to public health and medicine for strategies to reduce violence (Lee, 2017a, 2017b). In terms of physical health, there are three broad approaches to disease control: (1) eliminate the disease (Dowdle, 1998); (2) prevent the spread of the disease (Gordon, 1983); and (3) treat those individuals who have the disease.

The first approach to disease control, *elimination*, can be achieved through vaccination. The WHO has certified the global eradication of two infectious diseases: in 1979 smallpox was declared eradicated, followed in 2011 by rinderpest (*cattle plague*), an infectious viral disease which affected cattle, domestic buffalo, and various other species. The second approach, *prevention*, is concerned with helping people to avoid disease. A preventative approach may seek to change cultural practices, such as tobacco smoking or unprotected sexual activity through which diseases such as lung cancer and sexually transmitted diseases occur. The goal of prevention may also be achieved by directing resources at basics such as sanitising drinking water or promoting widespread vaccination programmes. Finally, *treatment* is concerned with medical intervention for the sick individual to enable them to recover from the disease.

If these three strategies for disease control are applied to reducing inter-personal violence, then the following options emerge: (1) totally *eradicate* the causes of interpersonal violence through legal and societal change; (2)

prevent the likelihood of interpersonal violence through legal measures and environmental control to reduce the likelihood of violence for high-risk groups; (3) *treat* the violent person to reduce the likelihood of future violent behaviour.

In similar manner to the WHO, the Institute of Medicine identified three ways to reduce mental, rather than physical, illness: (1) *universal*, targeted at a whole population; (2) *selective*, targeted at "at risk" groups; (3) *indicated*, targeted at those with the specific problem (Mrazek & Haggerty, 1994).

Eradication/prohibition

Is it possible to take steps totally to eradicate the causes of interpersonal violence? This option borrowed from health does not translate easily to reducing violence. While it may literally be possible to eradicate the biological causes of a disease the same is plainly not true of human behaviour. The behavioural analogy to eradication is to *prohibit* behaviour and so this term will be preferred here. An example of a prohibitive approach to changing behaviour on a large scale lies in the effort made in the mid-2000s to improve public health by significantly restricting the smoking of tobacco. Thus, laws were introduced to prohibit smoking in public places synonymous with smoking such as bars and restaurants; mass advertising on the perils of smoking, some specifically aimed at children and adolescents; and financial measures in raising the cost of tobacco. The number of people who have stopped smoking since the ban came into force is difficult to estimate. It is the case however that tobacco sales have fallen and surveys suggest that there are fewer people smoking. A specific effect of the ban is that it has been effective in reducing secondary smoking, as for example with bar staff in a smoke-filled pub.

Any attempt to introduce widespread societal change will, perhaps rightly in some instances, provoke opposition and even a backlash against the new legal measures. These attempts at societal change are best understood within their historical context: what we take today as being self-evidently correct may not have been the case at the time the changes were introduced. This point is illustrated by the attempts in the 19th century to prohibit the ill-treatment of children.

In Victorian times children were a ready source of cheap labour in the ferment of industrial activity stoked by the industrial revolution. Children were readily put to work in coal, tin, and lead mines as *putters*, pushing trucks of coal along the narrow mine tunnels, and as *trappers* responsible for opening and shutting wooden doors to allow air to pass through the tunnels. A trapper boy or girl would sit alone for hours each day with just a small candle for light. Children working in mines could start work at 2 a.m. and remain below ground for 18 hours. As well as labouring in the mines children were also put to work sweeping chimneys or toiled in dangerous factory conditions. Children were in demand by industry because their size meant they could access small spaces in factories or mines, they were easy to control, and, of course, as they were paid less than adults they were a cheap source of labour.

The wages children earned as labourers could help to support their families but at the cost of their education. In the 1830s Parliament became concerned about the exploitation of child labour and passed a series of Acts intended to improve the lot of young children. The 1833 Factory Act was intended to improve conditions for children working in factories. The Act stated there should be no child workers under 9 years of age, children aged from 9 to 13 years were to work no more than 9 hours a day, and those aged 13 to 18 years no more than 12 hours a day. Further, children would not be allowed to work at night and they should receive a mandatory 2 hours schooling each day. In a similar fashion the 1834 Chimney Sweeps Act made it illegal to employ a child below 10 years of age, while no child under 14 years of age could be engaged in cleaning chimneys.

The introduction of legislation strongly favourable towards child welfare met with strong opposition, mainly on the grounds of its effects on profits. There were many attempts to repeal the laws in Parliament and some employers sought to flout the new legislation. To enforce the law, the government set up various inspectorates – the Factories Inspectorate, followed by the Mines Inspectorate and then the Quarry Inspectorate – to scrutinise these places of work and ensure that the law was followed.

From a modern standpoint, we may think that the steps our forbears took to safeguard children are to be commended and we express disapproval of countries where children are still put to work. However, the debate about child welfare continues in other arenas: for example, in the UK the Children Act 1989 strengthened the rights of children with respect to those who held parental responsibility for their safety and wellbeing. As will be discussed in the following chapter, legislation intended to eradicate the corporal punishment of children has led to disputes like those seen with changes in child labour laws.

In the following chapters prohibition will be considered by looking at how the relevant legislation is enforced and by reviewing, where possible, the effectiveness of the legislation.

Prevention

While the notion of prevention makes sense in a medical context there are difficulties in transposing it to a behavioural framework. First, a major problem with prevention of behaviour lies in knowing exactly which high risk individuals will actually carry out the specific behaviour and so where to focus resources. A risk is an estimation of the *likelihood* that an individual will act in a certain way: for example, rather like a 100–1 shot winning the Derby while the odds-on favourite loses, some adults at *low* risk for, say, hitting children will hit while others at *high* risk do not. Thus, directing preventative measures to those at a high risk of hitting children may reduce behaviour by those who would hit but is wasted on those who would not. In addition, a focus just on high-risk groups alone will miss those at low risk who nonetheless will hit children.

Another problem with prevention is that it runs the risk of *net widening* (Ezell, 1989). As Smyth (2011) explains:

> Net widening is a term most commonly used to describe a phenomenon whereby a program is set up to divert youth away from an institutional placement or some other type of juvenile court disposition but, instead, merely brings more youth into the juvenile justice system who previously would never have entered. Instead of shrinking the "net" of social control, one actually "widens" it to bring more in.
>
> *(p. 159)*

The issues surrounding prevention – including measurement of risk, unnecessary intervention with some high-risk individuals while missing some low risk individuals, and the potential of net-widening – suggest that prohibition and treatment are more likely to be used to reduce interpersonal violence. Thus, from a conceptual point of view, there is a clear distinction between the legally driven process of prohibition of interpersonal violence and the psychological treatment of the violent individual. However, prevention is intertwined with prohibition and treatment. As prohibition is manifest across society it may influence the behaviour of high-risk groups and so has the potential to prevent interpersonal violence. At the level of the individual, treatment aims to prevent further instances of violence by those who have acted violently and so also serves a preventative function. While there are difficulties in this context in clearly delineating prevention, there are some clear examples of strategies that are additional to legal sanctions and which are intended to prevent interpersonal violence. As these instances arise they will be considered as appropriate within a given context.

Psychological treatment

The use of psychological theory and practice to change antisocial and criminal behaviour, including interpersonal violence, has been evident since Freud and the advent of psychoanalysis (Hollin, 2012; Marshall & Hollin, 2015). A gamut of psychological theories – from Gestalt to radical behaviourism, transactional analysis to cognitive therapy, education and vocational training to family therapy, and therapeutic communities to cognitive-behavioural programmes – have all been employed with offenders (Hollin, 2001a). The treatment option of working constructively with those who have committed violent acts to bring about psychological and behavioural change to reduce their future involvement in violence is a well-trodden path (McGuire, 2008a; Polaschek & Reynolds, 2011).

Treatment and risk

The decision to deliver psychological treatment will necessarily be influenced by the risk posed by the individual. When the treatment is effective it will reduce risk and therefore the likelihood of recurrences of the behaviour. Thus, the aim of reducing interpersonal violence may be achieved by targeting those deemed to be at high risk of repeated violence. A study by Castellanos-Ryan et al. (2013) provides a perfect example of focusing treatment on high risk groups to reduce later behaviour. Castellanos-Ryan and colleagues targeted their intervention at a group of six-year-old disruptive kindergarten boys. As disruptive behaviour at an early age is a risk factor for substance use in adolescence, the targeted intervention should act to prevent, or at least reduce, the children's use of substances in later life. At follow-up the intervention was successful in reducing the children's substance use in their adolescent years.

The Castellanos-Ryan and colleagues study is an example of early intervention intended to have a beneficial effect in later years. While this study could focus on a known childhood risk factor for substance use, an issue for interpersonal violence lies in the precise identification of risk factors used to indicate who is most "at risk". If risk is understood as the likelihood of some future event there are two related elements to consider: first the identification of the factors which contribute to the risk; second, how the level of risk is established in each individual case.

In practice, an individual's level of risk may be gauged in one of two ways, either through practitioner experience or by use of an empirically developed assessment measure. In the former, estimation of the level of risk is based on clinical judgement; in the latter, risk level is based upon measurement using evidence-based scales. The relative merits of these two approaches to assessing risk have been much discussed in the literature (e.g., Dawes, Faust, & Meehl, 1989; Meehl, 1954).

The empirical approach to risk assessment typically establishes the identity of the relevant risk factors for the specific behaviour, then uses actuarial methods to produce a scale or an inventory to measure risk. There are many actuarial risk assessment instruments for violent behaviour: for example, the Risk Matrix 2000 assesses the risk of sexual reoffending (Barnett, Wakeling, & Howard, 2010; Thornton et al., 2003); the Spousal Assault Risk Assessment (SARA) Guide may be used to inform assessments of the risk of inter-partner violence (Kropp & Hart, 2000); and the Violence Risk Appraisal Guide (VRAG) for use with male violent offenders (Quinsey et al., 2006).

The risk factors used in these actuarial scales may be classified as *dynamic risk factors*, such as problem drinking, which, by definition, can be changed; and *static risk factors*, such as number of previous convictions which, again by definition, cannot be changed. (There is a third type of criterion, such as age, which naturally changes slowly: in practice age is generally taken to be static in nature.) Of course, risk factors do not always occur in isolation, the general rule is that the greater the number of risk factors in a given case so the greater the overall cumulative risk becomes (Andershed, Gibson, & Andershed, 2016). There is a substantial body of research given to consideration of the use of risk instruments with violent populations (Prell, Vitacco, & Zavodny, 2016; Singh et al., 2014; Singh, Grann, & Fazel, 2011), their relative accuracy (Campbell, French, & Gendreau, 2009; Yang, Wong, & Coid, 2010) and their use in practice (Buchanan, 2013).

As Cooke has pointed out (Cooke, 2016; Hart & Cooke, 2013), the efforts to refine actuarial measures of risk have led to research which is dominated by statistical, rather than psychological, thinking. The net effect of this focus on methodology, Cooke argues, has been to neglect the fact that while actuarial measures may say whether a person is a member of an at-risk group, they cannot say that a specific individual within that group will be one of those who reoffends. The psychological reasoning that should inform decision-making at the individual level has become lost in the mists of "statistical ritual" (Cooke, 2016, p. 84). The middle road of *structured professional judgement* offers a blend of the application of empirical research on known risk factors with traditional clinical skills to focus on the likelihood that an individual will behave violently. This approach, used by scales such as the HCR-20 (K. S. Douglas et al., 2013), has prompted a fresh wave of thinking about practice (Falzer, 2013).

Protective factors

A risk factor increases the likelihood of a given behaviour, however there are other factors that appear to counter risk. Klepfisz, Daffern, and Day (2017) note that these mitigating factors "Are increasingly being referred to as 'protective' factors, but are denoted by various other terms including 'strengths', 'promotive factors', 'stabilizers', and 'desistance factors'" (p. 80). A body of research has revealed the complexity of protective factors: for example, there are protective factors for children in the community (Li, Godinet, & Arnsberger, 2011); for young offenders they may vary by age (Fontaine et al., 2016); for adult prisoners some protective factors may prove to be stronger than others (Ullrich & Coid, 2011); protective factors may vary according to the nature of their effect on behaviour and in their relationship with risk factors (Hemphill, Heerde, & Scholes-Balog, 2016; Lösel & Farrington, 2012).

There has been interest in protective factors from the perspective of reducing criminal behaviour (Kewley, 2017). The basic premise holds that if offenders can be encouraged to apply their personal strengths in a constructive manner they will be able to gain legitimately what they want in life. The Structured Assessment of Protective Factors for Violence Risk (SAPROF; de Vries Robbé et al., 2011) is intended to assess protective factors for violence in adult offenders. The 17-item SAPROF considers both individual factors, such as empathy, coping, and self-control, alongside environmental support factors such as a stable intimate relationship and social support which is negative towards criminal behaviour. In addition, there is evidence to show that from early adolescence to adulthood higher intelligence can function as a protective factor (Ttofi et al., 2016).

Strong assessment protocols help to identify high risk individuals and groups so that steps can be taken towards prevention. The preventative measures may involve, for example, welfare services, education, or psychological treatment. A contemporary treatment approach to reducing interpersonal violence is informed by understanding the individual's actions in a social context, a *situated transaction* in Luckenbill's terms. Thus, in a potentially violent situation how does the individual's social cognition function? What distinguishes their perception of the situation and their appraisal of the other people present? How do their social problem-solving skills, alongside their moral values and beliefs, influence their behaviour? In addition, is there a need to consider the influences of alcohol, mental disorder, and high emotionality? These various factors will appear as strategies to reduce a range of types of interpersonal violence with different populations are considered in the following chapters.

3

REDUCING 'EVERYDAY VIOLENCE'

Violence against animals

The starting point is violence against animals, not in itself an act of interpersonal violence but, as shown below, a very close relative. The ways in which we are cruel to animals know no bounds: we test cosmetics on animals, we hunt and kill animals for pleasure and profit (some to the point of extinction), we cause animals to suffer in the name of farming, we displace animals from their natural habitat, and we are cruel to the domesticated animals with which we share our homes. I have considered this topic in detail elsewhere (Hollin, 2012) but from the perspective of reducing interpersonal violence is there any association between animal cruelty and interpersonal violence?

Petersen and Farrington (2007) note that cruelty to animals is often mentioned as a feature of the childhood histories of violent offenders and so may be associated with interpersonal violence. This suggestion is reinforced by research showing that cruelty towards animals in childhood is a strong indicator of other childhood problems such as conduct disorder, aggression, and antisocial personality disorder (Dadds, Turner, & McAloon, 2002; Gleyzer, Felthous, & Holzer, 2002). Yet further, Flynn (1999) found that students at an American university who admitted that as a child they committed some form of animal abuse were more likely than their non-abusing peers to have attitudes supportive of spanking children and of a husband slapping his wife. The weight of evidence shows that a child, typically male, who observes or perpetrates acts of violence against animals may grow into a violent adult (Holoyda & Newman, 2016; Levitt, Hoffer, & Loper, 2016) or, in extremis, even a serial murderer (Wright & Hensley, 2003).

It is not unreasonable to suggest that if there was a reduction in cruelty to animals there would be a concomitant reduction in interpersonal violence (and the animals would benefit too). How might levels of animal cruelty be reduced?

Animal cruelty: prohibition

Given that cruelty to animals is such a long-standing and pervasive aspect of life it is highly unlikely that it will ever be eliminated. However, there have been attempts to place restrictions on some forms of animal cruelty. In the UK, the *Cruel Treatment of Cattle Act 1822* was one of the first attempts to legislate to improve animal welfare, since when there has been a succession of Acts of Parliament which seek to improve the lives of animals. The most recent Act, the Animal Welfare Act 2006, specified the conditions necessary to promote the welfare of animals and protect them from harm. In addition, in England and Wales the Hunting Act 2004 banned the hunting with dogs of wild mammals, principally foxes, deer, hares, and mink. Of course, other countries have similar concerns and similarly seek to limit harm to animals.

The arguments opposing the Acts prohibiting cruelty to animals are typically based on protecting the countryside from vermin. Thus, cruelty to animals, as with hunting, is defended as a time-honoured sporting tradition, while those who object are depicted as being from those parts of society who do not understand and appreciate the ways of genuine country folk. In the same manner, advocates of bullfighting, popular in several parts of the world, defend it as an art form which is part of their cultural heritage.

It is the task of the police to deal with those instances, such as fox hunting, where the law has been broken. However, there are various organisations in the UK, such as the *Royal Society for the Prevention of Cruelty to Animals* (RSPCA) and the *League Against Cruel Sports* (LACS), which are involved in protecting the rights of animals and instigating prosecutions where they find that the law has been broken. There are small bodies, such as the *Animal Cruelty Investigation Group* (ACIG), and large, international organisations such as *Greenpeace* which take as their remit the protection of animals, ranging from the humble fox to whales and other marine life as regulated by international law, together with the shrinking habitat of animals in areas such as the rainforests in the Amazon and in Indonesia.

It is impossible to gauge the effect of prohibitive legislation. It is true that the effects of some campaigns, such as those to save endangered species, can be estimated with some degree of accuracy. However, a great deal of animal abuse undoubtedly remains unreported and so any attempt to extrapolate the effects of legal provision on animal welfare to reductions in interpersonal violence would require a large-scale research effort.

Animal cruelty: treatment

If a child is suspected of harming animals there are several assessment instruments with which to attempt to establish the type, frequency and degree of the cruelty. These assessments include the Children and Animals Assessment Instrument (CAAI; Ascione, Thompson, & Black, 1997), the Cruelty to Animals Inventory (CAI; Dadds et al., 2004), and the Children's Treatment of Animals Questionnaire (CTAQ; Thompson & Gullone, 2003). The information gleaned from the assessment can be used to inform treatment planning by, say, establishing the targets for change during the intervention.

Table 3.1 gives illustrative examples of items from the CAAI and the CTAQ.

While assessment may help identify which children are likely to abuse animals, it is less certain exactly which of them, as either children or adults, will commit acts of interpersonal violence. Walters (2013) reported a meta-analysis which

TABLE 3.1 Illustrative items from the Children and Animals Assessment Instrument (CAAI; Ascione, Thompson, & Black, 1997) and the Cruelty to Animals Inventory (CAI; Dadds et al., 2004).

CAAI	CAI
(i) Sometimes, kids and grownups treat pet animals in ways that are not good or ways that are mean. Can you remember a time when you were mean to a pet animal or hurt a pet animal?	(i) Have you ever hurt an animal on purpose?
(ii) Who were the other people who were mean to the pet animal?	(ii) Do you treat animals cruelly in front of others or by yourself?
[The same questions are asked about pet animals and wild animals.]	(iii) If you purposely hurt an animal, do you feel very sorry for it and feel sad that you hurt it?

showed that, for male offenders, animal cruelty was associated with both non-violent *and* violent offending. This finding opens the possibility that the relationship between animal cruelty and offending is in fact part of a larger pattern of antisocial and criminal behaviour.

Given the evidence for the overlap between cruelty to animals, child abuse, intimate partner violence, and elder abuse (Becker & French, 2004; Peak, Ascione, & Doney, 2012), can cruelty to animals within a household serve as a "red flag" for the risk of violence between family members (DeGue & DiLillo, 2009)? Yet further, as cruelty towards animals is likely to be dealt with by agencies such as the RSPCA, is there a case for cross-agency reporting such that animal charities inform, say, local Children's Services?

In agreement with Tiplady, Walsh, and Phillips (2012), Monsalve, Ferreira, and Garcia (2017) point out that veterinarians are also likely to see cases of animal cruelty. Monsalve and colleagues suggest that while vets are well placed to play a role in animal welfare and public health some training is required:

> The involvement of veterinarians in this area is crucial for the protection of people and animals. Therefore, veterinary colleges must offer appropriate training to their students. The limited number of published studies in the field of veterinary medicine reflects the lack of recognition of the role veterinarians play in preventing and intervening of cycle of violence.
>
> *(p. 24)*

On the other side of the coin, in instances of family violence where there are pets in the house, should animal welfare agencies be alerted by the police or social services of the potential risk? While there are organisational issues to resolve in developing protocols for cross-agency reporting, there are examples of risk markers for child welfare and animal abuse being used to inform multi-agency work (Risley-Curtiss, Zilney, & Hornung, 2010). Thus, as Lunghofer and Shapiro (2014) explain, the association between cruelty to animals and domestic violence has led 25 American states to enact legislation which allows for the safety of pets where there is a domestic violence protection order. In addition, some domestic violence shelters work in collaboration with animal welfare organisations to offer shelter for pets both to encourage the victim to leave the abusive situation and for the safety of the animal. However, this use of risk markers is not widespread in practice and so its potential is not fully realised (Risley-Curtiss, Rogge, & Kawam, 2013).

In terms of treatment of animal abuse, there is a marked absence of evidence-based treatments informed by rigorous outcome studies for (Haden & Scarpa, 2005; Miller, 2001). In the absence of an evidence base several approaches have been attempted including animal welfare education, counselling, and empathy development, and several programmes have also been developed, such as the AniCare Programme (Shapiro et al., 2013). It is possible that elements of treatment for conduct disorders (e.g., Bakker et al., 2017) would address aspects of child and adolescent functioning related to animal cruelty.

Bullying

The vulnerability of the victim when faced with the power of the aggressor is an aspect of animal cruelty that is to be found in several forms of interpersonal violence. The next type of everyday violence, bullying, is certainly a case in point. The act of bullying, either between children at school or between adults in the workplace, can be a cause of great distress to the victim. The psychological health of those who are bullied may suffer significantly, sometimes to the point of depression, self-harm, and even suicide; social relationships with friends and colleagues may be adversely affected; and in some cases victims suffer varying degrees of physical harm. These adverse experiences may culminate in post-traumatic stress disorder (PTSD): Nielsen et al. (2015) reported that there were strong associations between experience of bullying and PTSD symptomatology in over one-half of child and adult victims of school and workplace bullying.

Bullying at school

As well as the immediate problems it creates, bullying at school can have long-term consequences. Involvement in bullying at school, as an aggressor or a victim or both, is a significant predictor of violence later in life (Ttofi, Farrington, & Lösel, 2012). Bullying can bring disorder to a child's educational progress: the bullied child may refuse to go to school, truant, or even drop out of education; the bully may be suspended or expelled from school. In either case, dropout or expulsion, there are likely to be adverse consequences for the child as their life unfolds (e.g., Farrington, 1996; Hibbett & Fogelman, 1990; Rocque et al., 2017).

While bullying is one form of violence found within schools, others include the use of weapons, vandalism, and assaults on staff (Eisenbraun, 2007; Valdebenito et al., 2017). These different forms of violence may require different types of intervention to those intended to reduce bullying (e.g., Fahsl & Luce, 2012; Farrington et al., 2017). The magnitude of the problem of bullying (e.g., Raynor & Wylie, 2012) has led to attempts to reduce this form of interpersonal violence.

Bullying at school: prohibition

The closed environment of a school (or workplace) means that everyone within that setting is potentially at risk of being bullied. In turn, the circumscribed nature of a school offers the possibility of eradication of bullying within the restrictions of that environment. Thus, anti-bullying policies and programmes are ideally not selectively applied to certain pupils but are manifest across the whole of the school setting so that, like smallpox, the problem can be totally removed.

The design of policies and procedures to reduce bullying should, of course, be informed by knowledge of the risk factors for bullying. A systematic review by Álvarez-García, García, and Núñez (2015) considered many risk factors for bullying and classified them as individual factors, school factors, family factors, or community factors. The large quantity of risk factors associated with bullying raises the question of both the content of anti-bullying programmes and what they can realistically be expected to achieve. It is clear, for example, that a school-based programme can do nothing about static risk factors such as parental education or dynamic factors such as inequalities in family income. It follows that when set against the powerful forces of family and community factors it is realistic to anticipate modest gains from school-based anti-bullying programmes.

Bullying at school: treatment

Cognitive-behavioural interventions, which seek to change how a person thinks, feels and acts, encompass a wide range of techniques such as impulse control, anger management, moral development, and social skills training. The evidence strongly favours a cognitive-behavioural approach to treating violent behaviour generally (McGuire, 2008a) and in schools specifically (Barnes, Smith, & Miller, 2014). In this tradition there are multi-modal programmes, such as *Aggression Replacement Training* (Goldstein, Glick, & Gibbs, 1998; Goldstein, Nensén, Daleflod, & Kalt, 2004), which draw together several cognitive-behavioural elements into a cohesive whole and can be used with the individual child.

Aggression Replacement Training (ART)

The *ART* programme, developed by Arnold Goldstein and colleagues (Goldstein & Glick, 2001; Goldstein, Glick, & Gibbs, 1998; Goldstein et al., 2004), incorporates the three elements of skills training, anger control, and moral reasoning training. With its roots firmly in a cognitive-behavioural approach (Hollin, 2003), *ART* has been used in several countries with school children as well as young offenders and adult offenders.

Koposov, Gundersen, and Svartdal (2014) used *ART* successfully with school children in Russia to reduce problem behaviour and increase the children's social skills. In Norway, Gundersen and Svartdal (2006) report an evaluation of an intervention "based on Aggression Replacement Training (ART)" with children and young people with behavioural problems. A pre-post assessment of social problems and social skills showed that compared to a no-treatment control those participating in *ART* showed an indicated significant improvement in social skills and a reduction in behavioural problems.

While individual treatment of the highly aggressive bully is an option, the more widespread approach is to use a behaviour change programme to reduce levels of school bullying. These programmes encompass a wide diversity of measures ranging from a focus on levels of school discipline and classroom rules, to changing pupils' attitudes to bullying and to providing information about bullying for parents (e.g., Baldry & Farrington, 2004; Lund et al., 2012; Muijs, 2017). The high levels of programme diversity create difficulties in establishing the overall effectiveness of anti-bullying programmes (Fox, Farrington, & Ttofi, 2012).

Ttofi and Farrington (2011) examined 44 evaluations of school-based anti-bullying programmes (see also Ttofi & Farrington, 2012). As may be expected, the various anti-bullying programmes differed in their effectiveness with an average decrease in bullying of 20–23 per cent and a decrease in victimisation of 17–20 per cent. However, the involvement of peers in efforts to reduce bullying – through strategies such as peer mentoring and encouraging involvement to prevent bullying – were contra-indicated in that they made matters worse not better. In support of this conclusion, Frisén, Hasselblad, and Holmqvist (2012) reported that very few former victims of bullying said that the bullying had stopped because of peer support. On the other hand, there is support for involving parents in prevention programmes (Axford et al., 2015).

In summary, Ttofi and Farrington (2011) state:

The most important program elements that were associated with a decrease in bullying were parent training/meetings, improved playground supervision, disciplinary methods, classroom management, teacher training, classroom rules, a wholeschool anti-bullying policy, school conferences, information for parents, and cooperative group work.

(p. 41)

The findings of another review of the evidence, reported by Barbero et al., (2012), were in accord with the central conclusion reached by Ttofi and Farrington (2012) but emphasised different elements as having a critical effect in reducing bullying. They state that the "most effective interventions appear to be those aimed at improving social and interpersonal skills and modifying attitudes and beliefs" (p. 1656). However, Barbero and colleagues' review included interventions to reduce aggression and violence in schools while programmes with these aims were explicitly excluded from the Ttofi and Farrington review.

Bullying in the workplace

As with school bullying, workplace bullying may be carried out by an individual or a group and consist of either or both verbal and overt aggression (Samnani & Singh, 2012). The verbal aggression may consist of malicious gossip, belittling personal jokes and insults, the withholding of important job-related information, and being told to leave one's job. Overt bullying may include inflicting excessive workloads, excessive monitoring of work activity, high levels of criticism, blocking opportunities for training and career advancement, and even physical and sexual aggression. There are forms of workplace violence, including criminal violence and homicide (Nowrouzi & Huynh, 2016; Schmidtke, 2011), which are more extreme than verbal and physical bullying although they would not be perceived as "everyday".

Again as with school bullying, workplace bullying may have serious individual and social consequences for the victim (Hogh & Viitasara, 2005). These personal costs can be exacerbated by economic hardship if the bullying forces the victim to leave their employment. In addition, in some settings bullying can lead to an increased likelihood of workplace accidents.

Bullying in the workplace: prohibition

In employment law, it is recognised that bullying (in this context sometimes referred to as *harassment*) in its various forms can occur within the large number of settings in which people work. The exact definitions and associated legislation will differ from country to country: in the UK the relevant legislation, which favours the term harassment, is the Equality Act 2010. This Act defines harassment as "Unwanted conduct related to a relevant protected characteristic, which has the purpose or effect of violating an individual's dignity or creating an intimidating, hostile, degrading, humiliating or offensive environment for that individual". The protected characteristics noted in the Equality Act include age, disability, race, religion, and sexual orientation. However, the Act is inclusive as it is an offence to treat a person *as if* they had a protected characteristic. In addition, an employee may be bullied at work because of their gender (Lippel et al., 2016; Salin, 2015).

At an individual level, an employee who exhibits personal qualities such as appearing anxious, showing high levels of agreeableness, or low self-esteem, is at risk of bullying. These qualities may signal a vulnerability to which bullies respond (Samnani & Singh, 2012).

Accepting that there is no easy answer to workplace bullying (Schindeler & Reynald, 2017), the onus is on employers to maintain legal working conditions including prevention of bullying. An organisation can manage the risk of bullying in several ways. The most obvious step is to provide employees with a clear statement of organisational policies and practice regarding how to deal with harassment. The policy can be reinforced by training personnel, at all organisational levels, with respect to these policies and procedures. However, a crucial step for any organisation is to develop a culture which is intolerant of harassment and which is modelled and reinforced by the organisation's leaders (Hoel et al., 2010).

When bullying occurs, there are avenues which the employee may follow, such as mediation or employment tribunals, to deal with the situation. The mediation agency known as ACAS (Advisory, Conciliation and Arbitration Service) has made available on its website a range of leaflets informing employers and employees of their rights, responsibilities, and potential courses of action. As a great deal of workplace bullying goes unreported it is impossible to know what effect, if any, legislation has on the frequency with which bullying takes place.

As the actions of the workplace bully mean that they have committed an offence, they will face the appropriate legal consequences rather than engaging in treatment. Those employees who have suffered at the hands of the bully may be offered counselling or a rehabilitative period to ease their return to work.

A more recent form of bullying, *cyberbullying*, involves the use of advances in technology to hurt other people.

Cyberbullying

The use of social media such as *Facebook* to bully others is increasingly widespread, particularly so among children and adolescents (Baldry, Farrington, & Sorrentino, 2016; Kwan & Skoric, 2013; Zych, Ortega-Ruiz, & Del Rey, 2015) although adults may also engage in this form of bullying (Jenaro, Flores, & Frías, 2018). Cyberbullying can assume many diverse forms: El Asam and Samara (2016) distinguish "Flaming, harassment, impersonation, outing and trickery, exclusion and ostracism, denigration, defamation, and cyberstalking" (p. 129). Indeed, cyberbullying is just one type of cyber-interpersonal violence (Choi & Lee, 2017), a topic which will be considered further in Chapter 5.

There are several types of cyberbully. First, as might be expected, those who bully face-to-face may also be cyberbullies; second, there are victims who seek recompense for being bullied by themselves cyberbullying; third, a distinct group who are just cyberbullies and may also be victims of cyberbullying. From the bully's perspective, social media bullying via the internet and the mobile telephone holds several advantages over face-to-face bullying: it does not rely on physical prowess; it allows anonymity; posts may remain accessible for long periods of time; and the posted material can reach a wide audience.

Given the overlap between cyberbullying and traditional bullying it is not surprising that the characteristics of the two types are very similar (Baldry, Farrington, & Sorrentino, 2015; Kowalski & Limber, 2013). Baldry and colleagues (2015) draw on the distinction between static and dynamic risk factors for cyberbullying in identifying risk factors for cyberbullying and victimisation. Thus, for cyberbullying the predominant static risk factor is being a male alongside dynamic factors such as low school achievement, poor parental support, impulsivity, and a lack of empathy and morality. The principal static risk factors for becoming a cyberbully victim are being female accompanied by dynamic factors such as poor social skills, a lack of parental control and peer rejection.

Cyberbullying: prohibition

In a review of the extant legislation, El Asam and Samara (2016) point to several shortcomings when current laws such as the Protection from Harassment Act 1997 and the Telecommunications Act 1984 are applied to cases of cyberbullying. These shortcomings include the lack of an agreed definition of cyberbullying, issues in showing intention to harm, and problems when the cyberbullying is across legal jurisdictions. In this respect, cyberbullying is simply another example of the inevitable lag between technological advances and the development of controlling legislation. The issue of the formulation and enactment of legislation to prohibit cyberbullying is of concern in many parts of the world. In Qatar, for example, as Foody et al. (2017) explain, enactment of legislation is hampered by a general lack of awareness of cyberbullying and its consequences.

Mishna et al. (2009) conducted a systematic review of interventions to prevent and reduce cyber abuse, focusing on three interventions in detail. First, the *I-SAFE Curriculum* which includes lessons in areas such as cyber community citizenship, maintaining cyber security, ensuring personal safety, and predator identification (Chibnall et al., 2006). Second, the *Missing Program*, contains an interactive computer game to encourage the development of safe use of the internet (Crombie & Trinneer, 2003). Finally, the HAHASO programme which is aimed at both face-to-face and cyberbullying and based on teaching in the five areas of "Help, Assert Yourself, Humor, Avoid, Self-talk, Own it" (Salvatore, 2006). Mishna and colleagues summarise their findings as showing that:

> Results so far provide evidence that participation in cyber abuse preven-
> tion and intervention strategies is associated with an increase in Internet
> safety knowledge. The findings suggest however, that participation in
> cyber abuse prevention interventions may not be significantly related to
> Internet risk attitudes and behavior.
>
> *(Mishna et al., 2009, p. 33)*

Thus, while the programmes increase participants' knowledge, this growth in understanding does not lead to significant changes in behaviour. A null finding, as Mishna and colleagues note, not uncommon in public health research.

It is evident that cyberbullying is not going to go away and that progress towards effective strategies to reduce its effects will demand attention to optimum methods of programme implementation (Della Cioppa, O'Neil, & Craig, 2015; Hendricks, Lumadue, & Waller, 2012), extending inter-ventions to parental involvement (Robinson, 2013), assimilating what is known about how young people cope with cyberbullying (Raskauskas & Huynh, 2015), and using technology to combat technology (Nocentini, Zambuto, & Menesini, 2015).

Corporal punishment of children

There are few issues connected with child development as likely to raise the temperature, perhaps particularly among parents, teachers and researchers (recognising that these are not mutually exclusive categories!), as the debate about whether it is right or wrong to hit children.

The corporal punishment of children is mainly carried out by parents and school staff. As Benjet and Kazdin (2003) succinctly state:

> Parents and teachers who have responsibility for the care of children, not to mention all those adults who once were children themselves, are likely to have a well formulated stance on whether children should be hit during discipline, the extent to which children ought to be hit, and the circumstances in which such hitting is appropriate.
>
> *(pp. 197–198)*

In this light, Knox (2010) makes a pertinent point in stating that while, rightly, there is condemnation of violence against women and there are laws against hitting adults, criminals, and prisoners, in the USA "The only humans it is still legal to hit are the most vulnerable members of our society – those we are charged to protect – children" (p. 103).

There are several arguments in favour of the use of corporal punishment – variously called *smacking, spanking, paddling*, and *whuping* (Brown, Holden, & Ashraf, 2018) – including its use as a parental strategy to improve the child's behaviour and so facilitate its development (Taylor et al., 2016). Those in favour of hitting children are not arguing for excessive and abusive physical force. However, it is not straightforward to say where corporal punishment ends and child abuse begins (Lee, Grogan-Kaylor, & Berger, 2014; Straus, 2000; Zolotor et al., 2008). This definitional point is illustrated by a study by Durrant et al., (2017) which examined the complexities of reaching a legal understanding of "reasonable force" in the Canadian courts.

The corporal punishment of children is not prohibited in Canada, rather the legal debate hinges on whether parents' punishment of their children falls within acceptable limits. Thus, the legal limits state that the force must be of a minor nature and that it must not involve the use of objects. Durrant and colleagues formed the hypothesis that the application of the criteria for reasonable force would clearly differentiate between cases of abusive and non-abusive force which were brought before the court. They reported that:

Each of the court's criteria defining reasonable force was actually met in most cases of substantiated child physical abuse. In fact, more than one in four … substantiated physical abuse cases did not exceed any of the Supreme Court's limits on reasonable force. These findings indicate that when judges use the court's limits to decide whether an act was reasonable, they will fail to identify many acts of physical abuse. As a result, caregivers will hear that their acts were justified under the law, perpetuating the beliefs that contribute to violence against children. Moreover, children will hear that they are not protected by the law, learning that their rights are not being upheld in Canada.

(Durrant et al., 2017, p. 9)

The reverse side of arguments in favour of corporal punishment is that it has detrimental short- and long-term effects on the child such as engendering an increased likelihood of aggression (MacKenzie et al., 2015) and leading to poor physical health (Afifi et al., 2013). In addition, parents who switch between harsh and lax punishment are also likely to create psychological problems for their children (Parent, McKee, & Forehand, 2016).

There is a large body of research on the topic of hitting children (e.g., Ferguson, 2013; Fuller, 2009, 2011; Gershoff, 2002, 2010; Gershoff & Grogan-Kaylor, 2016; Grogan-Kaylor, Ma, & Graham-Bermann, 2018; Knox, 2010; Larzelere & Baumrind, 2010), not all from a western perspective although reaching similar conclusions about the detrimental effects on the child (Okuzono et al., 2017). A point has been reached where the weight of evidence showing that corporal punishment has negative consequences has led some researchers to state confidently that the case against hitting children is proven (e.g., Durrant & Ensom, 2017; Grogan-Kaylor, Ma, & Graham-Bermann, 2018; Lee, Grogan-Kaylor, & Berger, 2014). Gershoff (2013) makes the forceful claim that "We now have enough research to conclude that spanking is ineffective at best and harmful to children at worst" (p. 134). MacMillan and Mikton (2017) suggest that it is time for research to move to issues such as changing social norms regarding methods of disciplining children, a point which equally applies to schools as well as parents.

There is no doubt that corporal punishment is used in schools round the globe with children of all ages (Gershoff, 2017; Jones & Pells, 2016; Mncube & Tshilidzi, 2014). In 2016 the Global Initiative to End All Corporal Punishment of Children (www.endcorporalpunishment.org) recorded that corporal punishment in schools is allowed in 69 countries. The arguments for corporal punishment in schools are generally couched in terms of maintaining school discipline in the face of serious student misbehaviour.

The case against corporal punishment is not only founded on empirical evidence. In sympathy with the views of Knox (2010), as noted above, Gershoff points to the moral as well as the empirical debate: "Although most Americans do not like to call it so, spanking is hitting and hitting is violence. By using the euphemistic term spanking, parents feel justified in hitting their children while not acknowledging that they are, in fact, hitting" (Gershoff, 2013, pp. 134–135). The question Gershoff asks of whether corporal punishment is morally defensible – regardless of intention, is it right that parents, caregivers, or teachers may inflict physical pain upon a child? – has been debated at length in many countries and jurisdictions (Gershoff & Bitensky, 2007). Indeed, Article 19 of the United Nations Convention on the Rights of the Child states that all children regardless of their nationality have the right to be raised without violence. These views have led to expressions of concern about hitting children from many countries including Egypt (Khalifa, 2017), India (Ghosh & Pasupathi, 2016; Muchhal & Kumar, 2016), Nigeria (Iguh & Nosike, 2011; Omoyemiju, Ojo, & Olatomide, 2015). In order to address these concerns a growing number of countries have prohibited the corporal punishment of children.

Corporal punishment of children: prohibition

The Global Initiative to End All Corporal Punishment of Children states that in 2017 worldwide a total of 52 states have prohibited all corporal punishment of children (including in the family home). A further 54 states have stated their commitment to full prohibition. In Europe, many countries followed Sweden's lead in 1979 by introducing prohibition of corporal punishment of children. However, in England and Wales parental corporal punishment of children is not prohibited by law and there is continued support for its use (Bunting, Webb, & Healy, 2010). As Fréchette and Romano (2017) note, corporal punishment remains legal in Canada and the USA.

The global movement towards prohibition has allowed studies to be conducted that compare the national effects of banning corporal punishment of children. Bussmann, Erthal, and Schroth (2011) compared five European countries – Austria, France, Germany, Spain and Sweden – which have introduced legislation banning the corporal punishment of children. In spite of the myriad of practical problems faced by researchers in this field,

Bussmann and colleagues compiled an extensive report concluding that prohibition does lead to a decline in violence against children.

Lansford et al. (2017) examined rates of reported use of corporal punishment and parents' views on its use in eight countries, one-half of which had introduced a ban. They found that in three countries belief in the need for corporal punishment decreased over time; the reported rate of the use of severe corporal punishment decreased in four countries. Thus, in some countries the enduring belief in and use of corporal punishment regardless of prohibition indicates the need for nationwide campaigns to promote the legal changes and for systematic education of parents in alternative forms of discipline.

Corporal punishment of children: treatment

Parents

There is a long list of cultural, economic, individual, religious, and social variables associated with the corporal punishment of children (e.g., Gershoff et al., 2010; Lansford, 2010; Litzow & Silverstein, 2008; Maldonado, 2004). Of these variables, an adult's experience of corporal punishment is a prominent factor in understanding their favourable views on hitting children. Those parents who themselves experienced physical punishment as children are likely to endorse its use; those parents who experienced severe corporal punishment are likely to use higher levels of punishment with their own children (e.g., Bussmann et al., 2011; Deater-Deckard et al., 2003; Dietz, 2000).

A basic theoretical principle in understanding interpersonal aggression is that if we make a hostile attribution of another person's words or actions then the likelihood of aggressive behaviour towards that person is increased. A study by Crouch et al. (2017) tested parents' responses to several vignettes which "Described the participant's child engaging in behaviors that were: messy, dangerous, lazy, irresponsible, rude, bossy, impatient, rebellious, cruel, dishonest, hostile, and greedy" (p. 16). The parents were asked about the degree to which they saw their child, at age 11 years, as first intending intentionally to cause them annoyance and second intending to be bad. They found that inter-relationships between several variables predicted harsh parenting (defined as screaming at the child and hitting): thus, those parents who believed in an authoritarian approach to parenting – "do as you're told", "be seen and not heard" – were also more likely to hold that their child was intentionally misbehaving or being annoying. These highly authoritarian parents also said they would experience more negative affect, such as irritation and anger, in response to their child's behaviour. Thus, high attribution of hostile intent accompanied by negative affect was associated with harsh parenting. Crouch and colleagues suggest that interventions to reduce the risk of aggressive parenting could adopt a multimodal strategy to: (i) challenge authoritarian parenting beliefs; (ii) train parenting skills to decrease dependence on harsh methods of discipline; (iii) refocus attributions to reduce hostile intent; and (iv) introduce ways to reduce negative affect and increase cognitive control. As seen in the examples below, the issues highlighted by Crouch and colleagues have been addressed in several recent studies.

The approach taken by Holland and Holden (2016) involved the use of motivational interviewing with mothers of children aged from three to five years. This approach aims to change the mother's attitudes to the use of corporal punishment and future intentions in managing her child's discipline. The motivational interviewing produced positive results and suggests a promising approach to engaging parents who may otherwise remain unmotivated to change.

The act of hitting a child may occur when a parent is anxious, or in a stressful situation, or when other types of violence take place within the home. Grogan-Kaylor et al. (in press) addressed the use of corporal punishment, through an intervention called *The Moms' Empowerment Program*, by mothers who were themselves victims of intimate partner violence. This programme uses group work to reduce stress by helping the women improve their self-esteem and providing resources and support to lower their distress. In addition, the programme expands the mothers' parenting skills, reinforcing positive parenting and the use of non-corporal methods of discipline, thereby enhancing their relationship with their child. At a follow-up of six to eight months the intervention had significantly lowered the rate at which the mothers used corporal punishment.

Altafim and Martins (2016) carried out a systematic review of child maltreatment prevention programmes in which they considered 16 different types of parenting education programme. These programmes, delivered in groups, were designed to promote positive parenting practices, such as the use of non-coercive discipline strategies, and parenting skills such as relationship building with the child. The findings of the review were positive in that "All of the studies showed some improvements in effective parenting strategies post-intervention. Additionally, the programs effectively improved child behavior in 90% of the studies that assessed this outcome" (p. 36).

However, as explained by Miller-Perrin and Perrin (2017), the approach taken to reduce spanking may have to be modified to take account of the political and religious views of the parents.

Schools

With regard to corporal punishment in schools, Gershoff (2017) makes the point that "Legal bans are not sufficient to completely eliminate school corporal punishment. True behavior change by teachers and school administrators will require education about the harms of corporal punishment and about alternative, positive forms of discipline" (p. 234). However, there are relatively few examples of school-based interventions to reduce teachers' use of corporal punishment. Gershoff cites promising work from Africa, including Ghana, Kenya, Mozambique, and Uganda, and makes the point that if corporal punishment is removed from a teacher's repertoire it will need to be replaced with something else. Positive teaching practices to mirror positive parenting practices, perhaps.

4

REDUCING VIOLENCE AT HOME

Family violence

The majority of instances of interpersonal violence within the home are between family members, be they children, adolescents or adults. These acts of violence may serve to develop and reinforce interpersonal violence generally (Labella & Masten, 2018), particularly with a cumulative effect as, for example, when there is violence between adult partners alongside adult abuse of children (Maneta, White, & Mezzacappa, 2017). As with interpersonal violence generally, acts of violence between family members may be associated with alcohol, drug use, and mental health issues (Labrum & Solomon, 2016).

The physical abuse of children

The abuse of children takes several different forms – emotional, physical, and sexual abuse; physical and emotional neglect; and commercial and other forms of exploitation – that may occur concurrently and which have harmful short- and long-term effects for the child (Radford et al., 2016). While it is important to understand each of these different forms of abuse, it is a sad fact that combinations of the types of abuse may occur concurrently, giving rise to poly-victimisation (Debowska et al., 2017).

Two aspects of physical abuse will be considered here: first, an act of commission where the adult harms the child by hitting them with their hand or an object; second, an act of omission where the child's well-being is threatened by physical neglect or by the withdrawal of adult care and attention. Social learning theory offers an explanation for the child's experience of being hit leading to a continuation of violence as the child hits others (Bandura, 1978). However, as Bland and Lambie (2018) suggest, there are several potential explanations for the association between childhood neglect and violent behaviour in adulthood. The explanations range from biological factors, including the effect of neglect upon brain development and childhood psychopathologies as well as physical and social environmental factors.

Physical abuse: hitting

The physically abusive hitting of a child, which may be carried out by either parent, acting individually or together, is distinguished from corporal punishment (although the lines can become blurred) by the degree of force used and the consequent level of harm to the child. The estimates of the prevalence of child physical abuse can, of course, only be based on what is known through official figures and surveys. These official estimates will invariably be underestimates, the true prevalence of abuse is always likely to be greater than the number reported. A survey carried out in the UK found that just under 1 per cent of children, both males and females, over the age of 11 years had experienced severe physical abuse at the hands of their parents (Radford et al., 2016). In the large majority of cases the abuse was carried out by the father. In the USA, Zolotor and Shanahan (2011) state that for male and female children, with the majority under the age of 5 years, "An estimated 381,700 children are physically abused annually for a rate of 5.7 children per 1000" (p. 11).

Zolotor and Shanahan describe the types of injury which can result from physical abuse: the injuries are mainly to the face, head and neck, the abdomen, skeleton (broken bones), and skin (bruises and burns). Physical maltreatment may lead to brain injury and impaired brain development (Crozier et al., 2011). The practice of genital disfigurement of young females, carried out using different types of cutting, leaves lasting physical mutilation (Bennett, 2011).

Shaken Baby Syndrome

It is not uncommon for a baby's behaviour to lead parents to lose control and fiercely shake their child. The pattern of intracranial injuries and broken bones resulting from the shaking gave rise to the notion of an identifiable cluster of injuries with profound consequences for the child's well-being (Caffey, 1972). The familiar pattern of injuries, now called *Shaken Baby Syndrome* (SBS), has attracted a variety of terms: Tang et al. (2008) note other terms: "abusive head trauma, shaken brain trauma, pediatric traumatic brain injury, whiplash shaken infant syndrome, and shaken impact syndrome" (p. 237). As head trauma has various causes other than physical assault, typically an accident of some sort (Kemp, Trefan, & Summers, 2015), so it can present in a variety of ways. There is some debate within the medical profession as to the diagnostic accuracy of the injuries (subdural haematoma, retinal haemorrhages, and encephalopathy) used to detect SBS (Lynøe et al., 2017). In the baby's later life, the brain damage may have profound effects during childhood and adulthood. The seriousness of the harm to the child's head caused by physical abuse may lead to significant financial costs in treating the brain injuries (Boop et al., 2016; Peterson et al., 2014).

In a minority of cases of physical abuse, the level of harm inflicted on the child may result in death, so precipitating further investigation (Parrish et al., 2017). In England and Wales this statutory function is carried out by local Child Death Overview Panels which report directly to central government (Sidebotham et al., 2011). There have been several cases in England where parental physical abuse and neglect of young children has resulted in a great deal of publicity and precipitated public inquiries. The investigations into these cases – including the murders of Maria Colwell in 1973, Jasmine Beckford in 1984, Tyra Henry in 1984, Kimberly Carlile in 1986, Victoria Climbié in 2000 and Peter Connelly in 2007 – led to national changes in child protection practice (Brandon et al., 2008).

In the longer-term, physical abuse in childhood may be associated with a range of adverse outcomes including engaging in both violent and non-violent antisocial behaviour (Braga et al., 2017) and further victimisation in adolescence (Benedini, Fagan, & Gibson, 2016).

Physical abuse: neglect

As Long et al. (2014) note, the term *neglect* is notoriously difficult to define given that it may vary according to its frequency, intentionality, and chronicity. Horwath (2007) makes distinctions between the neglect of the child's medical care, their educational requirements, their nutritional needs, emotional needs, physical needs, and a lack of supervision and guidance. It is tempting to see neglect as a deliberate act, but as Dubowitz (2011) explains:

In most cases, parents do not intend to neglect their children's needs. Rather, problems impair their ability to adequately meet these needs. Even the most egregious cases, such as those where parents appear to willfully deny their children food, probably involve significant parental psychopathology; labeling such instances "intentional" may be simplistic.

(p. 29)

As is often the case, the effects of alcohol misuse, at times in conjunction with low income, contribute to the parental problems associated with neglect (Lloyd & Kepple, 2017).

Given the definitional issues with the concept of neglect, reaching an exact description of chronic neglect is even more problematic. Jones and Logan-Greene (2016) address the issue by suggesting that chronic neglect: "refers to multiple and repeated incidents of child neglect over time. Families experiencing chronic neglect are often facing multiple and complex issues, and children in these families may experience not just neglect but incidents of child physical or sexual abuse" (p. 212).

As with other forms of child abuse within the family, it is impossible to know precisely how many children are neglected. A meta-analysis of data collected in several countries reported by Stoltenborgh, Bakermans-Kranenburg, and van Ijzendoorn (2013) gave an estimate that more than 15 per cent of children suffer from neglect. In the UK, based on data collected in a national survey, Radford et al. (2016) suggest that for children under 11 years of age, there is a 5 per cent incidence of neglect.

Neglect may have both short- and long-term adverse effects on the child. In the short-term neglect can mean the child is deprived of basics such as food and social interaction; in the long-term the child's psychological, emotional, social, and educational development is threatened (Black & Oberlander, 2011). The neglected child is also at an increased risk of other forms of abuse, including physical and sexual abuse (Cohen et al., 2017).

As with "cycles of violence" where violent behaviour is characteristic of successive generations of the same family, it may be that, notwithstanding the methodological complexities in gathering data (Thornberry, Knight, & Lovegrove, 2012), neglect leads to neglect (Bartlett et al., 2017). It follows that attempts to reduce neglect may have benefits not only for the short term in relieving the child's suffering but also in sparing future generations from the misery of neglect.

Physical abuse: prohibition

There are laws prohibiting the maltreatment of children in most countries with various agencies charged with monitoring the welfare of children to ensure their safety and well-being. In England and Wales the task of protecting children from physical abuse and neglect falls primarily to social workers, generally within the structures of Local Authority Children's Services. Thus, guided by the relevant legislation (e.g., *the Children Act*), the role of child protection social workers is to work constructively with families to attempt to resolve their difficulties and keep the family intact. There are other agencies involved in child protection, such as schools and medical services, and it is expected that these agencies will work together in a coordinated manner through multiagency Local Safeguarding Children Boards to ensure the child's best interests are served (HM Government, 2015). The term *safeguarding* is used here in a wider sense than child protection in that it covers protection from maltreatment, prevention of harm to health and development, and seeking to ensure that children live and grow up in a safe environment. Thus, while child protection is an important constituent of safeguarding, the overall aim is to be constructive as well as protective.

When maintaining an intact family is not possible the children will be removed from their home to live either with relatives or in residential care. Although it may be that residential care is not a haven from bullying and violence (Mazzone, Nocentini, & Menesini, 2018). In cases of serious maltreatment the child protection agencies will alert the police to determine if a criminal offence has been committed and whether there are grounds for prosecution. An American study of arrests for child maltreatment reported by Eldred et al. (2016) found that factors such as the age of the child, evidence in addition to the child's testimony and any concurrent offences may influence the decision as to whether to prosecute in a given case. As discussed by Cross and Whitcomb (2017), it is difficult to secure a conviction when the case depends solely on the child's testimony.

Child protection arrangements comparable to those in England and Wales are in place in other countries in the UK and, to a greater or lesser extent, in some other countries. On an international scale, there are organisations such as *Save the Children* and the *United Nations Children's Fund* (*UNICEF*), which endeavour to protect and rescue children from maltreatment.

Physical abuse: treatment

In order to address the relevant risk factors to change the behaviour of parents who physical maltreat their children it is necessary to consider the characteristics of the individuals who commit the abuse.

Abuser characteristics

Stith et al. (2009) conducted a meta-analysis of risks for child maltreatment. The strongest risk factors included the child being perceived as a problem by a parent, a poor parent–child relationship, the parent being quick to anger, and parental and family conflict. Jones and Logan-Greene (2016) note a range of family characteristics associated with physical abuse: these include low income and poverty; other forms of violence within the family such as intimate partner violence; the parent's mental health and drug and alcohol misuse (particularly for neglect), and a lack of social support leading to social isolation. In addition, the abusing parent may have a reduced understanding of their child's needs and poor parenting skills. Finally, in some instances a parent may have a criminal record; however, it is a moot point as to whether this is an independent risk factor for child maltreatment (Austin, 2016). It is as well to state that risk factors are precisely that: characteristics of the people and the situation that make the violence more likely but *not* inevitable. Thus, for example, the presence of protective factors such as parent education and high levels of social support may counter other risk factors (Li, Godinet, & Arnsberger, 2011).

It is evident that some parents are struggling to raise their children in far less than optimum environmental, financial, social, and individual conditions. Indeed, there is a significant association between a family's disposable income and the likelihood of child maltreatment (McLaughlin, 2017). Thus, any attempt to reduce child abuse is arguably more likely to be effective if it can introduce significant social and economic changes, alongside addressing mental health and substance use problems (Patwardhan et al., 2017). In the absence of wide-ranging societal change, there are interventions which may be applied to reduce physical child abuse.

Adolescents

As well as adults, it should not be forgotten that adolescents, male and female, may also be involved in violence within the family as both perpetrators and victims. As perpetrators, adolescents may act violently, at times using weapons (Khan & Cooke, 2013), towards their parents and, most commonly, their siblings (Khan & Cooke, 2008; San Kuay et al., 2016). As with other acts of violence, the adolescent who acts violently towards their sibling may also be violent to others, including animals, as well as experiencing mental health problems (Phillips et al., in press). Finally, the violent adolescent is also likely to be a victim of assault, particularly wounding, to the extent that they require hospital treatment (Rivara et al., 1995).

There are many interventions of varying types aimed at reducing violence among adolescents generally (e.g., Cassidy et al., 2016; Matjasko et al., 2012). However, while there are examples of treatment initiatives (e.g., Caffaro & Conn-Caffaro, 2005; Reid & Donovan, 1990), sibling violence specifically appears not to have received a proportionate degree of attention.

Parent-child treatment

It is important to state at the outset that working with parents who abuse their children typically means taking into account the parents' own histories of abuse alongside any current mental health or substance abuse problems (Simon & Brooks, 2017). In cases where the parents have such issues of their own a clear strategy is needed at the onset as to how to direct resources most effectively (Hartney & Barnard, 2015).

Kolko and Kolko (2011) make several points in a review of interventions to reduce physical child abuse: (1) there are a variety of styles of treatment, with cognitive behaviour therapy and parenting skills training the most popular; (2) treatment has been directed at a wide range of targets such as stress management and anger management; (3) treatment has been used both individually and in combination with physically abused children, and with abusing parents, and the families where abuse occurs.

The individual treatment of physically abused children is typically aimed at helping them to cope with the problems associated with their abuse, such as anxiety and depression, and to maintain peer group relations. Informed by their review of the evidence, Leenarts et al. (2013) suggest that trauma-focused cognitive-behavioural therapy is the optimum approach. While the wellbeing of abused children is imperative, it is clearly preferable to reduce or eliminate the abuse. As is evident from the reviews of the field (e.g., Kolko & Kolko, 2011; Landers et al., 2018; Levey et al., 2017; Poole, Seal, & Taylor, 2014; Runyon et al., 2004; Vlahovicova et al., 2017) a substantial investment has been made in efforts to reduce physical abuse.

A good example of these efforts is to be found in the *ACT Against Violence – Parents Raising Safe Kids Programme* (ACT-PRSK) developed by the American Psychological Association. As Knox, Burkhart, and Hunter (2011) explain: "Through ACT-PRSK, groups of parents and caregivers of young children are trained in effective parenting, including nonviolent discipline, child development, anger management and social problem-solving skills, effects of media on children, and methods to protect children from exposure to violence" (pp. 57–58). Knox and colleagues report an evaluation conducted with 117 caregivers, 92 of whom completed the programme. They found that the programme was successful in reducing harsh parenting behaviours and attitudes and improving parents' use of constructive methods to teach their children nonviolent social skills. The programme was also successful in reducing the frequency of physical violence towards the children. This positive finding was replicated by Knox and Burkhart (2014) who also reported that older parents were more likely to complete the programme.

However, not all the evaluative research has been of the same quality. It is generally taken that a randomised control trial (RCT) is the premium research design providing the highest level of internal validity. Levey et al. (2017) carried out a systematic review of RCTs (eight in all, seven American and one UK) which investigated interventions intended to reduce child abuse (neglect, psychical, and sexual abuse) in high risk families. They cautiously concluded that the evidence "indicates promising possibilities for decreasing child abuse" (p. 55).

A UK study by Barlow et al. (2007) used an RCT to compare the standard service given by health visitors with the standard service augmented by the Family Partnership Model which promotes positive interactions between parent and child. The study showed positive effects of the enhanced service but the magnitude fell short of significance. As Barlow and colleagues suggest, this null finding may reflect a lack of power in the execution of the research; or that the intervention does not work, meaning that it should therefore be disregarded. Barlow and colleagues used Intention to Treat (ITT) analysis which may also explain their non-significant findings. The use of ITT analysis in programme evaluation is discussed in detail in Chapter 7.

Following their systematic review of the literature, Poole et al. (2014) make note of the strong effects of the American *Triple P System* (*Positive Parenting Program*). As described by Prinz et al. (2009):

This multilevel system includes five intervention levels of increasing intensity and narrowing population reach. The system was designed to enhance parental competence, and prevent or alter dysfunctional parenting practices, thereby reducing an important set of family risk factors both for child maltreatment and for children's behavioral and emotional problems.

(p. 2)

The Prinz et al. outcome study is notable for being a population trial, rather than a clinical trial, with the programme disseminated to an estimated 8,883 to 13,560 families across nine American counties. It is evident that a great deal of organisational effort took place in order to recruit and train those responsible for the delivery of the programme. In addition, the process of data collection, including telephone contact with participants, would have been both expensive and time-consuming. Any positive gains are not to be won cheaply.

Another approach to reducing violence within the home lies in the use of a family group conference (FGC). As Dijkstra et al. (2016) explain:

FGC is a decision-making model that focuses on the family and its social network, and which aims to gather all parties with an interest in the wellbeing of a child and his or her family to make a family group plan that teaches and supports active responsibility.

(p. 101)

Hollinshead et al. (2017) note that Family Group Conferencing (FGC) has grown in popularity and that there are now several variations on the theme. In some countries, including Ireland, the Netherlands and New Zealand, it is legally required that where appropriate families are offered the opportunity to formulate their own recovery plan which may include carrying out a FGC.

A lesson to be taken from the popularity of FGC, which will doubtless have involved a great deal of practitioner training, financial cost, and family time, is that popularity does not guarantee effectiveness. A Swedish study reported by Sundell and Vinnerljung (2004) involved a 3-year follow-up of 97 children involved with the Child Protective Services (CPS) who had taken part in FGCs compared with 142 children who had received the traditional service. They reported that FGCs had a negligible effect: "Contrary to the expectations, significantly more FGC-children were re-referred to the CPS authority during the 3-year follow-up period, thus indicating less stability in the lives of the FGC-children during the follow-up period" (p. 282).

Now, while Sundell and Vinnerljung rightly point to several explanations for the lack of effect of FGCs, their study proved to be a forerunner for a wave of similar null findings. For example, an American study by Hollinshead et al. (2017) failed to find an effect of FGCs on outcomes such as re-referrals to child welfare services or the need for placements outside the family home. A meta-analysis of 14 studies of the effects of FGCs, involving 88,495 participants, led Dijkstra et al. (2016) to conclude that: "The findings of the present study indicate that, overall, FGC does not outperform regular care in terms of less child maltreatment, reduction of out-of-home placements and less involvement of youth care" (p. 106). The obvious question to ask is why given the lack of empirical support do FGCs remain in use? The role of evidence to inform choices in interventions is addressed in Chapter 7.

Reducing Shaken Baby Syndrome

One approach to reducing the likelihood of SBS is to educate new parents, using video presentations, written material and discussion, about the dangers of shaking their infant. There is evidence to suggest that education can be successful in lowering the rate of SBS (Altman et al., 2011; Dias et al., 2005; Shanahan et al., 2011). The baby's crying can be a trigger for shaking and parents may need to learn to cope with their frustration, particularly when they are stressed or awoken from sleep. The American PURPLE programme (**P**eak of Crying, **U**nexpected, **R**esists Soothing, **P**ained Face, **L**ong-lasting, **E**vening or late afternoon) was applied in a multi-site study in London and Ontario, Canada (Charyk Stewart et al., 2011). In addition to the educational programme, parents also received home visits from Registered Nurses. The evaluation showed that parents said they found the programme to be helpful and their knowledge did significantly improve. As Charyk Stewart and colleagues state, the critical test is "Whether this program will ultimately lead to decreases in the incidence of SBS in our region has yet to be determined, but the positive findings presented herein are promising" (pp. 1806–1807). Ornstein et al. (2016) reported that PURPLE both increased the knowledge about crying for first-time mothers and significantly reduced the rate of abusive head trauma.

In England the *Coping with Crying* programme aims to reduce injuries to babies, including those resulting from shaking. The evaluation of *Coping with Crying* showed that in times of stress parents were behaving in a more positive manner towards their children and seeking help as necessary (Coster, Bryson, & Purdon 2016). However, as was also the case in the Canadian research discussed above, Coster and colleagues were unable to demonstrate a reduction in injuries given the methodological problems set by the low base rates for injuries of this kind.

Intimate Partner Violence

There are several terms in common usage, such as *family violence, violence against women* and *domestic violence*, which are used interchangeably. These terms are inclusive of several different forms of violence, such as child and elder abuse, and violence both inside and outside the home. The World Health Organization's report on violence and health (Krug et al., 2002) offered a definition of this specific form of violence: "Any behavior within an intimate relationship that causes physical, psychological or sexual harm to those in the relationship" (p. 89). This definition of Intimate Partner Violence (IPV) encompasses a variety of acts of violence such as physical aggression, emotional and psychological abuse, sexual coercion, stalking, and acts of social control such as isolation from friends or extended family.

The various acts of violence within an intimate relationship may have a range of short- and long-term adverse physical and psychosocial consequences, often the same as those associated with trauma (Pill, Day, & Mildred, 2017), and in some cases can result in death (Caman et al., 2017). Once again it is impossible to give exact figures on prevalence but there is no doubt that IPV is endemic. Drawing on the World Health Organization report, Thackeray and Randell (2011) state that:

> What is clear, however, is that IPV is a global health crisis. A review of 48 population-based surveys from around the world found that between 10% and 69% of women report being physically assaulted by an intimate partner at some point in their lives.
>
> *(p. 23)*

As with other acts of violence, IPV is a criminal offence and therefore is subject to the attention of the police and courts. As is the case with many other acts of violence, IPV is associated with high levels of recidivism (López-Ossorio et al., 2017; Richards et al., 2014) and therefore there is much to be gained in human, social, and financial costs, from reducing IPV. A particularly poignant possibility with a reduction in IPV lies in saving an unborn child from injury or death (O'Reilly, Beale, & Gillies, 2010).

At this point it is worth clarifying terminology. The terms *victim* and *survivor*, sometimes used interchangeably, are used here in the sense that at the time of the offence and its immediate aftermath the person is a victim; as they seek to cope with and recover after the event, so they become a survivor.

IPV prohibition

The physical abuse of an intimate partner is a criminal offence, prohibited by law, and may be dealt with through prosecution of the aggressor in the civil and criminal courts. The legislation may differ from country to country in two ways: first, with regard to the definition of IPV; second, the exact type of offence which has been committed. In the UK, IPV is viewed in the context of a wider definition of domestic violence: thus, Strickland and Allen (2017) state that "Any incident or pattern of incidents of controlling, coercive or threatening behaviour, violence or abuse between those aged 16 or over who are or have been intimate partners or family members regardless of gender or sexuality" (p. 4). This definition covers both heterosexual and homosexual partnerships inclusive of male and female victims within both types of partnership. It is also the case that definitions may shift over time within the same country: for example, in England and Wales the Home Office has issued guidance on changes in the definition of domestic violence and abuse specifically concerning young people (Home Office, 2013).

As listed in the *Domestic Abuse Guidelines for Prosecutors* (available on the Crown Prosecution Service website), there are a range of potential offences associated with domestic violence, from common assault and wounding to grievous bodily harm and rape, depending on the particulars of the case. When there is a prosecution involving adults it may be heard in Specialist Domestic Violence Courts. These courts seek to co-ordinate the work of the police, the legal profession, the probation service and specialist support organisations.

Domestic Violence Protection Orders

The introduction in England and Wales in 2014 of the Domestic Violence Protection Order (DVPO) enabled the court to begin the process of reducing IPV. As explained in a Home Office (n.d.) publication, DVPOs encompass two steps: (1) When the police believe that domestic violence remains a risk they may issue an emergency non-molestation and eviction notice, called a Domestic Violence Protection Notice (DVPN), which is effective from the time it is issued; (2) within 48 hours of the perpetrator being served with a DVPN the police make an application to a magistrates' court for a DVPO.

The court may issue a DVPO which is effective for a minimum of 14 days and a maximum of 28 days. A breach of a DVPO is punishable by a fine up to £5000 or a maximum prison sentence of two months.

Kelly et al. (2013) reported an evaluation of DVPOs in Greater Manchester, West Mercia and Wiltshire police forces. They cautiously conclude that DVPOs were effective in reducing the number of incidents when compared to the standard procedure of police arrest such that there were "On average, 2.6 fewer repeat incidents of domestic violence per victim-survivor compared to around 1.6 fewer incidents" (p. 6).

The tactic of legally prohibiting contact between the aggressor and the victim is a form of situational management which is also evident in attempts to reduce domestic violence. Prenzler and Fardell (2017) suggest that there are five types of security applications which can be used: (1) GPS tracking of the offender's whereabouts; (2) shelters which offer secure accommodation to victims; (3) home security where the offender leaves the home and home security is increased by installing measures such as alarms, security lighting, and door and window locks, finally, an emergency mobile telephone may be provided; (4) a one-touch pendant personal duress alarm, similar to the emergency systems for the elderly, can be used when a telephone is unavailable (offenders may cut telephone lines) to alert a call centre that assistance is needed at a given address; (5) combined home security and duress alarms.

As Prenzler and Fardell point out, these security systems have been used in various combinations as well as in conjunction with other measures such as protection orders. While evaluation of these security systems is less than straightforward given the problems with data collection, forming control groups and so on, there are positive indications that increasing security can lower rates of assault.

If the home cannot be made safe then the alternative is for survivors, both men and women, to leave the family home. The act of leaving the home may place the survivor, sometimes with their children, at grave risk of homelessness (Baker et al., 2010). In the first instance the need is for a safe place, a refuge, to enable the survivor to gather her forces. In the UK, for example, the charity *Refuge* is responsible for a network of emergency provision across the country: their website states that:

> A refuge is a safe house for women and children escaping domestic violence. The address is confidential and no men are allowed in the building. A refuge is a place where women can be sure they are safe, and where they can access emotional and practical support from staff who understand what they have been through.

Newberry (2017) notes that household pets can be forgotten or abandoned in cases of domestic violence. Indeed, some victims find solace in their pets and refuse to leave their home to go to a safe place if they have to leave their pet behind. However, some refuges will accept pets or arrange for their safe-keeping with a pet fostering service until they can be reunited with their owners. Once the initial crisis is over the survivor may move from an emergency refuge to transitional housing then to permanent accommodation as their survival unfolds.

It is possible that the aggressor will take part in a treatment programme, either in the prison or in the community, intended to reduce IPV. Of course, treatment programmes are available for the survivors of domestic and well as other forms of violence (O'Brien & Macy, 2016). It is also possible that, as with other forms of violence, IPV may be associated with issues such as anger (Ruddle, Pina, & Vasquez, 2010) and excessive use of alcohol (Foran & O'Leary, 2008). These issues will need to be dealt with either as part of a treatment programme or as an adjunct to it. It cannot be assumed that effective treatments will easily cross cultural boundaries. As Mallory et al. (2016) show, the risk factors for IPV vary across cultures, indicating that an effective treatment in one setting may not generalise to another setting.

IPV treatment

Dobash and Dobash (2001) make the point that before the 1970s men who were violent to their intimate partner were not perceived as offenders and were seldom charged and prosecuted. This situation began to change in the 1980s, as Feder, Wilson, and Austin (2008) explain, "The idea of counseling male domestic violence offenders developed directly out of the women's shelter movement where advocates, working with battered women, realized that the only way to stop the cycle of violence was to change the behavior of the abuser" (p. 4). The focus of these interventions was twofold: first, men should confront their sexist beliefs and accept responsibility for their abusive acts; second, the development of new prosocial behaviours through anger management and social and communication skills training. In the USA these interventions became known as *Batterer Intervention Programmes* of which the Duluth model is one of the best known (Pence, 1983).

As may be anticipated, some of the perpetrators proved difficult to work with and there were high dropout rates from batterer programmes. The next step was for the courts to make participation in treatment compulsory:

> In 1980, California became the first state to mandate treatment for men convicted of domestic violence .... Judges also saw this intervention as providing an alternative to prison (important during this period of extensive overcrowding) while simultaneously holding out the hope of breaking the cycle of violence.
>
> *(Feder & Wilson, 2005, p. 241)*

In the USA IPV court-mandated batterer intervention programmes remain in use; as Mills, Barocas, and Ariel (2013) state, "[h]undreds of thousands of convicted offenders are mandated to receive this treatment each year by U.S. judges" (p. 67).

In the UK, as Bowen (2011) notes, the first group programmes within the criminal justice system for men were developed in Scotland in the 1970s. This innovation set a trend both for the development of new pro-grammes and their wider use in several parts of England including Cheshire, London, and the West Midlands. The developments in the UK were in keeping with practice in Europe. A survey carried out by Hamilton, Koehler, and Lösel (2012) looked at 54 programmes for perpetrators of domestic violence delivered in 19 European countries. These programmes were principally cognitive-behavioural, psychodynamic, or profeminist in orientation; some programmes were government funded, others by client fees; most programmes were mainly for men and women, some were just for men and one was solely for women perpetrators. However, there was a dearth of high quality programme evaluations.

The second stage of the survey considered the state of the evidence from these 54 programmes (Akoensi et al., 2012). There were only 12 programme evaluations in place and for these evaluations there was limited documentation on programme methods and procedures and little evidence of the degree of programme integrity. The evaluations were not heterogeneous, encompassing a range of designs, method and types of data collection, and length of follow-up period. Akoensi and colleagues conclude that "Our findings resonate with the conclusions of reviews from North America, namely, that we do not yet know what works best, for whom, and under what circumstances" (p. 1220). This conclusion is in broad sympathy with the reviews of the outcome evidence (Babcock, Green, & Robie, 2004; Feder & Wilson, 2005; Feder, Wilson, & Austin, 2008): for example, Feder, Wilson, and Austin (2008) state that their meta-analysis "does not offer strong support that court-mandating treatment to misdemeanor domestic violence offenders reduces the likelihood of further reassault" (p. 18).

The extant evaluations have considered a range of outcome variables from the perpetrator's psychological and social functioning (Sheehan, Thakor, & Stewart, 2012) to changes in the assaulted woman's positive parenting (Howell et al., 2015). A fall in assaultive behaviour is a fundamental outcome measure in terms of reducing violence (Lila et al., 2014; Sartin, Hansen, & Huss, 2006). While the evidence for the effectiveness of treatment programmes in reducing violence is not compelling, this failing may be a function of an ineffective programme, or poor programme implementation and maintenance (Davis & Auchter, 2010), or an unsound evaluation. With respect to the final point, the evaluation of treatment programmes to reduce IPV is not a straightforward task. There are several obstacles facing evaluative research: (i) the impossibility of taking into account unreported instances of partner violence; (ii) it may be highly difficult to access police call-out data for reasons of confidentiality (a point which, as Bowen notes, is true in the UK even for government sponsored research); (iii) it can be problematic to gather sufficient data given problems such as high rates of programme attrition, obtaining comparable control groups, and in employing an experimental, rather than quasi-experimental, design (Dobash & Dobash, 2000; Gondolf, 2004).

Nonetheless, the growth in knowledge about programme evaluation generally and interventions to reduce IPV specifically has led to a new generation of studies (Mills, Barocas, & Ariel, 2013). A feature of these new generation of studies is their use of ever-more sophisticated styles of analysis to compensate for procedural issues. Hasisi et al. (2016), for example, evaluated a prison-based programme with multiple treatment modalities for offenders convicted of domestic violence. The perennial problem with non-randomised designs is that, despite case matching, there may be differences between treatment and control groups. Hasisi and colleagues used the technique of propensity score matching whereby the variables that predict selection for treatment, risk, criminal background and so on, are used with a pool of prisoners so that each has a propensity score. A propensity score, with a range of 0 to 1, is the likelihood of a prisoner participating in the treatment. When a prisoner is selected their "twin" with the identical or closest propensity score becomes a member of the control group. The evaluation showed significant differences in recidivism between those participating in the programme and the control group.

Children's exposure to IPV

Children living in a home where IPV occurs may be at risk of neglect and physical abuse. Alongside this risk it has become apparent that children, from infants to adolescents, may be harmed in both the short- and long-term by observing and being exposed to IPV within their home. The child's observations may take several forms, ranging from being told about the violence, to seeing or hearing the violence, or trying to intervene (see Holden, 2003). The effects on the child of observing familial violence are not dissimilar from those found in physically abused children and include PTSD symptomatology, such as anxiety and emotional dysfunction, alongside social and behavioural problems (Kitzmann et al., 2003; Van Horn & Lieberman, 2011). In later life there is a strong association between witnessing familial violence and a recidivistic violent criminal career (Fowler, Cantos, & Miller, 2016).

Children's exposure to IPV: prohibition

As knowledge has grown of the effects on children of witnessing violence in their home so legislative changes have taken place. In the UK, the Adoption and Children Act 2002 included the child's "impairment suffered from seeing or hearing the ill-treatment of another" as an extension to the definition of significant harm. In light of this move welfare policy and practice changed accordingly.

In the first instance it is necessary for practitioners to determine whether the child needs immediate medical care. The level of risk of harm to the child is then assessed and if this is judged to be high then steps to safeguard the child, as with procedures in child protection from physical abuse and neglect, are brought into play. The exact nature of welfare policies varies in different parts of the world but the aim is always to protect the child from harm (Cross et al., 2012).

Children's exposure to IPV: treatment

The *National Safe Start Initiative for Children Exposed to Violence* is an American initiative intended to reduce the harm experienced by children exposed to violence in their home. This ambitious programme took the form of a menu of possible interventions rather than a preordained set of procedures as seen in some intervention programmes. As Hickman et al. (2013) explain:

> All [programmes] included a therapeutic component, and in some cases the modality offered by the site varied by child age, with dyadic or family therapy for caregivers of younger children and group therapy for older children. Most programs also offered case management, and some

established or enhanced interagency service coordination for families. Some of the programs had other intervention components, such as family or child-level advocacy, parent/caregiver groups, or other services (e.g., assessment of family needs or inhome safety assessments). The intervention setting also varied with services delivered in families' homes, clinics, shelters, social service agency offices, or Head Start classrooms. The intervention length ranged from 3 months to more than 1 year, though most were 6 months. Eligible child age varied but most programs enrolled only young children and their caregivers/families.

(p. 303)

Hickman and colleagues looked at the effectiveness of the intervention, in terms of improved outcomes for both caregivers and children, using pooled data gathered from nine sites. The initial allocation of referrals to intervention or control group was randomised giving a randomised control trial (RCT): the advantages and disadvantages of RCTs in treatment evaluation are discussed in Chapter 7. The results failed to show that the intervention had any substantial effects on a range of outcome measures, such as PTSD symptoms and caregiver–child relationship, for either the caregivers or the children. Hickman and colleagues offer a range of possible explanations for this finding, including low dosage in the treatment condition (caused by dropout) and the alternative treatments received by those in the control group.

Thompson and Trice-Black (2012) make the case that given their welfare and counselling resources the school provides an ideal setting to work with children who have witnessed violence in the home. They describe a variety of approaches to this type of work, including play therapy and group-based interventions, which can be applied to ameliorate the effects of observing violence. The evidence for the effectiveness of these school-based approaches would be a welcome addition to the literature.

An et al. (2017) report an evaluation of a group-based intervention, the *Mantra Program*, for adolescents who have been exposed to family violence. The participants move through a 10-stage programme which includes sessions such as defining abuse and understanding power, responsibility for abuse and family changes, and conflict resolution style and anger. The intervention aimed to help improve the participants' understanding of domestic violence, the effects it may have on them, and how they could progress towards a healthy future. The evaluation showed that the programme had a positive impact on knowledge and understanding of domestic violence as well as on symptoms of depression; however, changes in anxiety and behaviour were at best only marginal. An and colleagues suggest that the addition of cognitive-behavioural components to the programme may make it more effective in the future. Thus, the *Mantra Program* provides an excellent example of using the extant research to construct an intervention to a multi-faceted problem then using the evaluative findings to attempt to improve the effectiveness of the programme.

5

REDUCING SEXUAL VIOLENCE

As sexual violence against children and adults is a criminal act it follows that the legal points covered in the previous chapter are germane in this context. However, unlike physical violence, the eradication of some types of sexual offence is possible: for example, changes in the age of consent can eliminate some sexual crimes. There are a range of interventions, including risk awareness training and sex offender treatment, encompassing medical as well as psychological intervention, which may be used with this population.

The exact legal definition of sexual violence varies from country to country. There is a range of sexual offences defined in UK law, classified under five broad headings: (1) *Non-Consensual Offences* such as rape and sexual assault; (2) *Offences Involving Ostensible Consent* such as offences involving children or vulnerable adults; (3) *Preparatory Offences* including sexual grooming and administering a substance with intent; (4) *Other Offences* such as sex with an adult relative, exposure, voyeurism, intercourse with an animal and sexual penetration of a corpse; (5) *Exploitation Offences* involving indecent photographs of children and abuse of children through prostitution and pornography (Sentencing Guidelines Secretariat, 2007). The question of why sexually assaultive behaviour takes place is a far-reaching and complex issue at individual, social, and cultural levels. There is, as Lussier and Cale (2016) note, four generations of research and theory across a range of disciplines given to attempting to understand sexually violent behaviour towards women.

The concern here is with sexually violent contact offences against children below the age of consent and with sexually violent contact offences against adults. It should be added that while it is expedient to separate sex offenders into those who offend against children and those who offend against adults, the real world is not so obliging. There is a group of sex offenders who cross boundaries of *age*, committing offences against both adults and children; or *gender* with offences against females and males; or *relationship* with offences against family members, acquaintances, and strangers (Heil, Ahlmeyer, & Simons, 2003; Kaseweter et al., 2016; Stephens et al., 2017). Cann, Friendship, and Gozna (2007) estimate that, based on a sample of 1,345 adult male sex offenders in English and Welsh prisons, that almost one-quarter of their sample had a criminal history that showed evidence of crossover. Of the crossover offenders, about one-half crossed the relationship boundary, with the remainder similarly divided across age and gender. A much smaller group, about 5% of the total sample had crossed two boundaries, most commonly age and relationship; and seven of the 1,345 sex offenders had crossed all three boundaries. The crossover offenders were of a significantly higher risk of reoffending than the non-crossover offenders.

There are commonalities between offences against children and against adults such as the setting in which the abuse occurs. As with other forms of interpersonal violence, alcohol is likely to be involved in sexual abuse. Thus, for example, Abbey (2002) suggests that alcohol is involved in about one-half of sexual assaults in the college student population. The role of alcohol in sexual abuse is complex given its effects upon physiological, psychological, and social process before, during, and after the assault (Lorenz & Ullman, 2016).

Sexual abuse of children

There are a range of definitions of child sexual abuse including legal definitions and statements from august bodies such as the Council of Europe (Lalor & McElvaney, 2010). While it may be expedient to consider different types of child abuse individually, the fact is that more than one type of abuse can occur either concurrently or sequentially (Witt et al., 2016). In the UK Radford et al. (2016) found that for the children under 11 years of age in their sample the rate of sexual abuse was 0.3 per cent. This figure rose over time to 1.4 per cent of the sample by age 18 years. Across all the age groups higher rates of sexual abuse were reported by females than by males. Radford and colleagues also found that when compared to children who had not been abused, the risk of sexual abuse was significantly higher for children, particularly those aged between 11 and 17 years, who had experienced physical violence from someone other than a parent or guardian. Thus, the experience of physical abuse acts to heighten the risk of later sexual abuse, with girls at greater overall risk than boys.

The consequences of sexual abuse can be profound for the developing child in terms of their mental health (Amado, Arce, & Herraiz, 2015; Fergusson, McLeod, & Horwood, 2013; Turner et al., 2017), an increased risk of further victimisation (Papalia et al., 2017a) and behavioural problems including violent and sexual criminal acts (Papalia et al., 2017b). Sexual abuse can happen at any point between very early childhood and adolescence and may have different consequences for the physical and mental health of males and females (Daigneault et al., 2017; de Jong & Dennison, 2017). Alongside emotional and behavioural disruption (Schreier, Pogue, & Hansen, 2017), the siblings of the sexually abused child may also be at risk of an elevated risk of offending (de Jong & Dennison, 2017). The deleterious effects of childhood abuse may become manifest in adult life in areas such as education, employment, relationships and parenting (de Jong et al., 2015).

The sexual abuse of older children is particularly prevalent among those adolescents who are vulnerable because of homelessness, drug use, imprisonment, and through working in and being exploited by the sex industry (Finkel & Sapp, 2011). In addition, as well as the sex industry, children can be exploited sexually in other ways such as via the internet through dissemination of child pornography, engagement in chat rooms, and cybersex (Broughton, 2011) and when in residential care (Allroggen et al., 2017).

There is a substantial list of risk factors associated with the various forms of child sexual abuse: Whitaker et al. (2008) suggested six classes of risk factor, family factors, externalising behaviours, internalising behaviours, social deficits, sexual problems, and attitudes/beliefs, with numerous individual risk factors within each type. The range of potential risk factors is expanded when adolescent perpetrators of child sexual abuse are included (Letourneau et al., 2017). It is impossible for any one approach to bringing about change to address all the risks, so for maximum efficacy several agents of change are required across the full spectrum of cultural, social, familial, and individual factors.

Child sexual abuse: prohibition

It is, of course, illegal to engage in any sexual practice with a minor and detection, arrest, and prosecution can lead to a long jail sentence. It is unlikely that all acts, even the majority of acts, of child sexual abuse are detected. The attempts to detect child sexual abuse, thereby reducing child sexual abuse, will be influenced by the nature of the abuser's behaviour. This point is exemplified by some of the efforts made to uncover child exploitation.

Child exploitation

Child exploitation, including sexual exploitation, was once thought to be focused on girls but it has become apparent that boys can also be drawn into this world (Mitchell et al., 2017; Moynihan et al., 2018). Reducing the harm brought about by exploitation of young people has become a pressing contemporary issue. Bourke, Prestridge, and Malterer (2016) describe an American multi-agency strategy, the *Interdiction for the Protection of Children Program* (IPC), designed to reduce child exploitation. The strategy under-pinning the programme involved training traffic law enforcement officers to improve their performance in three areas: (i) to identify high risk individuals with regard to children; (ii) to identify those children being trafficked, exploited, or abused; (iii) to detect at-risk children such as those who have been abducted or who have run away from home or care. Bourke and colleagues explain that the programme arose from the observation that:

> 57,472 reports of children were recorded as having gone missing in Texas in 2008. In that year DPS [Directorate of Public Safety] troopers initiated 2,891,441 traffic stops, during which they recovered 1812 stolen automobiles, seized 69,063.99 lb of marijuana, arrested 12,615 wanted fugitives, and seized $16,351,102 related to illegal activity. Despite the nearly three million contact stops, not one missing or at risk child was reported rescued.
>
> *(p. 70)*

Thus, the training was designed to sharpen the awareness of the law enforcement officers to enable them to detect and intervene when they suspected child exploitation. The IPC programme has now been applied in several US states.

In Texas the programme showed positive results in two domains. First, while stopping vehicles for investigation, the IPC-trained officers detected several hundred known sex offenders and so were able to verify whether these offenders were in compliance with their legal registration requirements. Second, over 200 children were rescued from abduction or exploitation and the number saved from abuse continues to rise. Given the paradox that child exploitation takes place on a global scale (Dubowitz, 2017) but there is a poverty of effective strategies to reduce its frequency it is evident that programmes such as IPC must have a role to play.

Child sexual abuse: prevention

Patno (2011) makes the point that there are various approaches to the prevention of child sexual abuse: (i) to concentrate on the effectiveness of *external* agencies, such as the criminal justice system which can, for example, place legal restrictions on the movement of known child sex offenders (Colombino et al., 2017); (ii) to work with families by teaching parents about grooming and internet predators; (iii) teaching children how to detect and avoid potentially abusive situations and individuals; (iv) change the psychological functioning of the abuser. Mendelson and Letourneau (2015) make a similar point in suggesting that preventative efforts can concentrate on different levels of social organisation from the individual to family, neighbourhood, and the wider cultural context.

The application of preventative strategies across these levels of social organisation leads to the approaches to prevent child sexual abuse shown in Table 5.1.

Those who sexually (and physically) abuse children will seek to take advantage of any situation where there are groups of children. A typical scenario is that the offender gains a position of authority such as a teacher, sports coach, scout leader, and so on, then uses that position to identify vulnerable children and groom them for later sexual abuse. There are various external agencies who may become involved in preventing child sexual abuse. The obvious candidates are parts of the criminal justice system, action groups, schools, sports clubs, and religious organisations. As discussed below there are strategies which may be applied with some or all of these agencies to reduce the likelihood of sexual assault.

External agencies

Criminal justice system

The principal role of the criminal justice system is to detect crimes, prosecute, and deliver the appropriate penalty. The detection of crimes and

TABLE 5.1 Organisational scheme for preventative strategies for reduction of child sexual abuse (after Mendelson & Letourneau, 2015)

Justice system restrictions	Criminal justice system curtailment of liberty, e.g., prison and probation.
Advocacy and media campaigns	These campaigns are intended to raise public awareness. In the UK, NSPCC is an example of a body who might use the media in this way.
Youth-serving organisations	There are places where young people gather, such as sports clubs, youth clubs, and churches where preventative strategies may be appropriate.
School-based programmes	Schools may provide the setting to teach young people how to avoid sexual abuse, both directly and online, and how to respond if necessary.
Treatment of offenders	The application of psychological treatment to known sex offenders to reduce the likelihood of reoffending.
Treatment of victims	Treatment of victims may, as well as alleviating the pain of abuse, reduce the risk of the victim becoming an offender in later life.

gathering evidence to enable a prosecution to proceed is the responsibility of the police. In a small number of instances police officers are involved in inappropriate sexual conduct.

Police

Stinson, Liederbach, and Freiburger (2012) reviewed 771 sex-related arrest cases over the period 2005 to 2008 involving 555 American police officers. The most common sexual offence was rape, against both adult and child female victims, with the majority of victims under the age of 18 years. A similar study by Stinson et al. (2015) reviewed 548 arrest cases involving police officers in the District of Columbia, USA. They found that the majority of sexual crimes by the police officers, all male, involved a female victim, and children accounted for over 40 per cent of cases.

There is a correspondingly small number of cases of sexual misconduct by British police officers (National Police Chiefs Council, 2017). A report from

Her Majesty's Inspectorate of Constabulary recorded 117 public complaints involving allegations (not all of which will be proven) of sexual assault against police officers in England and Wales between March 2015 and March 2016 (HMIC, 2017).

Multi-Agency Public Protection Arrangements (MAPPA)

The criminal justice system can have a preventative aspect in legally restricting sex offenders' access to children. The incarceration of child sex offenders is an obvious example of this type of prevention. However, the imprisonment of offenders serves to protect children only for the length of sentence. There remains the issue of what can be done to prevent the offence in the first place and to reduce the chances of known offenders committing further offences after their release from custody.

The introduction of Multi-Agency Public Protection Arrangements (MAPPA) in 2001 was an attempt by the criminal justice system in England and Wales to manage the risk posed by some offenders in the community (Kemshall & Maguire, 2001; Ministry of Justice, 2016). There are offenders of all ages in the community who are a risk of inflicting serious harm on other people. These offenders may engage the attention of several agencies such as police, social services, psychiatric services and the probation service. To increase the efficacy of communication between these various agencies with a view to managing risk, MAPPA are guided by the categories and associated levels of management outlined in Table 5.2. Similar systems to MAPPA are in place in Northern Ireland and in Scotland and encompass young as well as adult offenders (Sutherland & Jones, 2008).

Wood et al. (2007) reported an evaluation of the effectiveness of MAPPA arrangements. The findings were positive in terms of the process of controlling offenders' movements and encouraging them to engage in rehabilitative programmes. However, the recommendations presented by Wood and colleagues specifically stressed the need for progress in the management and treatment of child sex offenders. A later Ministry of Justice evaluation (Peck, 2011) looked at the 1- and 2-year reconviction rates of seven annual cohorts (with about 9,500 offenders per cohort) of offenders released from custody between 1998 and 2004 who were eligible for MAPPA. When compared to 1998–2000 there was a fall in reconviction rates, by just under 3 per cent, among sexual and violent offenders released between 2001 and 2004. It appears that MAPPA arrangements are achieving their aim of managing risk and improving public safety.

TABLE 5.2. MAPPA categories and levels of management (after Ministry of Justice, 2016)

MAPPA categories	*Category 1.* Registered sexual offenders previously convicted of a serious sexual offence, including rape and sexual assault, and who are required to notify the police of their name, address and other personal details, and any changes.
	Category 2. Violent offenders convicted of a serious violent offence and sentenced to custody for 12 months or more, or who have been detained under a hospital order. This category includes those sexual offenders without the notification requirements which apply in Category 1.
	Category 3. Dangerous offenders who do not fall into Categories 1 or 2 but have been assessed as currently posing a risk of serious harm and who may require continued surveillance. High profile cases in the media may fall into this category.
Levels of management	*Level 1: Ordinary Agency Management.* This level is applied to those offenders covered by the usual management arrangements for the lead supervising agency. Information may be exchanged between agencies, such as police and probation services, but formal multi-agency meetings are not required.
	Level 2: Active Multi-Agency Management. These are offenders who require the active involvement of several agencies. The risk management plans are monitored by regular multi-agency public protection meetings.
	Level 3: Active Multi-Agency Management. As with offenders at Level 2, several agencies will be involved: in addition, the risk of Level 3 offenders requires the involvement of senior staff from the agencies involved to authorise the use of additional resources when necessary.

Advocacy groups

The agencies concerned with the prevention of child sexual abuse will vary from country to country. In the UK there are various agencies involved in prevention: Local Authority Children Services are the lead agency alongside several voluntary agencies and charities. These voluntary agencies, such as the National Society for the Prevention of Cruelty to Children (NSPCC),

Childline, and Action for Children, offer a range of services and are familiar for their media campaigns which seek to educate and inform the public about the risks and consequences of abuse.

A major obstacle facing preventative work in child sexual abuse (as well as other forms of abuse) lies in what Jeremiah, Quinn, and Alexis (2017) call "the culture of silence". A culture of silence is where any or all of those involved, the victim and their family and friends, contrive to remain quiet about the abuse. As Jeremiah, Quinn, and Alexis report, there are several reasons why those involved in the abuse maintain silence including fear of further victimisation, shame, and a normalisation and social acceptance of violence.

Schools

An example of developmental crime prevention in schools is provided by Averdijk et al., (2016) with a randomised trial, conducted in Zurich, Switzerland, involving 56 schools and 1,675 children aged 7 and 8 years, of the social-emotional skills programme Promoting Alternative Thinking Strategies (PATHS) and the cognitive-behavioural Triple P parenting programme. A follow-up when the children were 13 and 15 years looked at 13 outcome measures related to antisocial behaviour delinquency, and substance use. There were just two notable effects: (1) the PATHS programme led to a reduction in contacts with the police compared with controls; (2) there was a difference in conflict resolution skills in the combined PATHS Triple P condition but, contrary to prediction, the treatment group were *less* proficient than the controls.

While schools have potential opportunities to detect abuse, such as regular contact with the child and observing changes in their behaviour, they do not always capitalise on these advantages (Greco, Guilera, & Pereda, 2017). Walsh et al. (2015) carried out a systematic review of school-based programmes intended to prevent child sexual abuse. The review encompassed 24 individual studies with 5802 school children aged 5 to 18 years in primary and secondary schools in Canada, China, Germany, Spain, Taiwan, Turkey, and the United States. The programmes were delivered under a variety of names including *body safety, personal body safety, child assault prevention, child protection education, personal safety education*, and *protective behaviours*. While there are significant variations in length and mode of delivery across programmes, Walsh and colleagues note that the content of the programmes has much in common: "Programme content covers themes such as body ownership; distinguishing types of touches; identifying potential abuse situations; avoiding, resisting, or escaping such situations; secrecy; and how and whom to tell if abuse has occurred" (p. 7). In addition, most programmes emphasise the child is not to blame for the abuse; the blame ultimately lies with the perpetrator.

The critical question is whether the programmes are effective. There are two ways of addressing this issue: (1) are the programmes effective in increasing the children's knowledge and influencing their behaviour? (2) do the programmes achieve their purpose of reducing levels of child sexual abuse? As with content and delivery Walsh and colleagues noted large variations in the design of studies such as the way in which children's retention of knowledge was assessed, the length of follow-up, and the use of control groups. These procedural differences make it difficult to compare across studies and reach general conclusions from the evidence they provide. It follows that for the two questions above firm statements can only be based on a relatively small subset of the studies. The short follow-up periods preclude any measurement of the long-term effects of a programme.

Walsh and colleagues are confident in stating that *protective behaviours*, such as not interacting if approached by a stranger, improved significantly but there was no evidence regarding retention of the behaviours over time. A similar conclusion was drawn with respect to *knowledge attainment*: the children retained knowledge at the end of the programme but with equivocal evidence regarding long-term retention. The children taking part in a programme were more likely to disclose abuse than those in the control group and a small number of children reported previous and current sexual abuse. Of course, the child's disclosure is a critically important step towards reducing sexual abuse (Topping & Barron, 2009).

Davis and Gidycz (2017) conducted a meta-analysis of school-based child abuse prevention programmes. While they were able to draw conclusions about age effects, number of sessions and other process variables their telling conclusion was that:

> A shortcoming of all the evaluation studies utilized in this meta-analysis is that they did not objectively assess whether abuse prevention was actually achieved. The majority of the investigations evaluated program effectiveness using attitude and knowledge scales. Indeed, the effect size calculated in this meta-analysis can only provide a measure of knowledge and skill gains in program participants. Although the effect size is large, it does not indicate that program participants are less likely to be sexually abused.
>
> (p. 264)

The outcome of any programme intended to reduce behaviour can only be meaningfully evaluated if treatment fidelity has been maintained, that is, if the programme is delivered in terms of content and order of sessions in the way its design intends. Lynas and Hawkins (2017) found a lack of attention to programme fidelity in the majority of the school-based child sexual abuse prevention programmes they reviewed. They conclude that "Fidelity across research involving school-based child sexual abuse prevention programs will allow more meaningful interpretations of treatment effects and increase confidence that changes attributed to the intervention are due to the intervention itself, rather than variability in its implementation" (p. 19).

Sports clubs

Interpersonal violence can touch the lives of many people involved in sport, from athletes and their relatives to coaches and spectators (Parent & Fortier, 2017) and even young children (Vertommen et al., 2018). Vertommen et al. (2017) carried out a survey in Belgium and the Netherlands of interpersonal violence against children, males, and females in a sporting context. They recorded three key findings: (1) just over one-half of the children said that they had experienced an assault by more than one perpetrator; (2) most perpetrators were male; (3) the perpetrators were mainly coaches or athletes who were members of the victim's peer group.

Vertommen and colleagues make several suggestions based on their findings to help reduce violence in the context of sport. The first suggestion is that those applying for the position of a coach are subject to a criminal history check. However, as they note, criminal history checks can only be effective for convicted offenders; non-apprehended and first-time offenders cannot be detected in this way.

As with other employers, such as schools, in the UK a sports club can apply for Disclosure and Barring Service (DBS) check, formally known as a Criminal Records Bureau (CRB) check. This check will give information about an individual's criminal history. A DBS application is typically taken at the point of employing or engaging the services of a coach, teacher, and so on. There are three levels of DBS check: (1) a *standard check* which gives information on spent and unspent convictions, cautions, reprimands, and final warnings; (2) an *enhanced check* that gives the same information as a standard check along with any further relevant information held by the local police; (3) an *enhanced check with barred lists* provides the same information as an enhanced check and states if the individual is on the list of people barred from that specific role.

Vertommen and colleagues secondly suggest that coaches are educated to understand the vulnerability of some children and trained in the correct procedures to follow should they suspect violence. Third, it should be made clear to the children that if anything happens or they suspect it has taken place then it is safe to tell an adult about their experience. Children should know which adult to report a negative experience to and be aware that there are procedures in place to assist with any queries, complaints or disclosures of violence. Finally, these procedures should be drawn together to form an organisational policy which underpins a safe environment.

The Church

The once unthinkable situation of widespread sexual abuse of children by members of the church has, since its detection, developed into a large-scale scandal. It is apparent that the abuse is prevalent in several religious denominations, including the Anglican Church (Parkinson, Oates, & Jayakody, 2012) and the Catholic Church (Farrell, 2009), and across countries as diverse as Australia (Astbury, 2013), Germany (Rassenhofer et al., 2015), Ireland (Randall et al., 2011), and the USA (Flam, 2015).

Guerzoni and Graham (2015) called the Catholic Church's initial response to accusations of child sexual abuse by members of the clergy "Janus-faced". They state that in its opening responses "The Church shifts between a position of compliance and endorsement of the law, to a denial of responsibility to report to authorities and an appeal to higher loyalties when challenged on its stance towards confidentiality and collaboration with authorities" (p. 69).

The same point regarding denial of responsibility, a response not at all uncommon among sex offenders, was made by Spraitz and Bowen (2016) following their analysis of Catholic priests' responses to accusations of abuse. In addition, Spraitz and Bowen note that priests accused of sexually abusing children used problems with alcohol and mental health problems to excuse their behaviour.

While arguably slow to believe victims and to take appropriate action (Death, 2012, 2013), churches have made progress to reduce and prevent sexual abuse with the development of safeguarding procedures akin to those in other organisations (Wurtle, 2012). Steps have also been taken towards using psychometric assessment procedures to inform the church about any potential risks a cleric may pose (Jack & Wilcox, 2018) and developing programmes to reduce abuse by members of the clergy (Heydt & O'Connell, 2012).

Nurse (2017) reports an evaluation of an American programme, *Protecting God's Children*, aimed at informing adults about child sexual abuse and designed for use in the Catholic Church and allied organisations such as schools. The programme covers three broad areas: (i) the prevalence and effects of child abuse and the strategies used by offenders to engage children; (ii) how to make organisations safer through selection procedures such as background checks for volunteers and employees; (iii) how the participants can play a role in reducing the risk of abuse. Nurse records that the programme improved the participants' knowledge and understanding of the issues and that the improvements were maintained at a six-month follow-up. The effects of the programme were also seen to generalise with participants both talking about child sexual abuse with their own children and sharing information with other adults.

Finally, working across organisational boundaries, Rheingold et al. (2015) reported a trial of a programme called *Stewards of Children* which is designed to train childcare professionals, including those working with young people in the community in day-care centres, churches, and schools, to recognise and respond to child sexual abuse. The programme consists of a two and one-half hour workshop delivered either live or over the web. A follow-up of 267 professionals three months after they completed the training showed that the programme was effective in enabling participants to limit opportunities for child sexual abuse. It was also found that both modes of training, live or web-based, were equally effective.

Family

There are two ways in which families, particularly parents and guardians, can be involved in reducing child sexual abuse. First, they can become knowledgeable about the risks of abuse faced by their children and how they can manage such risks. Second, when the abuse is within the family they can engage in interventions to reduce the abusive behaviour.

One of the effects of sexual abuse is that the child may behave in a sexualised manner both in words and actions. It appears that not all parents can recognise these behaviours as indicators of abuse. Marriage et al. (2017) found that while able to recognise their child's age appropriate sexualised behaviour, some parents were less able to detect signs of the child's harmful behaviour which may be indicative of abuse. There are various programmes designed to teach and inform parents about child sexual abuse. Rudolph et al. (2018) suggest that parents can reduce the risk of their child's sexual abuse by both strong parenting in terms of supervision and involvement in their child's activities and by promoting their child's strength in terms of their social competence, self-regard, and well-being.

Dating violence

As children grow into adolescence so they develop romantic relationships with their peers. These adolescent relationships may be a setting within which interpersonal violence takes place. While males are frequent perpetrators of dating violence, there are indications that females may be aggressors at an unusually high rate (Lewis & Fremouw, 2001) and are more likely than males to perpetrate this particular type of interpersonal violence (Kaukinen, 2014; Theobald et al., 2016).

When it occurs the effects of dating violence, as with other forms of interpersonal violence, can be grave in terms of the psychological, psychical, and social consequences for the victim (Banyard & Cross, 2008). It may also be the case that perpetrators continue the violence in their adult relationships (Noonan & Charles, 2009). The predictors of male sexual aggression during dating include sexual abuse victimisation and attitudes supportive of rape (Moyano, Monge, & Sierra, 2017) alongside the familiar risk factors of substance abuse, emotional state (particularly depression), and symptoms of trauma (Kaukinen, 2014; Wolitzky-Taylor et al., 2008). These predictors of violence towards a romantic partner are similar to those found in sex offender populations; indeed, Sjödin et al. (2017) suggest that perpetrators of dating violence are no different to other violent offenders albeit with a particular victim.

As physical bullying has evolved to include cyberbullying, so dating violence has similarly assumed a technological face. In its electronic form violent communications are used to argue, to monitor or control a partner's activities and to express emotional aggression (Zweig et al., 2013). An American study by Reed, Tolman, and Ward (2017) asked 703 high school students about their experiences of electronic dating abuse. They found that males and females said they experienced this form of abuse at comparable degrees of frequency, with the exception of sexual coercion, such as pressure to send naked pictures or to have sex. Reed and colleagues conclude that while electronic abuse is potentially harmful for males and females, it may particularly be so for young women.

Another American study by Smith-Darden et al., (2017) also found high levels of electronic dating abuse among a sample of 727 male and female middle and high school students who reported that they had dated in the past year. They found that 38 per cent of the students said they had perpetrated at least one act of electronic dating violence with 17 per cent admitting to cyberstalking. An aversive childhood experience, such as witnessing parental violence or being abused, was highly predictive of the perpetration of electronic dating abuse. On the other hand, high levels of parental involvement, such as parents knowing their child's movements and strong emotional bonding between parent and child proved to be protective factors against perpetration of electronic abuse. Smith-Darden and colleagues suggest that further understanding of the nature of parental involvement in this context could potentially enhance interventions to reduce both teen dating violence and electronic dating abuse.

It is not the case that young people stumble blindly into or are unaware of sexual, including dating, violence. Cody (2017) interviewed 47 young people from Albania, Bulgaria, and England about the topic of sexual violence. The young people were aware of the issues and saw, in the main, that they had a role to play in preventing violence. There are advantages to including young people in preventative efforts as they bring a relevant perspective to discussions and can provide helpful advice on content. It could well be that allowing young people to contribute may be one strategy by which to build on the tentative findings discussed below by De La Rue et al., (2017).

Treatment of dating violence

A systematic review reported by Fellmeth et al. (2013) found little support for the effectiveness of interventions aimed at reducing relationship and dating violence. They concluded that:

> Studies included in this review showed no evidence of effectiveness of interventions on episodes of relationship violence or on attitudes, behaviours and skills related to relationship violence. We found a small increase in knowledge but there was evidence of substantial heterogeneity among studies. Further studies with longer-term follow-up are required, and study authors should use standardised and validated measurement instruments to maximise comparability of results.
>
> (p. 2)

A systematic review of the dating violence literature by Jennings et al. (2017) describes a wide range of types and styles of treatment encompassing therapeutic work in schools and communities. These interventions include several formalised treatment programmes such as the *Safe Dates Program* (Foshee et al., 2005), the *Fourth R: Skills for Youth Relationships Program* (Wolfe et al., 2009), and the *Ohio University Sexual Assault Risk Reduction Program* (Gidycz et al., 2001). The evaluative evidence was mixed with some positive findings, some ineffective treatments and others only effective in the short-term. Taylor, Stein, and Burden (2010) similarly reported mixed findings regarding the effectiveness of intervention to reduce dating violence. In a cautionary note Taylor point out that with the generally positive findings there is a possibility that interventions could *increase* the perpetration of dating violence.

Leen et al. (2013) reviewed nine programmes intended to reduce dating violence. As with the other reviews, Leen and colleagues found mixed results: some interventions reported little effect, others a positive effect but limited evidence of durability or replication. De La Rue et al. (2017) conducted a meta-analysis of 23 studies of school-based programmes that addressed dating violence. The meta-analysis showed increases in knowledge and positive changes in rejecting rape myths, alongside a moderate improvement in resolving interpersonal conflict. There was a small decrease in the incidence of dating violence measured pre-post intervention but this change was not maintained at follow-up. In summary, De La Rue and colleagues conclude that their findings "tentatively support the use of dating violence prevention programs in schools" (p. 22). The promising findings, they suggest, could be enhanced if schools systematically formulated comprehensive and effective policies to combat dating violence.

Child sexual abuse: treatment

While clinically necessary it is perhaps not immediately apparent how treatment of the abused child acts to reduce interpersonal violence. However, drawing on the notion of *cycles of violence* (Widom, 1989a, 1989b) alongside the association between aversive childhood experiences and later criminal behaviour (Craig et al., 2017; Malvaso, Delfabbro, & Day, 2016), if the child can be turned away from behaving in a violent manner then there is a strong chance of reducing later interpersonal violence. An example of the possibilities is provided by Kimber et al. (2018) who considered the link between a child's experience of interpersonal violence and their own violent behaviour. Kimber and colleagues conclude that: "Our synthesis reveals a significant and positive association between child exposure to physical IPV and the perpetration of physical IPV in adulthood" (p. 284). It may be argued that a successful intervention would reduce the likelihood of perpetuation of the cycle of violence.

There are two aspects to treatment: (1) the treatment of the abused child; (2) treatment of the offender. The treatment of the child is discussed below; offender treatment in the next chapter.

The effects of sexual abuse on children are well documented and include mental health problems, increased risk of further victimisation, and a range of behavioural problems that includes violent and sexual crimes. A substantial body of clinical research has evolved on the treatment of the sequelae of sexual abuse. Kim, Noh, and Kim (2016) give a summary of this research in which they refine the literature according to set criteria such as the victim being under the age of 18 years and interventions based on psychological principles. Thus, from a starting point of 670 studies, Kim and colleagues identified 18 as meeting the inclusion and exclusion criteria. One-half of the studies used an experimental design, the remainder a quasi-experimental design. Cognitive behavioural therapy was the most frequently reported type of intervention (9 studies), followed by group therapy (5 studies), with various one-off studies including psychotherapy, play therapy, eye movement desensitisation and family therapy. The most common targets for treatment were behavioural problems, psychosocial functioning, negative emotions, self-concept, and, most frequently, trauma-related symptoms. The review concluded that "CBT was the most promising type of CSA intervention, reporting substantial improvement and the maintenance of positive effects in diverse aspects of psychosocial functioning" (p. 609).

A meta-analysis of the psychological treatment of child sexual abuse was reported by Sánchez-Meca, Rosa-Alcázar, and López-Soler (2011). The analysis focused on a range of mental health outcomes, including anxiety, depression and self-esteem, and revealed that "that the best improvements in children's psychological wellbeing are achieved by combining trauma-focused CBT, supportive therapy and, to a lesser extent, psychodynamic therapy" (p. 85). Macdonald et al. (2012) are in broad agreement with Sánchez-Meca and colleagues although they state that in practice effective treatments are not widely available. The reference to symptoms of trauma as a consequence of violence is in keeping with research showing a direct relationship between involvement in violence, as both aggressor and victim, and traumatic symptomatology (Welfare & Hollin, 2012, 2015). The evidence favouring CBT approaches for violence-related trauma is in accord with the effectiveness of this approach with a range of child populations (Dorsey et al., 2017). The juxtaposition of these two empirical findings – that child sexual abuse may lead to traumatic symptomatology and the effectiveness of CBT in treating this effect of abuse – has led to innovative approaches as exemplified by the *Be Brave Ranch* (Silverstone et al., 2016). The *Be Brave Ranch* is a residential facility for sexually abused child aged 8 to 18 years who voluntarily take part in a 28-day trauma-focused cognitive behavioural therapy programme. A preliminary analysis based on 35 children who completed the programme showed positive changes in PTSD symptoms and mood. As Silverstone and colleagues suggest, a full-scale evaluation is a necessary next step.

Sexual abuse of adults

Adult sexual abuse: prohibition

The sexual abuse of adults is perpetrated by men and women upon men and women. Sexual abuse in its various forms is a criminal act and therefore prohibited and punishable by law. Of course, exactly how the law is applied from country to country depends on executive decisions concerning resources, political priorities, and so on.

A government crime statistics report notes that, based on data from the 2009/10, 2010/11 and 2011/12 Crime Survey for England and Wales, females were much more likely than males to report being a victim of all categories of sexual offence (Ministry of Justice, Home Office, & the Office for National Statistics, 2013). In all, 2.5 per cent of females and 0.4 per cent of males report suffering some form of sexual offence in the last 12 months, with males much less likely to report being a victim of a serious sexual offence. The report extrapolates from the reported figures to state that:

> Based on these prevalence rates, it is estimated that there were between 430,000 and 517,000 adult victims of sexual offences in the last year over these three survey periods ... Of these, it is estimated that there were between 366,000 and 442,000 female victims and between 54,000 and 90,000 male victims. With regard to the most serious sexual offences, the survey estimated the number of females who were victims ranged between 68,000 and 103,000 and male victims between 5,000 and 19,000 per year.

(pp. 11–12)

The widespread sexual abuse of women is one manifestation of violence to women generally (Krahé, 2018). In 2016 the UK government published its strategy for ending violence against women and girls (HM Government, 2016). (As an aside, unless the tide of human history can be reversed, "ending" violence is an impossible target; "significantly reducing" is arguably much more realistic.)

As is the case with children, only a minority of sexual offences against adults are reported to the police, detected, and then prosecuted. Hoare and Jansson (2007) estimated that only 11 per cent of victims of serious offences such as sexual assault and rape reported the crime to the police. Victims of sexual offences give various reasons for not reporting the crime: they may feel humiliated by events and not want to draw attention to their involvement in a sex crime; they may think that the police are not able to help; they may not want to be questioned about the crime; or they may be afraid of reprisals if they do report the crime. The victim may not perceive what has happened as a crime, even blaming themselves for the assault. To emphasise the point about non-reporting, at time of writing there is a great deal of public scandal and condemnation resulting from revelations that men in positions of power, including celebrities and members of government, had over the years been sexually abusing their junior colleagues.

There have been concerns that police investigations of sexual assaults and rape could be compromised by police officers' belief in rape myths (Parratt & Pina, 2017). If decisions about investigating a reported rape are influenced by an officer's belief that the woman was "asking for it" or that women "falsely allege rape out of spite to overcome guilt after a sexual encounter" (beliefs by no means restricted to members of the constabulary), it seems likely that this will prejudice the investigation and likelihood of prosecution. Further, by maintaining the stereotype of males as perpetrators and women as victims, rape myths act against an understanding of men as victims of rape.

The inhibiting effects of rape myths on the legal process can be countermanded in several ways. While police training is an obvious starting point, the values nurtured during training can only come into effect within a supportive organisational culture. Thus, many police forces have acted by having officers specifically trained to work with victims of sexual offences, designated interview suites, and working alongside specialist services. After the police investigation the Crown Prosecution Service (CPS) is the next link in the legal chain that leads to court. The role of the CPS is to determine whether the evidence is strong enough to allow a realistic chance of a successful prosecution. The CPS devotes a section of its website (www.cps.

gov.uk) to giving guidance on dispelling societal myths which impede the investigation and prosecution of rape and sexual offences.

The large number of victims of sexual offences does not correspond with a large number of convictions. Indeed, in cases of rape, England and Wales have the lowest rate of conviction in Europe (Hohl & Stanko, 2015). The government report cited above gives a figure for 2011 of 5,977 offenders found guilty of sexual offences; within this overall figure there were 1,058 offenders found guilty of rape of a female and 95 guilty of rape of a male. The statistics indicate a rise in the number of offenders guilty of rape over the past seven years. There has been a substantial increase in the numbers of rape and sexual assault of a female; the number of convictions for rape of a male have also increased, although convictions for sexual assault on a male decreased over the same period. A conviction for a sexual offence may lead to one of several outcomes ranging from a life sentence to an order served in the community. However, the rising number of reported and known sexual offences, especially against women, suggests that legal sanctions are not having a prohibitive effect.

A problem with prohibition is that, as Colombino et al. (2017) state with reference to American criminal statistics, "Most new sex crimes are not committed by recidivistic offenders. In fact, over 95% of all sexual offense crimes (measured by new arrests) are committed by first time offenders (or those not on a sex offender registry)" (p. 161). A similar point regarding low rates of recidivism among sex offenders based on an analysis of crime data from England and Wales has also been made (Friendship & Thornton, 2001; Friendship et al., 2001).

It follows that efforts to reduce sex offences among known sex offenders face the practical issue of discriminating the low number of future recidivists from the larger population of first-time sex offenders. The low recidivism baseline sets the additional methodological problem of evaluating the effectiveness of measures intended to reduce sex offences.

There are several practical strategies which can be put into place to reduce the likelihood of sexual offences (against both adults and children). These strategies include legally restricting the offender's movements in terms of geographical location, such as being near a particular residence or school; or prohibiting personal contact with a particular person, say an ex-partner.

Again, as with children, treatment is available for both the abused and the offender: the former is considered below, the latter in the next chapter. However, unlike the potential for reducing violence in children through treatment, this is an unlikely possibility with adult victims of sexual assault.

Nonetheless, there are ways in which interventions with adults can act to reduce the likelihood of violent behaviour.

Adult sexual abuse: treatment

Witness care units

The victim of a sexual assault may decide to report the offence to the police. A successful investigation and prosecution will result in the offender being subject to a penalty which may reduce the chances that they commit further offences. The woman who chooses to engage with the criminal justice system may well step into a world with which they are totally unfamiliar. They will be required to give a full and frank account of what happened to them, reliving the pain of the crime. It is the task of the police to establish the facts of the case and so the questioning may appear intrusive or unfeeling. After questioning, the wheels of justice can be slow to turn so that victims' stress is exacerbated by not knowing what is happening with their case or how to find out.

From a legal perspective, victims and witnesses are a crucial element in successful prosecutions and it is important that measures are taken to try to prevent their withdrawal from the case. In particular, vulnerable victims such as children or people with a physical or mental incapacity may require support. In England and Wales, the development of Witness Care Units, jointly run by the police and the CPS, aimed to relieve victim stress by providing a single point of contact for victims and witnesses. There are Witness Care Units specifically for children and young people (Plotnikoff & Woolfson, 2007). A publication giving details of the working of Witness Care Units is available from the Criminal Justice Joint Inspection (2009). The service provided by the units operates from the opening to the resolution of a case. Thus, it should be straightforward for the victim to obtain information about their case and to minimise the stress of attending court. The units are staffed by witness care officers whose statutory role is to guide and support victims through the criminal justice process. This task has two basic parts: (1) to attend to practical details such as telling the victim whether they will be called to give evidence, whether the accused is on bail, the dates of the court hearings, provide information such as the *Witness in Court* leaflet, and explain the court judgment at the conclusion of the trial; (2) to attend to and review the victim's personal needs including any particular support needs, to enable them to get to court and give their best evidence, to provide information about the final outcome, ensuring their contribution is valued and guaranteeing post-case support is available when required.

Reducing victimisation

There are steps that may be taken to reduce the likelihood of rape. These steps necessarily mean that the potential victim changes some aspects of their everyday behaviour. However, it is important that the victim does not blame themselves for any assault or attempted assault; it should be made absolutely clear that the responsibility for the crime lies with the offender not the victim, no matter what the circumstances may be.

There are steps that can be taken to reduce the likelihood of sexual and other assaults. An online search reveals a wealth of advice as summarised in Table 5.3.

TABLE 5.3 Strategies to reduce the likelihood of sexual assault

Outdoors

Stay with friends.

Remain in areas with good lighting.

Avoid disappearing from sight as with taking shortcuts through parks and alleyways.

When driving keep the doors locked and check fuel before setting off.

Always carry a charged mobile telephone.

Park in areas with good street lights avoiding underground and enclosed car parks.

On returning to the car have the key to hand to enable a quick entry.

If being followed, try to note the other car's make and licence number.

Do not drive home, go to the nearest police or fire station and on arrival sound the horn; alternatively, go to an open petrol station and call the police.

Never get out of the car if there is any doubt about being able to enter the building safely.

Giving lifts to hitchhikers is a very bad idea.

Indoors

Ensure all windows and doors in your home can be locked securely.

Use a security chain on the main entrance.

Use security lights, particularly at entrances.

Use a home security CCTV or wireless camera to check the identity of callers.

Always check their identification of any sales or service personnel before admitting them into the home.

If arriving home to find an open door or window and signs of forced entry do not enter and immediately call the police.

Despite taking precautions, someone may make an unwanted sexual advance. If this happens then firmly make it clear the attention is not welcome; being politely assertive is preferable to being passive, which can be taken as acquiescence. If the advances continue leave the situation quickly, with a friend if possible. If an assault begins is it wise to resist physically? A shout for help may alert others but could anger the attacker prompting increasingly violent behaviour; pushing the person away may be effective but it may intensify the attacker's use of physical force.

Wong and Balemba (2016) carried out a meta-analysis of the injurious effects of resisting during a sexual assault. They reported that the women who resisted, particularly when their resistance was physical, were more likely than those who did not resist to be physically injured beyond the effects of the sexual assault or rape. Wong and Balemba are clear regarding the limitations of their analysis:

> While the results demonstrate that reduced resistance might be the safer option for victims overall, the current study examined only one (narrow) aspect of the sexual assault event: the relationship between victim resistance and victim injury. We cannot from these findings suggest that all sexual assault victims should resist or that all sexual assault victims should not resist, because situations, offenders, and victims are heterogeneous. What the current study does provide is additional information for victims to consider when faced with a sexual assault. Arming potential victims with increased information regarding their potential for injury was one of the study goals.
>
> *(p. 10)*

While significant attempts have been made, including attempts at legal, cultural, and social changes, to reduce sexual violence in all its forms, it is true to say that much remains to be done. As DeGue et al. (2014) state: "Continued progress is needed toward the development and rigorous evaluation of effective, comprehensive, theory-based primary prevention strategies for sexual violence perpetration that address risk and protective factors at multiple levels of the social ecology" (p. 360).

6

REDUCING CRIMINAL VIOLENCE

Early intervention

The notion of an early intervention with both children and adolescents to forestall later anti-social and delinquent behaviour, including violent behaviour, has been in force for several decades. The practice of early intervention has increasingly been informed by the research that has established the risk factors which lead to delinquency (e.g., Farrington & Welsh, 2007a). These advances in what has become known as *developmental crime prevention* have led to the implementation and evaluation of a substantial number of programmes (Farrington, Ttofi, & Lösel, 2016; Homel, 2005).

Farrington, Ttofi, and Lösel (2016) point out that developmental prevention programmes for children and young people up to the age of 18 years have been introduced into a wide range of settings, including schools, nurseries, families, and child guidance centres. They note four broad programme classifications: these are (1) general, (2) individual, (3) family, and (4) school. General programmes are those such as nurse-family partnerships and the High/Scope Perry Preschool programme (e.g., Deković et al., 2011); individual programmes include child training using standard therapeutic approaches, such as skills training, cognitive-behavioural treatment, and psychodynamic therapy, aimed at reducing the child's aggressive behaviour (e.g., Lösel & Bender, 2012). The family interventions involve various approaches to family therapy, specialised Multisystemic Therapy, home visiting during pregnancy, and treatment foster care (e.g., Piquero et al., 2016). The school-based programmes encompass a wide range of interventions addressing targets ranging from anti-bullying and school violence, to programmes based on social information processing and cognitive-behavioural theory (e.g., Dymnicki, Weissberg, & Henry, 2011). Indeed, the interventions for pre-school (Lösel, Stemmler, & Bender, 2013; Schweinhart, 2013) and school pupils have addressed a wide range of targets including preventing school dropout (Christenson & Thurlow, 2004), reducing reincarceration (Blomberg et al., 2011), and the long-term reduction of generational cycles of violence (Chalfin & Deza, in press).

Farrington, Ttofi, and Lösel (2016) conclude their review by statistically considering the effectiveness of the four classes of intervention. They report positive results for all four with family interventions the most effective, then school, individual, and general programmes the least effective. The effects of early intervention are the positive effects of diverting children from anti-social and criminal behaviour and the consequent benefits for families. In addition, the financial savings in diverting potential offenders away from the criminal justice system run to millions of pounds of public expenditure (Welsh & Farrington, 2011, 2015).

The promise of developmental programmes has prompted efforts to refine the content of these interventions. In particular, the inclusion of protective factors – these may be thought of as variables that appear to mitigate risk factors – has received attention. Jolliffe et al., (2016) found that both individual factors, such as academic achievement, and social factors including non-delinquent peers, protected against involvement in anti-social and criminal behaviour. Vassallo, Edwards, and Forrest (2016) found that self-control and positive relations with school teachers were protective factors for adolescent interpersonal violence.

Adolescents

There are two primary approaches to reducing violence by adolescents. First, given the criminogenic consequences of involvement with the criminal justice system, to divert adolescents from contact with police, courts, and so on. Second, to engage adolescent offenders in treatment programmes to change the risk factors for violence.

Diversion

The potential of diversion for reducing crime has been recognised for several decades. Wilson and Hoge (2013) note that there are two types of diversion programme. The first relies on a diversionary caution to the adolescent, typically from the police, as to their future conduct. The second type, a formal diversion programme, requires the young offender to take part in an intervention such as community service, employment training or restorative justice. Once the programme is satisfactorily completed there is no further legal action.

Wilson and Hoge conducted a meta-analysis of 73 diversion programmes which included both types of diversionary programme. While the outcome was associated with a range of programme implementation variables such as the strength of the evaluative design, Wilson and Hoge conclude that: "Diversion programs, both caution and intervention, are significantly more effective in reducing recidivism than the traditional justice system" (p. 510).

Schwalbe et al. (2012) also conducted a meta-analysis of diversionary programmes, focusing on experimental evaluations of 28 diversion programmes published between 1980 and 2011. As with Wilson and Hoge, Schwalbe and colleagues reported various implementation variables, including the quality of implementation, which influenced outcome. They did not find an overall effect of diversion on recidivism although there were differences according to type of programme. The interventions based on youth courts, mentoring, and individual programmes did not reduce recidivism; however, family-based programmes were reliably associated with a statistically significant reduction in recidivism.

Prohibition

The majority of acts of interpersonal violence are forbidden by law and so by definition are prohibited. If apprehended perpetrators are liable to the punishment judged appropriate in a court of law. Thus, the first issue is how effective is punishment in reducing interpersonal violence? The second associated issue is whether any treatment can be offered to convicted offenders to reduce the likelihood of further violent behaviour.

An exception to punishment for a criminal act is made for both juveniles under the age of criminal responsibility and for those individuals who are legally deemed not to be responsible for their actions, typically because of a mental disorder. These three types of offenders – juvenile, convicted adults and mentally disordered – are each considered below.

Juvenile offenders

Of the many children and adolescents who engage in, mostly minor, antisocial behaviour, there are a minority who will continue to engage in antisocial and criminal acts after their adolescence. These young people who continue offending as they mature are termed *life-course persistent* offenders, as opposed to *adolescent-limited* offenders. As described by Jolliffe et al. (2017) the risk factors for life-course persistent offending are reasonably well established. Hawkins et al. (2000) group these risk factors into five types: (1) *individual*, such as holding attitudes favourable to antisocial behaviour; (2) *family*, including child maltreatment and family conflict; (3) *school*, including academic failure and truancy; (4) *peer-related*, including delinquent siblings and peers, and gang membership; (5) *community and neighbourhood* factors such as poverty and availability of drugs.

However, compared to delinquency generally with its preponderance of acquisitive crime, rather less is known about the risk factors which specifically predict persistent violent offending. Herrenkohl et al. (2000) looked at predictors of violence using longitudinal data gathered from over 800 American pupils. They found that the strongest predictors of violence at the ages of 10, 14, and 16 years were if the child was hyperactive, showed low academic performance, had delinquent peers, and lived in a neighbourhood where drugs were available. Those children exposed to multiple risks were significantly more likely to be involved in violence. On a note of caution, while the significant risk factors were characteristic of the group of children, their predictive accuracy for identifying exactly which child who would go on to commit violent acts was limited. The contrast between nomothetic statements, which provide general information about a social group, and ideographic statements which consider the uniqueness of the individual was originally made by the German philosopher Wilhelm Windelband (1848–1915). The difference between the two approaches is an issue in several areas of psychology as seen, for example, in contrasting the findings of experimental studies with groups and individual case studies.

While Herrenkohl and colleagues looked at a general population, it is known that specific childhood events increase the likelihood of later violent conduct. A Canadian study by Van Wert et al. (2017) considered the issue of which maltreated children are at greatest risk of later violent behaviour. Van Wert and colleagues analysed data from a total of 1,837 substantiated maltreatment investigations from the Ontario Child Welfare System. They found that 13 per cent of the sample of maltreated children, aged up to 15 years, were identified by child welfare workers as aggressive. In addition, 6 per cent of the sample were involved in the youth justice system: this figure stands in contrast to a national rate of less than 1 per cent of children involved in the youth justice system.

The maltreated and aggressive children were more likely to have experienced severe maltreatment as well as multiple and concurrent forms of maltreatment. The adolescents who displayed aggressive and criminal behaviour most often came to the attention of the authorities because of neglect and risk of abandonment as their caregivers were unwilling or unable to continue caring.

Against this backdrop of individual and social factors that culminate in youth violence, how can steps be taken to reduce the frequency and level of violence? There are two principle approaches to reducing criminal violence: first, punish the offender; second, intervene to counter the adverse risk factors, typically through some form of treatment.

Punishment

The question of whether punishment works is complicated as punishment may be intended to deliver several different consequences (Walker, 1991). The first consequence, based on the principle of *lex talionis*, "an eye for an eye", is that punishment acts as retribution for the crime. The "purist" view of punishment is that by breaking the law the criminal deserves to be punished, is punished, and that is the end of the matter. In contrast, the utilitarian position is that punishment should have an effect that leads to greater good by deterring both the individual and society at large from crime. The notion of deterrence underpins the criminal justice system in many countries (Kennedy, 2009).

As the current focus is on the individual not society at large, the question to ask here is whether punishment deters the offender from further acts of violence. The hoped for effect of punishment on the individual offender is called *special* deterrence as opposed to *general* deterrence where punishing criminals is held to discourage crime across the whole population.

The criminal justice system has a range of options for punishing violent young offenders, some delivered in the community, others in institutions. An example of a legal sanction delivered in the community lies in the imposition of a curfew to restrict a young person's movements at specific times of day. Fried (2001) reviewed the effects of curfews in reducing violence carried out by juveniles – including a study by McDowall, Loftin, and Wiersema (2000) which assessed the effectiveness of curfew laws in 57 cities in the USA with populations greater than 250,000 – and concluded that there is little evidence that curfews reduce violence. Wilson, Olaghere, and Gill (2016) carried out a systematic review of the effects of curfews on criminal behaviour by young offenders. In agreement with Fried, Wilson and colleagues concluded that: "Juvenile curfews appeal to common sense notions of how to prevent crime .... The empirical evidence, however, runs counter to these notions. Any effect of a curfew on crime, either positive or negative, is likely to be small at best" (p. 185).

If diversion and community sanctions have been exhausted or if the offence is serious the young person may be sentenced to a period of custody. In England and Wales, a young offender, defined as under the age of 18 years, may be detained in either a Secure Children's Home (SCH), a Secure Training Centre (STC) or a Young Offender Institution (YOI). A court can give a young person a custodial sentence if it is judged that the offence is so serious that there is no alternative option, or if the young person has previous offences, or they are seen to be a risk to the public.

There are 15 SCHs throughout England and Wales for young men and women aged between 10 and 17 years. These facilities are run by Local Authorities and Charities and provide residential care, education and healthcare. There are four STCs in England and Wales, all run by the private sector, for young men and women aged 12 to 17 years. Their purpose is to provide education for the young people. Finally, there are over 40 YOIs which accommodate mainly male offenders aged between 18 and 21 years, although some will hold offenders as young as 15 years. YOIs are run on lines not dissimilar to prisons, with lower ratios of staff to young people than SCH and STCs.

Do custodial sanctions reduce crime, including violent crime? The official statistics for 2014–2015 for young people aged 18 years and under highlight two relevant points (Ministry of Justice & The Youth Justice Board, 2015). First, with regard to type of offence, when set against the previous year, offending fell for most types of offence with the exception of crimes of violence against the person, criminal damage, and sexual offences. These figures suggest that rates of violent behaviour are relatively unaffected by legal sanctions. Second, in 2015 the rate of reoffending for young people had increased by 5.6 per cent since 2008 and by 1.9 per cent since 2013. Once more, these figures indicate that violent offenders are undeterred by the threat of legal sanctions.

There is very little, if any, support from either the research literature (Lambie & Randell, 2013) or the official figures for the proposition that punishing young people by removing their liberty has any positive effect in terms of reducing violent crime. This is not a revolutionary statement and does not mean that depriving offenders of their liberty fails to serve other functions such as protecting the public. The lack of evidence for the effectiveness of punishment on recidivism suggests two ways to proceed: (1) do even more of the same and do it harder; (2) find an alternative to punishment. The first option has led to various types of "punishment plus" regimes; the second is discussed later when treatment options are considered. There are two particular "punishment plus" regimes that have been designed for young offenders: these are Boot Camps and the *Short, Sharp Shock Regime*.

Boot camps

The notion of boot camps for young offenders began in the USA in 1983 when they were introduced in Georgia and Oklahoma. The thinking behind the boot camp regime is that forcing the offenders to live in a military environment will reduce offending. In boot camps the staff are given military titles, military uniforms are worn by staff and young offenders, there is strict discipline at all times, and a great deal of time is given to marching drills, physical training, and hard labour. The original idea caught on such an extent that by 1994 there were boot camps to be found in 36 American states.

MacKenzie et al., (1995) gathered data from across eight American states in conducting the first large-scale evaluation of boot camps. MacKenzie and colleagues reported that the custodial staff were highly enthusiastic about the regime, seeing their role as agents for positive change. The inmates found the regime's discipline and activities stressful, although their physical fitness improved and they were drug free, and they complained about abuse by staff (see Benda, Toombs, & Peacock, 2003). MacKenzie and colleagues found that compared with controls in other types of institution the recidivism rates for the eight boot camp inmates were lower in three states, higher in one state, and no different in four states. A characteristic of the boot camps with the lower recidivism rates was that they included rehabilitative elements and supervision post-release. As Meade and Steiner (2010) note, the initial enthusiasm for boot camps based on a military ethos soon dissipated. A "second generation" of boot camps emerged during the 2000s which switched their focus to include a rehabilitation and aftercare component.

Short, Sharp, Shock

Influenced by the American boot camps, the *Short, Sharp, Shock* custodial regime for young offenders was introduced in England in the early 1980s. (The term "Short Sharp Shock", taken from a Gilbert and Sullivan opera, refers to the act of beheading.) This regime was based on the notion that experience of a brief, unpleasant, and (inevitably) militaristic sentence would jolt the young offender out of a life of crime. A Home Office evaluation by Thornton et al., (1984) found no effect of the *Short, Sharp, Shock* regime on reconviction rates.

A similar idea to *Short, Sharp, Shock* was introduced in the 1990s at two English custodial institutions for male young offenders; these were the Thorn Cross High Intensity Treatment (HIT) regime and the Colchester Military Corrective Training Centre (MCTC). In both the institutions the environment was austere, with strict enforcement of rules, and the young offenders were allowed only a few personal possessions. The HIT regime was based on a fully programmed 16-hour day with military drills before breakfast followed by skills and vocational training, education, and an offending behaviour programme before the day ended at 10 pm. The MCTC regime was based on conditions for military prisoners with physical training, physical fitness, and, of course, marching drills. The MCTC was closed after a year's operation so that only a small number of offenders passed through the regime. The main evaluation was therefore focused on the HIT regime.

In bringing the regimes into operation – at a cost of several million pounds in building work alone – the government claimed that crime would be reduced by exposing the young offenders to a combination of deterrence, strict discipline, and training. Farrington et al. (2002) conducted a reconviction study of the MCTC and HIT regimes. As the MCTC regime was closed down after a year the evaluation was concerned with just a small number of young offenders. With due reservations given to this limitation, Farrington and colleagues conclude that "There was no evidence that Colchester YOI succeeded in reducing actual reconviction rates" (p. 60).

For the HIT regime Farrington and colleagues compared the actual and predicted reconviction rates of the offenders who had passed through the regime with a control group. They found that for the young offenders who experienced the regime the 1-year predicted rate of reconviction (47.2%) was significantly higher than the actual rate (34.7%). The young offenders in the control condition showed highly similar 1-year rates of predicted (56.1%) and actual (55.1%) reconviction. The 1-year fall in actual versus predicted reconvictions for the HIT regime offenders was not found at a 2-year follow-up with similar predicted (66.4%) and actual (65.1%) reconviction rates.

In recidivism studies a 2-year follow-up is taken to be an acceptable standard by which to judge the effects of an intervention. A notable 10-year follow-up of the HIT regime was reported by Jolliffe, Farrington, and Howard (2013).

The follow-up compared the reconvictions of 125 young offenders from the HIT regime with a matched group of 125 young offenders drawn from the original control group. It was found that over the follow-up period the offenders from the HIT regime committed significantly fewer offenses (15.6) than the controls (18.7) and had a lower rate of receiving custodial sentences (62.4%) than the controls (72%), although the difference was not statistically significant. There was no significant difference in the number of custodial sentences served by the HIT group (3.9) and controls (4.60), nor in average sentence length.

Is it possible that, as with boot camps, the juxtaposition of punishment and treatment accounts for the effect of the HIT regime in reducing reoffending? One of the selection criteria for the HIT regime was that the young offender was ready to address their offending behaviour. In the course of their sentence the young offenders participated in education which resulted in nationally recognised educational qualifications, cognitive-behavioural treatment, drug education, vocational training with community work placements, and planned reintegration into the community following release.

In conclusion, the literature offers little support that the militaristic elements of boot camps are effective in reducing recidivism. When boot camps include a rehabilitative focus they can have an effect in reducing reoffending. However, the fact that rehabilitation can be successful within a boot camp is not an argument for boot camps; there are other less costly and more efficient ways to offer rehabilitation. As Gültekin and Gültekin (2012) state: "Juvenile boot camps do not lessen costs or reduce recidivism, are not successful at changing the behaviors of the inmates" (p. 739).

If punishment is not having the desired effect, then perhaps more of it is needed. However, it is doubtful that moving from a *Short, Sharp, Shock* to a *Long, Sharp, Shock* would bring about any change in outcome. An American study reported by Winokur et al. (2008) looked at length of custodial confinement and recidivism in a large sample of juvenile offenders. They failed to find any consistent relationship between length of confinement and recidivism.

Convicted adult offenders

Convicted offenders may legally be punished through the enforced loss of some aspect of their life: they may lose some or all their liberty, or their assets, or access to their children, or their life in those criminal justice systems which have the death penalty. The imposition of a community penalty is a first step in curtailing an offender's movements and may take one of several forms.

Supervision in the community

In England and Wales a low risk offender may receive a Community Order with one or more requirements depending on the specific circumstances of the case. A Community Order may specify a range of alternatives more or less appropriate for different offenders: a *prohibited activity* bans the offender from, say, attending football matches or being in a public house; an offender with *specified activity* requirement must engage in events such as employment training, debt counselling, victim reparation, or drug treatment. Alternatively, a *curfew* may be imposed so that the offender must be at a specific location at a specified time. A community punishment may include electronic monitoring or *tagging* (Nellis, 2000). The formal monitoring of an offender's whereabouts through tagging may be of use with sex offenders who are required, for example, to stay away from schools (Gies, Gainey & Healy, 2016; Payne & DeMichele, 2010), or with driving under the influence offenders (Kubak, Kayabas, & Vachal, 2016).

Vanhaelemeesch, Vander Beken, and Vandevelde (2014) found that most of a sample of 27 Belgian offenders preferred electronic monitoring to prison. They suggest that the use of monitoring will reduce prison over-crowding while allowing the offender to maintain family links and reconnect to society.

Padgett, Bales, and Blomberg (2006) found that electronic monitoring reduced reoffending in a large sample of offenders. Killias et al. (2010) looked at outcomes for offenders randomly assigned to community service or electronic monitoring. They found that when offenders completed their sanction, the monitored group reoffended at a slightly lower rate than the community service group. Graham and McIvor (2015) reviewed the use of electronic monitoring in Scotland noting that it is significantly cheaper than imprisonment and that around 80 per cent of offenders completed their period of monitoring without a breach of order. Andersen and Telle (2016) reviewed the use of electronic monitoring in Norway and found that it had a positive effect in reducing reoffending over a 2-year period. The beneficial effects were strongest for offenders with no experience of prison or recent periods of unemployment, suggesting that avoiding prison and maintaining work may be important in reducing recidivism.

However, not all studies are supportive of the crime reduction potential of electronic monitoring. Finn and Muirhead-Steves (2002) reviewed the use of electronic monitoring specifically with violent offenders compared to a non-violent control. There was no effect of electronic monitoring on return to prison or time to reoffending, with offenders with drug problems returning to prison the quickest. However, the electronically monitored sex offenders were less likely to return to prison than their controls, while the sex offenders who returned to prison survived longer in the community than their controls. Renzema and Mayo-Wilson (2005) reviewed the use of electronic monitoring with high risk offenders and failed to find convincing evidence for its effects on recidivism. They concluded that "after 20 years, it is clear that EM has been almost desperately applied without adequate vision, planning, program integration, staff training, and concurrent research" (p. 230). An Argentinian study by Di Tella and Schargrodsky (2013) suggests that compared to prison electronic monitoring has a negative effect on recidivism.

Imprisonment

The court has a range of custodial options available for sentenced adult offenders, ranging from short sentences of a few months' duration to sentences up to and including life imprisonment. There is a debate about whether as well as their liberty prisoners should also lose their civil and human rights. The sensitive issue of prisoners' rights touches on international standards such as the Universal Declaration of Human Rights and the UN Standard Minimum Rules for the Protection of Prisoners (Coyle, 2008), a prisoner's right to vote, and even the use of cruel and degrading treatment.

It is not the case that prisons are "crime neutral"; they are after all institutions replete with potential offenders and victims. While a change in the prisoner's environment has taken place, their behaviour may well remain constant with similar, or *parallel*, behaviours inside prison to those seen outside security (Daffern, Jones, & Shine, 2010). Thus, prisoners incarcerated for violent crimes are more likely than those convicted for property crimes to commit violent acts in prison, including sexual violence, against both inmates and prison staff (Sorensen & Davis, 2011).

Bonta and Gendreau (1990) note that prisoners adapt to and manage the pains of custody in different ways, some functional, others not. The distress experienced by some prisoners can precipitate self-harm and suicide (Pratt et al., 2006). However, the pains associated with imprisonment do not affect all prisoners, nor can they be assumed to have an effect upon reoffending (Chen & Shapiro, 2007; Cook & Roesch, 2012). Indeed, it appears that the severity of sentence passed by the court has little or no impact on levels of crime (Doob & Webster, 2003; McGuire, 2008b) and can hardly claim to have a deterrent effect. In this light it is not surprising that a community sentence can be more effective in reducing recidivism than a short prison sentence (Wermink et al., 2010). Nonetheless, the trend in the UK is for an ever-increasing prison population. Allen and Watson (2017) provide an apposite summary:

> As at Friday 31st March 2017, the total prison population in England and Wales was just over 85,500. In Scotland the prison population was just under 7,700 as in the 2015/16 annual report (latest data). For the 2015/16 financial year the total average daily prison population was just under 1,600 in Northern Ireland.
>
> There is a general underlying trend of an increasing number of people held in prison. The prison population of England & Wales rose by about 90% between 1990 and 2016, an average rise of 3.5% per annum. In Scotland this increase was 62%. Between 2000 and 2015/16 the prison population of Northern Ireland increased by 49%.
>
> *(p. 3)*

Allen and Watson provide figures for the average cost per day for the penal detention of one person in 2014: in England and Wales it is £143.67, in Northern Ireland, £139.25, and in Scotland £155.14. Now, if England and Wales have a prison population of 85,500 at a cost of £143.67 per day, then the *daily* cost is £12,283,785. Given that several commentators have remarked that a prison sentence is a remarkably expensive way to achieve minimal change in the number of crimes (Marsh & Fox, 2008; Nagin, Cullen, & Jonson, 2009), there must be some powerful reasons for the growth in the use of incarceration.

Why does punishment fail to reduce offending?

Why does punishment have such a minimal effect on reoffending? There are two arguments to make in answering this question, one based on the principles of effective punishment from a theoretical perspective, the other to do with the reality of offenders' lives.

There are decades of behavioural research which have established the contingencies necessary to bring about a significant reduction in behaviour (Axlerod & Apsche, 1983). Thus, effective punishment *immediately* follows the behaviour, *inevitably* follows *every* occurrence of the behaviour, and is *intense* in its administration. It is not difficult to see how the punishment administered by the criminal justice system deviates from these basic behavioural principles. The typical offender commits many more crimes than those for which they are apprehended and sentenced, so punishment is by no means inevitable or immediate. An offender's first sentence is unlikely to be intense: it is more likely that he or she will progress the tariff from lenient to severe sentences.

As well as focusing on the behaviour to be reduced in frequency (i.e., punished), it is important to reinforce alternative behaviours which allow the individual to gain the same reward. For example, employment and robbery both provide money, so enabling the offender to obtain employment provides them with an alternative to gaining money illegally. If the offender can develop new behavioural repertoires in order to gain rewards legitimately this may act to reduce criminal behaviour.

The second point above referred to the reality of many offenders' lives. After leaving prison many offenders, juveniles and adults, return to a life characterised by socially dysfunctional families, criminal and drug-using peers, and poor employment opportunities. When in that familiar environment old patterns of behaviour, including interpersonal violence, are likely to reappear and so the cycle continues. As Cullen and Gilbert (2013) state:

> The punitive paradigm that had a grip on American corrections since 1982 is intellectually bankrupt. If hundreds of thousands of offenders are locked up, this alone will suppress the crime rate to a degree. But beyond this "incapacitation effect," little is gained – and much is lost.
>
> *(p. xiii)*

Psychological treatment in its many forms

The philosophy underpinning treatment, or *corrections* as it is also called, is that the offender can be helped to change in order so that they may live a life free from crime. The positive effects of treatment are of benefit both to the individual offender and the wider community (Raynor & Robinson, 2009). The idea of using prison in a constructive manner was at the heart of the prison reformers – such as Jonas Hanway (1712–1786), John Howard (1726–1790), and Elizabeth Fry (1780–1845) in Britain and Enoch Cobb Wines (1806–1879), Theodore William Dwight (1822–1892), and Samuel June Barrows (1845–1909) in America – who campaigned for humane conditions in prisons. These reformers argued the case that time in prison could be put to good use by improving the prisoner through education and training in work skills.

As the reform movement gathered pace in the early 19th century so psychology entered the field and psychological treatment became part of the reform movement (Hollin, 2001b, 2012). The type and style of treatment tracked developments in mainstream psychological theory and practice. The first interventions with delinquents were informed by the psychoanalytic tradition (e.g., Aichhorn, 1925/1955) and there remain contemporary examples of this approach such as the psychotherapeutic unit at Grendon Prison in England (Shuker & Sullivan, 2010).

As psychotherapeutic methods waned the next major step took place in the 1970s with the application of behavioural theory to inform the use of therapeutic interventions such as the token economy with offenders (Milan, 2001), teaching-parent residential homes (Kirigin et al., 1982) and social skills training (Henderson & Hollin, 1986). The third phase saw a move to cognitive-behavioural methods of change such as coping skills training and anger management (Hollin, 1990; Novaco, 1975, 2007, 2013; Ross & Fabiano, 1985).

Family therapy has also been used with delinquents (Kazdin, 1987). With *parent management training* the parents are taught skills to help them manage their child's behaviour and to reinforce desirable behaviour. In *functional family therapy* the focus is on changing the interactive processes inside the family to help all family members to solve their own problems effectively.

Nothing works

The progress of therapeutic work with offenders was halted by several reviews which were negative in tone (Bailey, 1966; Brody, 1976; Martinson, 1974). It was the Martinson review, based on a larger review of 231 studies by Lipton, Martinson, and Wilks (1975), which proved to have the greatest impact. Martinson argued that it remained unproven that treatment had any significant or sustained effect on criminal behaviour; this conclusion led others to the view that it had been shown to be the case that nothing works in offender rehabilitation. The acceptance that "nothing works" in offender rehabilitation led in the 1980s to punitive regimes underpinned by the notion of "just deserts" (Hudson, 1987). While the idea that nothing works was strongly challenged (Gendreau & Ross, 1979, 1987; Thornton, 1987) and, indeed, Martinson himself revised his views (Martinson, 1979), it was not until the 1990s that treatment returned to centre stage.

What works?

The nothing works position was a direct consequence of the reviewers reading and interpreting the extant literature. In this form of narrative review the conclusions are based on the reviewer's opinions and judgement; it is hardly surprising that different reviewers can reach different views of the same literature. The development of the statistical technique of *meta-analysis* changed the way in which reviews were conducted while, unlike the narrative review, offering a replicable methodology (Glass, McGraw, & Smith, 1981). Meta-analysis is a statistical technique for reviewing the accumulated results of a large number of primary research studies to produce an estimate of the outcome of an independent variable, such as treatment versus no treatment, on a specified outcome such as reoffending. A meta-analysis gives a statistic called an *effect size* from which the magnitude of the difference in outcome between treatment and control groups can be calculated (Marshall & McGuire, 2003). In addition, a meta-analysis gives control over variations between the primary studies, such as type of offender group, treatment setting, length of follow-up and type of outcome, allowing their impact on effect size to be gauged (e.g., Lipsey, 1992; Redondo, Sánchez-Meca, & Garrido, 2002). Meta-analysis is only limited by the number of primary studies and can distill a substantial literature: for example, Lipsey (1992) incorporated no fewer than 443 studies of offender treatment into his meta-analysis.

The first meta-analysis of offender treatment was reported by Garrett (1985) which proved to be the forerunner of over 70 meta-analytic studies of offender treatment (see McGuire, 2002). The offender treatment meta-analyses included different offenders such as men who are violent to their partners (Babcock, Green, & Robie, 2004), sex offenders (Hanson et al., 2009), and violent offenders (McGuire, 2008a), alongside treatment modality such boot camps, group therapy, and behavioural interventions. The meta-analyses yielded two main conclusions. First, with respect to recidivism there is a "net effect" of treatment of the order of a 10–12 per cent reduction in reoffending compared to no intervention or business as usual (Lösel, 1996). Second, it is possible to identify the characteristics of interventions that had both positive and negative effects on reoffending.

The high positive effect interventions were multi-modal, cognitive-behavioural, or skills-oriented; the most effective mode of delivery was through the use of structured programmes. The effective interventions were targeted at factors directly related to offending (which became known as *criminogenic needs*) and were carried out with offenders who had a high risk of reoffending. The effective interventions were delivered by trained and supported staff with high levels of treatment integrity in settings that offered high levels of organisational support. The negative effects came from punitive, deterrence-based interventions.

The accumulation of information about the qualities of high effect interventions led to the formulation of the principles of effective practice.

Principles of effective practice

Turning on the phrase "nothing works", the syntheses of the findings of the meta-analyses became known as *"What Works?"* (McGuire, 1995). As the evidence-base grew (Andrews, 1995; Gendreau, 1996; Hollin, 1999; Lösel, 1996; Smith, Gendreau, & Swartz, 2009) and engagement in offender rehabilitation was reaffirmed (Cullen & Gilbert, 2013), so the three principles of effective practice, shown in Table 6.1, were formulated.

The focus on risk, need, and responsivity led to the formulation of a formal Risk-Need-Responsivity (RNR) model of offender assessment and rehabilitation, currently the leading approach to offender rehabilitation (Andrews & Bonta, 2010; Andrews, Bonta, & Wormith, 2006) including violent offenders (Dowden & Andrews, 2000).

Risk and need

An offender's risk of offending is defined by their level of *criminogenic need*, that is the elements in their life directly associated with their likelihood of

---

TABLE 6.1. Principles of effective practice to reduce reoffending

1. *The risk principle.* Intensive services are needed for offenders with a high risk of reoffending; a lighter approach is sufficient for low risk offenders.

2. *The needs principle.* Interventions should target offenders' criminogenic needs, i.e., those factors directly related to the individual's offending. This principle does not advocate ignoring noncriminogenic needs, rather that clarity is required regarding the outcome an intervention can be expected to achieve. Those unqualified interventions that target noncriminogenic needs and do not reduce offending will be judged as treatment failures.

3. *The responsivity principle.* There should be high degree of correspondence between the delivery of the intervention and offender characteristics such as age, culture, intellectual ability, and gender.

committing crime. There are two types of criminogenic need: (1) *static criminogenic needs*, such as criminal history, which cannot be changed; (2) *dynamic criminogenic needs*, such as drug and alcohol use, which are amenable to change. The Level of Supervision Inventory (LSI; Andrews, 1982), later becoming the Level of Service Inventory–Revised (LSI-R; Andrews & Bonta, 1995), was designed as a measure of risk and need for use by practitioners. The 54-item LSI-R, completed through an interview with the offender and a file review, assesses the ten criminogenic factors shown in Table 6.2. The 54 items are marked to give a score for each area of need: the score for each dynamic need indicates where change is required to reduce risk; the total score for all ten domains, translated into low, medium, and high bands, provides an estimate of the individual's risk of reoffending. The LSI-R has been shown to be reliable and valid in jurisdictions as diverse as England (Hollin, Palmer, & Clark, 2003) and China (Zhang & Liu, 2015) and has passed through several changes as the literature grows (Wormith & Bonta, 2018).

Hollin and Palmer (2003) compared the needs of violent and non-violent prisoners as assessed by the LSI-R. The violent prisoners showed higher levels of need than the nonviolent prisoners on the four domains of Alcohol and Drugs, Companions, Criminal History, and Education and Employment. The violent prisoners gave a higher total LSI-R score thereby indicating their greater risk of reoffending. The prominence of drug and alcohol problems in the violent offenders is in keeping with the wider literature.

TABLE 6.2. Assessment Domains in the LSI-R

1	Accommodation
2	Alcohol/Drug Problems
3	Attitudes/Orientation
4	Companions
5	Criminal History
6	Education/Employment
7	Emotional/Personal
8	Family/Marital
9	Finance
10	Leisure/Recreation

Changing criminogenic need

A major impact of *What Works?* lay in the finding that high effect interventions were delivered in a structured format. The first of a new type of structured cognitive-behavioural intervention, called *Reasoning and Rehabilitation (R & R)*, for use with offender populations was developed in Canada (Ross, Fabiano, & Ewles, 1988; Ross, Fabiano, & Ross, 1989).

Reasoning and Rehabilitation (R & R)

R & R is based on empirical research showing an association between thinking and offending (Ross & Fabiano, 1985). *R & R* employs cognitive-behavioural techniques such as modelling, rehearsal, reinforcement, and role-play to assist the offender to learn ways of thinking that increase self-control, social problem-solving skills, social perspective-taking, and critical reasoning, and challenges the attitudes and beliefs that support their criminal behaviour. *R & R* may be delivered by trained personnel, including prison and probation officers, not just by professional therapists. A system for video monitoring of sessions enhances feedback to practitioners and helps maintain treatment integrity. *R & R* has been used, both in institutional and in community settings, in Australia, Canada, England and Wales, Germany, Scandinavia, Scotland, Spain, New Zealand, and the USA. The evaluations are positive results in terms of reduced offending (Antonwicz, 2005; Tong & Farrington, 2006).

One of the innovations that characterised *R & R* was that it was made available in the form of a treatment manual. The manual contained guidelines for the selection of participants, the contents of the sessions such as role-play exercises, and the order in which the sessions were to be delivered. While use of treatment manuals to guide treatment delivery was established in mainstream clinical psychology (Wilson, 1996) their use with offenders was a pioneering step.

Straight Thinking on Probation (STOP)

In Wales, Mid-Glamorgan Probation Service adapted the *R & R* programme for their own use (Knott, 1995). A 12-months follow-up of *STOP* participants found that the actual and the predicted rates of reconviction were the same for those allocated to treatment and the comparison group (Raynor & Vanstone, 1996). However, those offenders who *completed* the programme showed both a significantly lower reconviction rate than predicted and, if reconvicted, a significantly lower rate of custodial sentences.

The possibilities raised by structured interventions were seen as attractive within the criminal justice system principally for two reasons. They offered, first, an evidence-based route to reducing crime which, if effective, would ultimately pay for itself, and, second, the possibility of large-scale delivery using current staff rather than employing ranks of expensive therapists. The scene was set for a growth in what became known as Offending Behaviour Programmes (Hollin & Palmer, 2006).

Offending Behaviour Programmes

The English and Welsh Prison Service introduced a set of standards, termed *Accreditation Criteria*, by which to decide if an Offending Behaviour Programme (OBP) is fit for purpose (Lipton et al., 2000; Maguire et al., 2010). Once an OBP is judged to be of the right pedigree, the next step lies in its implementation, in particular highly trained and supervised staff to deliver the OBP are essential and these staff must have the full support of the organisation's management (Andrews, 2011; Dowden & Andrews, 2004; Gendreau, Goggin, & Smith, 2001).

As the field opened up so there was a flurry of new OBPs in the prison and probation services. Some programmes, collectively known as *cognitive skills programmes* (Hollin & Palmer, 2009), were intended for general use with offender populations which would have included violent offenders. In addition to the general programmes other specialist OBPs were designed specifically for different types of offender.

Cognitive skills programmes

The OBPs focused on cognitive skills were *Enhanced Thinking Skills (ETS)*, a cognitive skills programme similar to *R & R* but shorter in duration. The evaluations showed *ETS* to be effective in institutional settings with adult male offenders who complete the programme (Sadlier, 2010). The *Think First* programme is similar in approach and content to both *R & R* and *ETS* but with a more obvious focus on offending behaviour (McGuire, 2005).

The effectiveness of *R & R, ETS*, and *Think First* within the English and Welsh Probation Service was considered in a series of empirical studies (Hollin et al., 2008; Palmer et al., 2007; McGuire et al., 2008; Travers et al., 2011; Travers, Mann, & Hollin, 2014). The evaluations showed a positive effect of the cognitive skills programmes with a reduction in reoffending commensurate with the *What Works* literature. This conclusion was later extended by Koehler et al. (2013) in their survey of young offender treatment programmes in Europe. In addition, the evaluations also highlighted the utility of different research designs in this type of evaluation (Hollin, 2008) and highlighted the detrimental effects of programme non-completion and incorrect allocation to treatment on treatment outcome (Palmer et al., 2008, 2009). These findings informed the next generation of OBPs for offenders on probation in the community (Bruce & Hollin, 2009; Pearson et al., 2011), so adding focus to offender supervision and bringing the RNR model into mainstream probation practice (Bonta et al., 2008).

Alongside cognitive skills programmes, programmes based on the RNR model were developed in England and Wales for a range of offences including drink impaired driving (Palmer et al., 2012) and substance use (McMurran & Priestley, 2004). Of interest here are the programmes for intimate partner violence, sexual violence, and violent offending.

Intimate partner violence

As discussed in Chapter 3, there are a range of treatment programmes – principally cognitive-behavioural therapy, profeminist methods, and a psychodynamic approach – used with perpetrators of intimate partner violence (IPV) although in practice these approaches are often combined to give a hybrid form of treatment. In addition, there are influential programmes such as the American Duluth model (Pence & Paymar, 1993).

Bates et al. (2017) carried out a review of domestic violence perpetrator programmes in the UK. They note that the Correctional Services Advice and Accreditation Panel has reviewed and accredited four programmes for use with IPV offenders: these four are Building Better Relationships (BBR), Community Domestic Violence Program (CDVP), the Healthy Relationships Program (HRP), and the Integrated Domestic Abuse Program (IDAP). In commenting on both the low number of evaluations and hence the lack of empirical support for these programmes, Bates and colleagues remark on the problems of non-cooperation from programme providers and low treatment integrity which both blight empirical research.

The low success rate of treatment for IPV is endemic in the literature, including several meta-analyses (e.g., Arias, Arce, & Vilarino, 2013; Babcock, Green, & Robie, 2004; Bowen, Gilchrist, & Beech, 2005, 2008; Haggård et al., 2017; Seewald et al., 2018). There are some positive findings (e.g., Hasisi et al., 2016) but Haggård and colleagues lament "The frustrating lack of proven effective treatments for IPV offenders" (p. 1027). In a wide-ranging discussion of policy and practice, Babcock et al. (2016) offer a long list of recommendations, including programme characteristics, training, and systemic evaluation, for setting evidence-based standards in order to improve the effectiveness of treatment.

Sexual violence: biological treatment

The view of sexual violence as a sexual deviation, rather than a type of violent behaviour, prompted the biological treatment of sex offenders. This form of intervention with its reliance on drugs and surgery is the province of the medical profession (Thibaut et al., 2010). The two forms of biological treatment that have been most relatively widely used are *androgen deprivation* (sometimes referred to as *chemical castration*) and *surgical castration*.

Androgen deprivation, a form of pharmacological intervention (Khan et al., 2015), takes the form of a drug regime that acts to suppress the production and functioning of male hormones, principally testosterone (Houts et al., 2011). The reviews of the effectiveness of androgen deprivation were initially positive and suggested that physiological rather than psychological change was more likely to reduce sex offending (Bradford, 2000; Lösel & Schmucker, 2005; Rösler & Witztum, 2000). In a comprehensive review, Rice and Harris (2011) make the point that there was a quick acceptance of the crime reduction power of pharmacological intervention. They suggest that this acceptance may partially have been a consequence of offenders' statements about their high levels of sexual arousal. In addition, it is also feasible that the drug effect, endorsed by some practitioners, accorded with wider "common sense" views on the causes of sex offending.

Rice and Harris also note that the favourable evidence is based on samples which include offenders who volunteer for the treatment (see Amelung et al., 2012). These volunteers may be a low-risk group or may be ready to change their offending behaviour, increasing their likelihood of not reoffending. Studies of the effect of drugs on sex offenders who do not volunteer for treatment are lacking and so little is known about the effects of treatment with this group. Rice and Harris conclude that: "Clearly, much more research is needed before ADT has a sufficient scientific basis to be relied upon as a principal component of sex offender treatment" (p. 328).

The surgical castration of those who commit sexual offences has been widely practised throughout history (Stürup, 1972) including in European countries such as Denmark, Germany, the Netherlands, Norway, and Switzerland (Heim & Hursch, 1979; van der Meer, 2014) as well as some American states (Weinberger et al., 2005). There are two main issues with evaluating the use of surgical castration. First, the methodological problems in evaluation, including a paucity of follow-up studies, make its effect on crime reduction uncertain (Heim & Hursch, 1979; Meyer & Cole, 1997) as seen with mixed reviews regarding its effectiveness with sex offenders against children (Garcia et al., 2013; Långström et al., 2013). Implausible as this uncertainty may initially appear, castrated men can continue to engage in sexual, including sexually violent, behaviour (Heim, 1981). The second concern, which equally well applies to chemical castration, lies in the ethics and morals of this type of biological treatment administered either coercively or voluntarily. Does the state have the right to impose such a sanction; can the individual offender be rightly said to have freely consented to the procedures (Douglas et al., 2013; Oswald, 2013; Ratkoceri, 2017)?

Sexual violence: psychological treatment

The history of the psychological treatment of sex offenders has moved through treatment models including variants of behavioural, psychodynamic, and cognitive-behavioural therapies (Dennis et al., 2012; Hanson, 2014; Marshall & Hollin, 2015). A great deal of the treatment of sex offenders has taken place in custody as, arguably, the most serious sex offenders are incarcerated and so have the greatest need for intervention. In addition, it is more efficient (although not necessarily more effective) to deliver treatment to a captive group. Olver, Wong, and Nicholaichuk (2009) carried out an extension and long-term follow-up to an earlier study (Nicholaichuk et al., 2000) of sex offenders treated in a Canadian federal maximum-security correctional treatment facility using treatment based on the *What Works* principles. Olver, Wong, and Nicholaichuk found that:

> A significant treatment effect was observed after controlling for relevant risk-related variables with treated offenders demonstrating a lower rate of sexual reconviction than untreated ones over nearly 20 years follow-up. There was a clear separation of the survival functions of the two groups from the time of release to the end of the follow-up period, suggesting that the treatment effect was maintained for the duration of the entire follow-up.
>
> *(p. 531)*

Pérez and Jennings (2012) reported an evaluation of an American prison-based treatment programme for sex offenders. This programme used a combination of techniques drawn from cognitive-behavioural and relapse prevention approaches. The evaluation looked at outcome for three groups: (1) those who completed treatment; (2) those who started treatment but did not complete it; (3) no-treatment controls. The evaluation showed a lower rate of recidivism and a longer length of time to re-arrest for those offenders who completed treatment compared to non-completers and controls.

Grady, Edwards, and Pettus-Davis (2017) reported no effect of a prison-based cognitive-behavioural programme on the sexual and violent reoffending of a group of sex offenders followed up for periods of up to 10 years post-treatment.

In the English and Welsh prison service the Core Sex Offender Treatment Programme (SOTP) has been the primary intervention for sex offenders (Mann & Fernandez, 2006). In order to address issues of responsivity, there are versions of the SOTP for sex offenders of lower levels of intellectual functioning, high and low risk sex offenders, and a booster programme for offenders who may need further intervention. Where positive results in terms of sexual reconviction have been found, these have typically been among medium-low and medium-high risk men who have been responsive to treatment (Beech et al., 2001; Friendship, Mann, & Beech, 2003). An evaluation of SOTP was reported by Mews, Di Bella, and Purver (2017) which found that over an average 8.2-year follow-up: "More treated sex offenders committed at least one sexual reoffence (excluding breach) during the follow-up period when compared with the matched comparison offenders (10.0% compared with 8.0%)" (p. 3). Is it the case, as it appears from this finding, that the Core SOTP makes matters *worse* in terms of reconvictions?

Mews, Di Bella, and Purver give several explanations for this null finding which is out of step with both the previous evaluations of SOTP and most of the wider literature (see below). These explanations include methodological factors in conducting the research, such as the quality of the data available, and programme factors such as the unquantifiable quality of programme delivery. Mews, Di Bella, and Purver suggest that the programme could be improved by being "Modified in line with the latest evidence base …. In particular, it could include individual sessions as well as group sessions. It could also focus more on factors that have been established to predict reoffending" (p. 28). The need to update programmes has been discussed by Thornton (2013), although whether any updating will happen with SOTP is unknown: when the Mews, Di Bella, and Purver report was published the Home Secretary instructed that the programme be withdrawn from use.

There have been several reviews of a large body of literature which are cautiously optimistic regarding the effects of treatment on reducing sexual reoffending (Beech & Mann, 2002; Hanson et al., 2002; Hanson & Yates, 2013; Kim, Benekos, & Merlo, 2016; Mpofu et al., 2018; ter Beek et al., 2018; Walton & Chou, 2015). However, Grønnerød, Grønnerød and Grøndahl (2015) conducted a meta-analysis of 14 evaluations of treatment specifically for sex offenders against children and concluded, as did Långström et al. (2013), that there was no effect of treatment. The problem Grønnerød, Grønnerød and Grøndahl identified is that the outcome evidence generally fails to reach the accepted standards for robust scientific research.

In those analyses where a treatment effect is evident the preferred mode of therapy is cognitive-behavioural. It may be that other therapeutic approaches could be adapted to become more effective (Hoberman, 2016) but the extant evidence favours cognitive-behavioural approaches.

The Sex Offender Treatment and Evaluation Project (SOTEP) provides an example of an evaluation using a strong research design and cognitive-behavioural treatment. SOTEP, carried out in California, was distinguished by its use of a randomised control trial in the evaluation of a relapse prevention programme with sex offenders serving custodial sentences (Marques et al., 2005). The programme of relapse prevention, taken from the treatment of substance abuse, uses cognitive-behavioural methods to prevent the recurrence of the criminal sexual behaviour. The outcome over an 8-year period, for both offenders against children and offenders against adults, showed no effect of the treatment in reducing sexual or violent offending. An examination of the treatment group (negating the effects of randomisation) showed that the offenders who met the programme's treatment goals had a lower rate of reoffending than those who failed to meet the treatment goals. The utility of randomised designs in evaluating treatment generally is discussed further in the following chapter: see Marshall and Marshall (2007) and Seto et al. (2008) specifically for a discussion of randomised designs in sex offender treatment and the SOTEP.

The utility of approaches other than cognitive-behavioural and RNR in informing the treatment of sex offenders is discussed in Chapter 7.

Violent offending

There have been various attempts to reduce violent recidivism among convicted violent offenders. The examples discussed below include specialist prison treatment regimes, and the use of programmes originally intended for use with non-offender populations. There have been several attempts to introduce specialist regimes into prisons with the aim of reducing violent recidivism. In the UK, Smith (1984) notes "Grendon Underwood, the psychiatric prison in Buckinghamshire, the Special Unit at Barlinnie for prisoners who are hard to manage, and the Wormwood Scrubs Annexe for sex offenders and drug addicts" (p. 472). In 1998 a prison programme, the Rimutaka Violence Prevention Unit, was introduced into the New Zealand prison system. This programme was developed using contemporary research and is characterised by its high level of monitoring and evaluation.

Rimutaka Violence Prevention Unit (RVPU)

The RVPU is a purpose-built 30-bed medium-security unit, located at Rimutaka Prison near the city of Wellington. The programme is designed for male prisoners who are at high risk of violent reoffending and who are close to eligibility for parole. The RVPU takes referrals from all of the national prison system. The admission criteria are a violent index offence and an absence of major barriers, such as mental disorder, to participation in the programme. The treatment within the RVPU is cognitive-behavioural and delivered in modules which are: (i) the identification of individual risk factors; (ii) challenging offence-supportive thinking; (iii) mood management; (iv) victim empathy; (v) enhancing moral reasoning; (vi) building problem-solving skills; (vii) communication and relationship skills; (viii) post-release risk management planning (see Polaschek et al., 2005). The level of treatment is intense with four 3-hour group meetings a week over 28 weeks giving 336 hours of group work. Any relevant psychological issues that cannot be addressed in a group setting are given individual attention. After completing the programme, the majority of offenders appear before New Zealand's national parole board and are released on parole within days or weeks.

The first outcome data for the RVPU, reported by Polaschek et al. (2005), compared the treated men with a non-treatment control on nonviolent reconviction, violent reconviction and subsequent imprisonment over a 2-year or greater follow-up period. There was a positive outcome in that the treated offenders were less significantly likely to be reconvicted of a violent offense than the controls, while those in the treatment group who were reconvicted took longer to fail. The treated prisoners also showed fewer reconvictions for nonviolent offences and were less likely to return to prison.

A larger scale evaluation of the RVPU was conducted by Polaschek (2011). The rate of reconviction for a violent offence was 62 per cent compared to 72 per cent for the prisoners in the control condition. The time to reconviction for a violent offence was 576 days for the treatment group compared to 490 days for the untreated controls. The success of the RVPU led to its adoption on a wider scale across New Zealand prisons (Polaschek & Kilgour, 2013).

A feature of the RVPU evaluation was that more than one-half of the prisoners were New Zealand Maori. The configuration of treatments to maximise responsivity among indigenous populations has received growing attention in several countries including New Zealand as well as Australia, Canada, and the USA among others (Grant, 2016; Macklin & Gilbert, 2011). This point is given emphasis by the adoption of cognitive-behavioural treatments for violent offenders in countries such as China (Chen et al., 2014) and Singapore (Zhou et al., 2018) where high levels of responsivity to western treatments cannot be assumed.

Aggression Replacement Training (ART)

Discussed previously in relation to treating aggressive children, *ART* has been used with violent offenders. Hatcher et al. (2008) conducted an evaluation of ART with convicted male violent offenders under the jurisdiction of the English and Welsh Probation Service. The study employed one-to-one matching on important criminogenic variables across the experimental and comparison groups. There was a 13.3 per cent decrease in reconviction in the experimental group as compared to the comparison group. The programme non-completers were more likely to be reconvicted than both their matched comparisons and the programme completers. Holmqvist, Hill, and Lang (2009) used *ART* with young offenders in custody in Sweden, comparing its effects with other interventions including a token economy and relational treatment methods. There was no difference in outcome according to style of treatment although Holmqvist, Hill, and Lang made the comment that treatment integrity could not be assured across the participating institutions. Brännström et al. (2016) conducted a systematic review of 16 evaluations of *ART*. They concluded that weaknesses in research methodology, including the protocols of the randomised studies and limited follow-up, restrict confidence in estimating the effectiveness of *ART*.

Anger management

Anger management techniques have been used with a wide range of populations in the treatment of a variety of problems (Lee & DiGiuseppe,

2017). The association between anger and violence has led to the widespread use of treatment using cognitive-behavioural techniques with offender populations (Novaco, 2013). On a lesser scale, other approaches, such as dialectical behaviour therapy (Frazier & Vela, 2014), have been used with anger problems.

Henwood, Chou, and Browne (2015) reported a systematic review and meta-analysis of the effectiveness of cognitive-behavioural anger management with a focus on offender populations. The review included 14 studies where adult male offenders had participated in anger management. Henwood, Chou, and Browne conclude that their findings "indicate a decrease in re-offending especially when the focus is on violent reconviction" (p. 291).

Violence in prisons

Finally, the ultimate setting for interpersonal violence is surely one in which violent offenders are forced to live together in restricted, often intolerable conditions. In this light it is hardly surprising that prisons are characterised by a high incidence of violence. Auty, Cope, and Liebling (2017) carried out a systematic review of 21 psychoeducational interventions intended to reduce violence in prisons. The most favoured theoretical approach was cognitive-behavioural, typically with a comparison of treatment and control groups on measures such as institutional reports, prisoner self-report, observer ratings, or psychometric scales. The outcome evidence was mixed in that, while the majority of studies reported a fewer violent incidents in the treatment group compared to the control group, the magnitude of the difference often failed to attain statistical significance.

Mentally disordered offenders

The critical difference between mainstream offenders in the criminal justice system and the mentally disordered offender is that the latter is legally detained not for punishment but for treatment, medical and psychological, to address both the mental disorder and the offending behaviour, and so to reduce their risk to the community. In practice the division between health services and the criminal system is not absolutely clear cut. Given the complexities of treating and managing mentally disordered offenders, efforts are made to divert them from the criminal justice system (James, 2010; Slade et al., 2016). Nonetheless, some of the offenders in prison have a mental disorder: it is impossible to be exact but estimates suggest that in western countries about one in seven prisoners have a psychotic illness or major depression, while about one-half of male prisoners and about one-fifth of female prisoners have an antisocial personality disorder (Fazel & Danesh, 2002). The consequence of this situation is a steady flow of prisoners from the criminal justice system to mental health services.

In some instances the nature of the offence committed by the mentally disordered offender, alongside the risk they pose to the public, may require high levels of security. When security is required the mentally disordered offender may be detained for treatment either in conditions of high or medium security. In other cases, the risk is judged to be minimal so treatment in the community is possible. Whether in security or the community, the psychiatric treatment regime for mentally disordered offenders may involve a combination of medication and psychological therapy. The medications used to treat violent behaviour may include clozapine, known to be effective in reducing aggression (Citrome & Volavka, 2011) while the psychological therapies include anger management and cognitive change programmes (Kolla & Hodgins, 2013).

In common with other violent populations the violent mentally disordered offender may have comorbid problems with substance use, primarily alcohol, which is associated with serious violence, including homicide (Fazel et al., 2010). With regard to treatment of alcohol use, Gumpert et al. (2010) compared outcomes for 403 male mentally disordered offenders who had taken part in substance abuse treatment with a non-treated control. The offenders who had completed more than 6 weeks of treatment had a significantly reduced risk of committing another crime, including a violent crime.

The association between anger and violence is, like alcohol use, a feature of mentally disordered populations, as it is with mainstream offenders (Novaco, 1997). Anger is a strong predictor of assaultive behaviour within hospital (Novaco & Renwick, 1998) and its treatment is clearly indicated for the violent mentally disordered offender to reduce violent behaviour (Renwick et al., 1997). Two successful evaluations of anger control programmes in a high security hospital were reported by Jones and Hollin (2004) and by Braham, Jones, and Hollin (2008). The multimodal treatment used anger control, social problem solving, and social skills training – as would be seen in interventions for mainstream violent offenders (Hollin, 2018) – and varied the pace of delivery to the needs of the patients. In addition to the group programme, personal support was also available to patient groups.

The mainstream cognitive change programmes, such as *ETS* and *R&R*, have been adapted for use with forensic patients (Moore et al., 2018). Similarly,

Hornsveld et al. (2008) modified *Aggression Replacement Training* for use with forensic psychiatric populations. While the evidence base is small, there are indications that programmes to address cognitive functioning can be successful with mentally disordered offenders. This latter point also applies to those offenders labelled as *psychopaths*. This group of high-risk violent offenders were once held to be untreatable but there are suggestions that tailored treatments accompanied by rigorous evaluation may mean that progress can be made (Abracen et al., 2011; Polaschek & Daly, 2013; Reidy, Kearns, & DeGue, 2013).

High security hospitals

High security psychiatric hospitals are known as State Hospitals or Special Hospitals: in England the first special hospital, Broadmoor Hospital in Berkshire, opened in 1863, followed in 1919 by Rampton Hospital in Nottinghamshire; Ashworth Hospital near Liverpool is the third Special Hospital, formed from a merger of Moss Side Hospital, itself dating back to 1914 when it served "shell shocked" soldiers returning from the Great War, and Park Lane Hospital which opened in 1974 (Greenland, 1969). Carstairs is the State Hospital in Scotland and it also serves Northern Ireland. Each Special Hospital holds over a hundred, mainly male, patients.

Follow-up studies

High security hospitals are an expensive facility and while they serve the purpose of removing the risk to the public the question remains of their effectiveness in reducing violence. However, it is unusual for a patient to be released directly from high security into the community. There is likely to be a transition from high to medium security and then into a supervised community placement. Thus, the follow-ups of high security patients reflect the efficacy of the system rather than that of a particular hospital.

Black (1982) reported a 5-year follow-up study of 125 male patients discharged from Broadmoor Hospital. In all, 101 of the patients were not readmitted to a psychiatric hospital, 97 had no record of imprisonment, and 70 had no further appearances in court. Jamieson and Taylor (2004) conducted a 2-year follow-up of 197 patients discharged from Special Hospital: in the follow-up period 74 patients were convicted mainly for property and violent offences. Buchanan, Taylor, and Gunn (2004) took a sample of 40 discharged patients from English special hospital who were later convicted of a serious offence. When compared with a matched group of unconvicted patients, the convicted patients were significantly younger, had poor school attendance, were more likely to have a history of alcohol use and a diagnosis of psychopathic disorder, and had more criminal convictions.

The Special Hospitals are expensive to maintain and the financial costs, if nothing else, lead to two questions: (1) is high security necessary for all mentally disordered offenders? (2) what happens to patients after treatment when high security is no longer necessary? The answer which emerged was hospitals with a medium level of security.

Medium security hospitals

Initially known as Regional Secure Units (RSUs), medium secure hospitals were set up in England and Wales in the 1980s (Treasaden, 2018). The medium secure units can either receive patients transferred from high security or directly receive patients whose level of risk does not warrant high security. There have been follow-up studies of both types of patient.

Cope and Ward (1993) considered patients who had been transferred from high to medium security. They found that one-third of the patients were directly returned to high security while just over 10 per cent had a serious reconviction. Quinn and Ward (2000) reported a return rate from high to medium security of over one-quarter of patients and a similar rate of serious reconviction as in the Cope and Ward study. Blattner and Dolan (2009) followed up 72 patients who had moved from high to medium security and then to discharge into the community. There was a high level of failure with 46 per cent of the patients returning to high security; however the reconviction rate for serious offences was comparable with the previous two studies.

Maden et al. (1999) followed-up for an average of 6 years a group of 234 direct admissions to medium security. They reported that close to one-quarter of the patients had been reconvicted at a follow-up. In all, 33 of the reconvicted patients had committed a violent offence and 10 a sexual offence; 4 patients had committed arson which is an offence that can endanger life. Maden et al. (2004) followed up a sample of 959 patients over a 2-year period and found that 145 had been reconvicted, including 60 for violent offences.

Davies et al., (2007) followed up 550 patients discharged from the same medium secure hospital over a 20-year period. They found that almost one-half of the patients had been reconvicted and, following the Home Office (2002) classification of convictions as either "grave" or "standard list", 14 per cent had been reconvicted for a grave offence. Davies and colleagues made the point that not every offence leads to a conviction, which is particularly true for detained patients. Thus, they report "Within the first 2 years after discharge at least 28% of patients had exhibited violent behaviour not resulting in conviction and within 5 years this had increased to at least 42%" (p. 72).

The rates of homicide and of sex offending were examined for the cohort of patients in the Davies et al. (2007) study. Clarke et al. (2016) focused on the 49 patients who had committed homicide together with the 24 patients with an index offence of attempted homicide. At the end of the follow-up period just one of the 73 patients had been convicted of a further homicide. Duggan et al. (2013) looked at the rates of reconviction of a group of mentally disordered sex offenders over a 9-year post-discharge follow-up. While the sex offenders were as likely to be convicted for any offence, including a violent offence, as the non-sex offender controls, they were significantly more likely to be reconvicted for another sexual offence.

Coid et al. (2007) looked at the reoffending of 1,334 patients for 7 of the 14 medium secure forensic psychiatry services in England and Wales. The patients had been discharged for a variable length of time, ranging from a month to almost a decade with a mean of 6.2 years. The reconviction rate for a violent offence was 18.1 per cent for men and 5.1 per cent for women; the reconviction rate for a grave offence, including homicide, attempted murder, wounding, malicious wounding, robbery, aggravated burglary, rape, and arson, was 12.2 per cent for men and 6.2 per cent for women.

Community

The supervision of mentally disordered offenders in the community includes both patients from secure hospitals and those who have never been admitted to security. Developed in Wisconsin, the *Assertive Community Treatment* (ACT) programme involves an interdisciplinary team, a psychiatrist, psychiatric nurse, and social worker, monitoring and supporting in the community a small caseload of people with severe mental illness who are at high risk for rehospitalisation (Test & Stein, 1976). The ACT programme was adapted, as *Forensic ACT* (FACT) and *Forensic Intensive Case Management* (FICM), for use with mentally disordered and mainstream offenders (Lamberti, Weisman, & Faden, 2004). In a review of the use of ACT with forensic populations, Jennings (2009) concluded that "Despite the complexity and diversity of forensic programs, the field appears to be converging on the conclusion that ACT is ineffective or minimally effective with forensic populations" (p. 18). Jennings suggests that the variations on ACT applied to forensic populations have diluted the original model and led to a loss of treatment fidelity.

In California, Cusack et al. (2010) conducted a randomised clinical trial comparing FACT with treatment as usual for frequently imprisoned offenders with serious mental illness problems. They reported that at both 12- and 24-month follow-up the FACT participants were less likely to be jailed, had more outpatient contacts, and had fewer days in hospital. The programme was cost effective in that the increased costs of FACT outpatient services were partially offset by the decrease in costs for hospital inpatient and prison. Cusack and colleagues conclude that their findings offer support for the provision of appropriate health services to offender populations.

Risk assessment

While the public is protected by the secure hospitals when the offender is detained and where therapeutic work contributes towards reducing the risk of further offences (Ross et al., 2013; Sturgeon, Tyler, & Gannon, 2018), it is nevertheless the case that some patients will commit further offences after discharge. It would clearly be of benefit to know which offenders are at greatest risk of further offences and a body of work has examined the predictors of reconviction (Scott & Resnick, 2006).

Bonta, Law, and Hanson (1998) reported a meta-analysis of the recidivism of mentally disordered offenders and noted three classes of significant predictor: (1) *individual* variables such as being male, age, employment problems, family dysfunction, and substance, particularly alcohol, abuse; (2) *clinical* variables such as previous hospital admission and length of stay, and a diagnosis of antisocial personality disorder; (3) *criminological* variables such as convictions as a juvenile and as an adult.

The studies after Bonta, Law, and Hanson's meta-analysis have emphasised the strength of two particular dynamic predictors of violence. First, as with other violent populations, alcohol misuse is a powerful predictor of reconviction for a violent offence among mentally disordered offenders (Castillo & Alarid, 2011; Nilsson et al., 2011). Second, a diagnosis of schizophrenia is associated with the likelihood of violence (Bo et al., 2011; Hodgins, 2008; Hodgins & Riaz, 2011; Witt, van Dorn, & Fazel, 2013). Risk factors do not always act alone and, given that perhaps one-half of people with schizophrenia have a comorbid substance use disorder (Volkow, 2009), the combination of the two may produce a heightened level of risk of violence, although alcohol may be the most powerful (Elbogen & Johnson, 2009; Fazel et al., 2009). The amelioration of risk can be achieved through treatment although continued substance misuse acts against any treatment gains (Langeveld et al., 2014).

The development of risk assessment protocols for this population is an obvious step (Scott & Resnick, 2006) and there are instruments for the specific purpose including the Camberwell Assessment of Need-Forensic Version (CANFOR; Thomas et al., 2003), the Historical-Clinical Risk Management (HCR-20; Webster et al., 1997), the Violence Risk Assessment Guide (VRAG; Quinsey et al., 2006), and the online clinical prediction rule (FoVOx; Wolf et al., 2018). In addition, there are other assessment methods such as patient observation which may be used to identify the cues associated with the onset and maintenance of violent behaviour (Hornsveld et al., 2007).

7

COULD WE DO BETTER?

Societal change

Alcohol

There is overwhelming evidence for an association between alcohol and violence. It follows that attempts to reduce violence must pay attention to reducing alcohol intake by perpetrators of acts of violence. At the level of working with the individual, including the violent offender (McMurran, 2012, 2013; McMurran et al., 2011), there is a vast body of expertise given to treating problem drinking. It is arguable that any individual treatment for violent behaviour should include a screen for problem drinking (Booth et al., 2013; Watt, Shepherd, & Newcombe, 2008). To treat the violence and neglect the alcohol use is potentially to complete only half the task. However, if we move away from the individual and look at the wider picture, the question arises of whether anything can be done at a societal level to curtail levels of alcohol intake. There are familiar arguments to limit alcohol consumption on health grounds but there are also benefits to be had in terms of reducing violence.

There are two commonplace strategies to reducing violence through controlling alcohol (World Health Organization, 2009): (1) target specific locations where drinking and violence may coincide; (2) employ a widespread curtailment of access to alcohol.

Local restrictions

At some major sporting events which attract large crowds, particularly where there is a fierce, even hostile, rivalry between opposing fans, various tactics may be used to restrict drinking. An early kick-off, say at noon rather than the traditional mid-afternoon, reduces time for drinking. The trains carrying supporters to the match do not sell alcohol, public houses near to the ground remain closed, and alcohol is not sold inside the stadium.

There is a contrast to be made in crowd behaviour at different types of sport. At football access to alcohol may be restricted while at cricket and rugby matches it is sold (typically at exorbitant prices) before and during and after the game. Whether this variation in crowd behaviour is due to the nature of the sport being watched or the type of individual who watches the different sports is a moot point (Jewell, Moti, & Coates, 2011).

Another local restriction lies in changing opening times for the purchase of alcohol. There is ample evidence that extending and reducing opening times for on-premise sales, even by as little as one hour, can have significant effects on the rate of night-time violent assaults (Kypri et al., 2011; Rossow & Norström, 2011).

Targeted policing

In most cities there are "hot spots", defined in terms of place and time, for alcohol-related crime. Some of these hot spots are obvious, such as bars and nightclubs at weekends; others, such as taxi ranks and fast food outlets, perhaps less so. These "hot spots" are often seen in the context of the night-time economy, the mainly pleasure and entertainment-related transactions that take place in cities, especially at the week-end, and which are strongly associated with excessive drinking (Lovatt & O'Connor, 1995; Moore et al., 2007). The issues posed by hot spots for violence in the night-time economy are prevalent in other parts of the world (e.g., Liu et al., 2016) and may also be associated with tourism (Evans, 2012). The deployment of police officers to these hot spots is a partial solution to the problem of violence but, of course, there are others who could play a role in reducing violence.

The Tackling Alcohol-Related Street Crime (TASC) project in Cardiff, the capital city of Wales, provides a good example of involving a range of players to diffuse violence at hot spots (Maguire & Nettleton, 2003). With a multifaceted, multidisciplinary approach, TASC was built upon the creation of a Licensees Forum to facilitate discussion between the police and representatives of the licensed trade. The project involved a range of initia-tives: (i) improving the conduct of door staff; (ii) encouraging changes in local licensing policy and practice; (iii) publicising the problem of alcohol-related violent crime; (iv) police resources targeted at "hot spots"; (v) the availability of a cognitive-behavioural problem drinking programme for repeat offenders; (vi) a training programme in managing altercations for bar staff; (vii) alcohol education in schools; (viii) support for victims of alcohol-related assaults who attend hospital.

As described by Maguire and Nettleton, the evaluation of the project was positive:

> A comparison of the first 12 months after the launch of the project with the previous 12 months indicated an overall decrease of four per cent in incidents involving alcohol-related assaults. This occurred despite a ten per cent increase in licensed premise capacity in central Cardiff. During the same period, incidents of violence against the person rose elsewhere in South Wales. The researchers' best estimate is that, during its first year, the project helped to reduce the expected level of violent incidents by eight per cent: that is, it prevented about 100 assaults. If it is assumed that just one (or more) of these incidents would have involved a serious wounding, cost-effectiveness analysis suggests that the project represented "value for money".
>
> *(p. vi)*

Minimum pricing

Whether we can afford to purchase a commodity depends on its availability and its price. If goods are scarce they will be expensive and sales will be low; if goods are cheap we can buy them with impunity. When it comes to alcohol there is, in many countries, no problem with availability. In the UK we can have all the alcohol we want and if the government proposed to move from ready availability to controlled availability of alcohol through prohibition it would be committing political suicide. However, price manipulation is a different proposition to prohibition: we are used to price changes through government action – at every budget we brace ourselves for a rise in the price of alcohol, tobacco, and petrol – so the strategy of price changing to reduce consumption is altogether less contentious. Thus, the introduction of minimum pricing for alcohol is intended to reduce sales of cheap alcohol and hence limit harmful drinking (Boniface, Scannell, & Marlow, 2017). Yet further, early exposure to alcohol, including the mother's drinking during pregnancy, is one of several childhood health risk factors that may act to increase the risk of childhood aggression and adult violence (Liu, 2011). A reduction in the level of the population's drinking will certainly be of serendipitous benefit in reducing interpersonal violence.

In actively considering the issue of minimum pricing, the Scottish Government website notes that, at current Scottish prices, sufficient alcohol to exceed the lower risk health guideline of 14 units per week can be purchased for less than £2.50. At the time of writing the Scottish Government is proposing to introduce a Minimum Price per Unit (MPU) of 50 pence per unit of alcohol. They note that this minimum price would have little if any effect in pubs where alcohol is sold well above the proposed minimum price. The force of the MPU legislation would be most evident in raising the price and therefore influencing the sales in retail outlets of drinks such as cheap white ciders and own-brand value spirits which have a high alcohol content. In England and Wales the issue of minimum pricing for alcohol remains under discussion pending reviews of its effects in Scotland (Woodhouse, 2018).

The introduction of a minimum price per unit (MPU) may have the net effect of reducing alcohol consumption across the retail market although the effect may vary by type of drink. A Canadian study by Stockwell et al. (2012) found that a 10 per cent increase in MPU had an overall effect of a 3.4 per cent reduction in consumption: however, alcoholic sodas and ciders fell by 13.9 per cent, wine by 8.9 per cent, spirits and liqueurs by 6.8 per cent, and beer by 1.5 per cent. Yet further, the overall reduction is a *net* effect as some consumers may decide to pay more and keep on drinking, others may continue to drink intermittently, and some may cut down or stop. Thus, the effects of minimum pricing will not be equally spread across society but will vary according to disposable income and socioeconomic class (Chalmers, 2014; Holmes et al., 2014).

In Chapter 1 the example was given of 19th-century opposition to the introduction of legislation in favour of child welfare on the grounds of its effects on profits. Well, *plus ça change*, the attempt to introduce MPU for alcohol has met similar 21st-century opposition, in this case from alcohol producers and retailers. The opposition is manifest in three ways. First, when government legislation is proposed it is covered in the media giving both sides in the debate the opportunity to influence public opinion. Katikireddi and Hilton (2015) consider the debate, including media presentations, about Scotland's proposal to introduce MPU. Katikireddi and Hilton analysed and compared articles about MPU published in 10 national newspapers (3 Scottish; 7 UK) over a 7-year period, alcohol policy documents, transcripts of evidence submitted to the

Scottish Parliament's Health and Sport Committee alongside 36 confidential interviews with policy stakeholders. As shown in Table 7.1, Katikireddi and Hilton framed three aspects of the debate, each with their respective supportive and opposing views, which emerged from their analysis of national newspaper coverage.

One of the many points raised by Katikireddi and Hilton, which will be returned to below, was about the use of evidence to inform the debate. It may be thought that in a rational world empirical evidence would play a significant role in making important policy decisions. After all, if the evidence shows that an initiative has no effect then it would be prudent to change tack and try something different; if the initiative has been shown to work then this strengthens the argument in favour of its use. Katikireddi and Hilton make the comment that those who were against MPU refused to engage with the research evidence. They quote an academic who had given a presentation at a public health interview and later voiced surprise at the critics' reply to his evidence:

> Academic: The only thing that occurred to me is just in terms of how the industry engage with the evidence. I found it surprising how willing they are to be wrong in the sense that they are willing to stand there after I've given a presentation saying, "there is a link between price and harm and here is a systematic review of fifty studies showing clearly that link exists", for someone to stand up from the industry five minutes later and say "there is no evidence of a link between price and harm". Not to engage with what I'd said but just to deny I even said it. And I found that a very strange way of them actually entering the debate.
>
> (p. 130)

What of the people most directly affected by MPU, those who drink heavily? O'May et al. (2016) interviewed 20 heavy drinkers, median weekly consumption 130.7 units (range 28–256.3 units), who lived in Edinburgh and Glasgow. The drinkers were somewhat confused about what MPU would entail, with some saying they would switch to cheaper brands, not grasping that they would pay a minimum for *each* unit in a drink, which precludes a financial benefit from buying a different drink. Some interviewees said they would be forced to reduce their drinking but worried about the effect this would have on them; others said that to afford alcohol they would have to reduce their household bills, even doing without heating and cutting back on buying food. If more money was needed,

TABLE 7.1 Pros and cons in the press regarding the Minimum Price per Unit (MPU) debate; after Katikireddi and Hilton (2015)

	Pro MPU	*Con MPU*
Focus of debate	Alcohol-related harm, health and social disorder problems	Pricing will not work, avoid discussing causes and evidence
Causes of problem	Cheap alcohol, irresponsible marketing	Problem drinkers, attitudes to alcohol
Arguments about MPU	Targets cheap drink and irresponsible marketing, targets alcohol misuse, reduces health and social problems	No evidence of effect, Punishes responsible drinkers, punishes the poor, will harm businesses, will lead to illicit trading, it is against the law

others said, they would borrow money from family or friends or find some other form of debt. One interviewee, rather ominously, said he did not know how he would find the money to procure his alcohol but "I think it will be drastic, what I would go to, to get what I need" (p. 4).

It is not just through the media and attempts to influence public debate that arguments about policy decisions are won and lost. The second form of manipulating the debate takes the form of lobbying the policy-makers. In this regard, McCambridge, Hawkins, and Holden (2013) quote a very senior politician's words to a national newspaper: "According to David Cameron, before he became UK Prime Minister: 'We all know how it works. The lunches, the hospitality, the quiet word in your ear, the ex-ministers and ex-advisers for hire, helping big business find the right way to get its way'" (p. 3).

Through a mixture of interview and documentary analysis, McCambridge, Hawkins, and Holden identified six strategies by which lobbyists engaged UK politicians and policy-makers between 2007 and 2010. Their first strategy is to build a long-term relationship with the key decision makers, this connection may be built by providing information and promising to achieve policy aims and outcomes through systems of co-regulation and self-regulation. Their second strategy is to seek to engage a full range of policymakers including Members of Parliament, irrespective of their political persuasion, Government Ministers and Shadow Ministers, ministerial special advisers and top civil servants. The engagement is by every means possible, and there are many ways, including email, text, tweets, and personal contact at party conferences and Parliamentary All-Party Groups.

The third strategy is to maintain maximum access to policymakers by attending regular formal meetings throughout the policymaking process and, the fourth strategy, to cultivate informal personal government contacts. The fifth strategy is to achieve a position where policymakers will consult informally before and after official policy consultation events so that, strategy six, the lobbyist becomes a key stakeholder in the policy process and, as a matter of course, is consulted on policy developments.

In a comment that chimes with the academic quoted above by Katikireddi and Hilton, McCambridge, Hawkins, and Holden consider the alcohol industry's claim to be committed to evidence-based policy:

> Yet they consistently opposed the international research community consensus that the policies most likely to be effective in reducing alcohol-related problems in the population are increases in the price of alcohol, and restrictions on availability and marketing …. Documentary submissions to the Scottish Government consultation failed to engage with the research literature in any depth, although made no shortage of claims about it. This and other tactics in relation to evidence are used by industry actors elsewhere. Strong evidence was misrepresented and weak evidence promoted when comparisons were made with the expert summary of the peer-reviewed literature. Unsubstantiated claims were made about the adverse effects of unfavoured policy proposals and advocacy of policies favoured by industry was not supported by the presentation of evidence.
>
> *(pp. 2–3)*

Hawkins and McCambridge (2014) present a case study of the tactics employed by a major multinational brewing and beverage company as they sought to promote their pro-alcohol arguments. These tactics included sponsoring "independent think tanks" who produce and then promote evidence supporting the brewer's position. This evidence is not subjected to standard research procedures such as peer review, thereby "leading to the formation of a methodologically flawed and highly biased but internally consistent parallel literature to the international peer-reviewed scientific literature" (p. 1366). Alongside producing its own evidence, Hawkins and McCambridge claim that the brewing industry may in its own interests play a role in academic research by sponsoring research-funding organisations and supporting university-based researchers. It is not just the evidence concerning MPU which is subject to the attention of the alcohol agency. Savell, Fooks, and Gilmore (2016) describe the similar strategies used by the alcohol industry to influence marketing regulations.

Finally, the alcohol industry is not the only commercial enterprise that seeks to defend its territory when under scrutiny for risk to health. Ulu-canlar et al. (2014), for example, provide an analysis of the representation of evidence by tobacco companies in the consultation about the standardised packaging, i.e., removing all brand imagery and text, other than the name, and replacing them with standard shaped and coloured packs with pictorial health warnings. Ulucanlar and colleagues' investigation bears some remarkable similarities with those of the alcohol industry.

The third form of opposition to MPU came in the form of a legal challenge to the legislation. A brief overview of the legal contest serves to emphasise the point that reducing harm can be a hard-fought battle. In Scotland a legal challenge to MPU was begun in 2012 by the Scottish Whisky Association who claimed that MPU is contrary to EU law, would be ineffective in tackling problem drinking, and would penalise responsible drinkers. The challenge was heard in the European and Scottish courts and was unsuccessful. The Scottish Whisky Association then lodged a complaint with the European Commission and sought judicial review with the Scottish Court of Session. In 2013, the Court refused the Scottish Whisky Association's petition, stating that MPU lay within the powers of the Scottish Parliament and the measure was not incompatible with European Union law. In 2014, following an appeal from the Scottish Whisky Association, the Scottish Court of Session ruled that the case should be referred to the European Union's Court of Justice. In 2015, the Advocate General to the European Union Court of Justice said that MPU could only be justified to protect public health if no alternative, for example a tax increase, could be found. The European Court of Justice added that this issue was for the Scottish Courts to decide. In 2016, the Scottish Court of Session upheld its earlier decision to refuse the Scottish Whisky Association's petition for a judicial review and so the Scottish Whisky Association appealed to the UK Supreme Court. In 2017, the Supreme Court said that the MPU did not breach EU law and that it was a "proportionate means of achieving a legitimate aim".

In some parts of the world, the next topic, gun control, makes the introduction of MPU legislation look like the proverbial stroll in the park.

Weapons

It is self-evident that the availability of a weapon increases the likelihood of a quarrel becoming a serious crime. The deadlier the weapon – from a blunt object to a knife, to handguns and fully automatic machine guns – the greater becomes the likelihood of injury and fatality.

Knives

One of the many problems with carrying knives is the belief held by some young people that they can reduce the risk of life-threatening injury by targeting the knife, of which there are many types from penknife to flick knife, at the victim's stomach or buttocks (Palasinski & Riggs, 2012). Needless to say, as testified by those serving prison sentences for serious wounding or homicide, this strategy is not a guaranteed success. In their review of knife crime, Eades et al. (2007) point to four strategies to reduce the use of knives: these are (1) the national knife amnesty; (2) stop and search; (3) increased prison sentences; (4) education and awareness-raising.

A knife amnesty can be a local affair, such amnesties have for example been held in several London boroughs, or it can be a national affair. Eaves and colleagues note that in the 2006 national amnesty that ran for 5 weeks, a total of 89,864 knives were surrendered to the police. While this appears to be a success Eaves and colleagues calculate that based on an estimate of the number of knives in England and Wales, "The amnesty has been successful in removing 0.0041 per cent of knives that might be used in crimes" (p. 27). To which they add: "Moreover, unlike guns, once a knife has been disposed of it merely takes a trip to the kitchen drawer to get another. As long as there is unsliced bread, opportunities for 'knife crime' will exist" (p. 28).

The term "stop and search" refers to the statutory police powers, which can be traced back to the 19th-century Vagrancy Act, to stop and physically search a person. A search needs to be on the grounds of "reasonable suspicion", typically on the basis of intelligence received, that the search will expose an illegal activity or possession of an illegal item. The use of stop varies but it can be widely used: McCandless et al. (2016) state "At its peak, in the final quarter of 2008/09, a search was undertaken every 20 seconds on average nationwide" (p. 2). In keeping with American research (Rosenfeld & Fornango, 2014), McCandless and colleagues found little effect of a stop and search initiative, called Operation BLUNT 2, on levels of weapon crime in a London borough.

The use of stop and search powers by the police is not a neutral act. There are accusations that these powers are disproportionately used against both ethnic minority communities (Bowling & Phillips, 2007) and against minors (Flacks, in press). The local discord and resentment of the police fostered by this police activity are a high price to pay for a less than certain outcome.

The effectiveness of increased prison sentences for convicted offenders has been discussed and shown to be of doubtful value in reducing crime. Nonetheless, in 2006 through the *Violent Crime Reduction Act 2006* the government increased the maximum available sentence for unlawfully carrying a knife in public from two to four years. This was another step towards increased punitive sentencing for knife crime (Stone, 2015). As Eades et al. (2007) state:

> Relying on the implausible view that increased sentence length will have a deterrent effect, it seems unlikely that the government's chosen policy will have an impact on knife carrying in public. This is particularly the case because such behaviour is most common among children and young people who are less likely to foresee the consequences of their actions.
>
> *(p. 19)*

Away from the criminal justice system, the fourth option for reducing knife violence lies in education and awareness-raising. The project *Fear and Fashion* (Lemos, 2004) and *No Knives, Better Lives* (Foster, 2013) provide examples of a multi-disciplinary educational approach which includes presentations to school pupils by the police, the development of weapons awareness courses, and mentoring programmes. There have been local evaluations of this type of initiative to reduce knife crime but, as Eades and colleagues note, more systematic evaluation is needed.

Firearms

The laws on gun control vary significantly from country to country. However, there is one major fact to take into consideration: a substantial proportion of the research looking at the association between gun ownership and associated injuries and fatalities has been carried out in the USA. In this regard, McPhedran (2016) observes:

It must also be highlighted that the USA is unique among developed nations in its approach to firearm ownership, and stands alone in enshrining in its Constitution the right to bear arms. Given this very specific cultural context, findings from the USA about firearm legislation and homicide may not, therefore, be applicable to (or relevant for) other countries.

(p. 65)

Thus, while the aim of reducing interpersonal violence may be the same, in the USA the context and magnitude of the issue is very different to elsewhere in the world. Hahn et al. (2005) indicate the scale of the matter: "Approximately 4.5 million new (i.e., not previously owned) firearms are sold each year in the United States, including 2 million handguns" (p. 40). In that light it is hardly a surprise that firearms-related injuries are the second leading cause of mortality in the USA with over 30,000 deaths each year attributable to guns.

Hepburn and Hemenway (2004) found that in high-income countries with more firearms, excluding the USA, men and women are at higher risk for homicide, particularly homicide involving a gun. The same picture is found in the USA with a significant gun prevalence–homicide association. The inevitable conclusion is that no matter where the firearm is used it causes the same damage to the victim.

Does firearms legislation influence levels of violence involving guns? This type of legislation may seek to achieve several aims: (i) to ban the sale and ownership of certain types of firearm and ammunition; (ii) to introduce limitations through background checks and waiting periods at the point of sale on who can purchase handguns; (3) to specify how guns must be unloaded and securely stored; (4) to increase the severity of legal sanctions for firearms-related crimes. The scale and complexity of the issues make it extremely difficult to estimate accurately the effects of such legislation. Thus, on the basis of their review, Hahn et al. (2005) suggest that insufficient evidence makes it impossible to gauge the effects of legislative changes to reduce firearm related violence. However, other studies have drawn cautious conclusions about the force of firearms legislation.

Santaella-Tenorio et al. (2016) considered data from 130 studies conducted in 10 countries in looking at the association between firearm legislation and firearm-related injuries. They found that in some countries the implementation of laws restricting firearms, such as control over the purchase of guns (for example, background checks), and regulations regarding access to guns, such as safe storage, are linked to reductions in firearm deaths.

Makarios and Pratt (2012) conducted a meta-analysis of approaches to reduce gun violence. In sympathy with Hahn and colleagues they noted the problems of data collection and weak designs and methodologies in the original studies. Nonetheless, Makarios and Pratt concluded that there was little evidence showing that banning guns was effective in reducing violence. Similarly, prosecutorial strategies had a slight effect although policing strategies did have a moderate impact on firearms violence. Koper and Mayo-Wilson (2006) offer qualified support for the effect on gun crime of police action against illegal gun carrying.

Fleegler et al. (2013) considered the relationship between the strength of firearms legislation in 50 American states and state mortality rates. They concluded that the higher number of firearm laws there are in a state the greater the association with a lower rate of firearm homicides. However, in Australia, McPhedran (2016) reviewed the effect on homicide rates of 1996 legislative changes in firearm control. There was no evidence that the changes had a statistically significant impact on homicides. However, another Australian study by Taylor and Li (2015) reported that one and two years after the controlling legislation there was a significant fall in armed robbery and attempted murder.

Hahn and colleagues stated that in the 1998–1999 school year, 3523 students were expelled for having a firearm in school. The issue of school shootings in America, as seen, for example, at Columbine High School in Colorado, attracts international attention. While writing this book there was a shooting in a school in Florida where 17 people, pupils and school staff, were killed and others physically injured. While shocking, these incidents are not isolated: the websites of American news channels carry details of the annual numbers of school shootings. Thus, for example, the CNN website (https://edition.cnn.com/) comments that after nine weeks into 2018 there have been 14 school shootings in the USA; these figures include accidental discharge of a firearm and single shot incidents. These are the truly remarkable statistics: not just that the dreadful major incidents occur, rather that school shootings are so frequent as almost to be commonplace.

How to reduce the numbers of school shootings is an issue that raises strong words from both sides on the debate. There is a movement among young people, as seen with the 17-minute (17 people were killed in the Florida shooting) school walkout and associated public demonstrations to force changes in gun laws. The National Rifle Association (NRA), which claims 5 million members, provides the main resistance to proponents of gun control. The NRA's defence of the legal status quo has two pillars, the political and the pragmatic, which they use to reinforce their image of the defender under siege.

The political defence rests on the constitutional right to bear arms, to wish to take away that right is to want to make Americans less free. Those in favour of gun control are portrayed as politically motivated – i.e., left-wing or as the NRA have been quoted "European socialists" – opportunists who do not care about children but use the school shootings cynically to further their own agenda. After the Florida shooting several major corporations announced an end to loyalty and discount schemes for NRA members. In keeping with the role of the innocent party, the NRA said these corporations' actions were cowardly and unfair in punishing NRA's law-abiding members for the school shootings which, in their eyes, were caused by failures in school security, in the American mental health system, in the National Instant Check System and in federal and local law enforcement.

The pragmatic solution to stopping school shootings offered by the NRA is to use greater numbers of armed security personnel in schools. President Trump has supported the possibility of arming school staff, floating the idea of an enhanced payment for bearing arms. President Trump tweeted that "Armed Educators (and trusted people who work within a school) love our students and will protect them. Very smart people. Must be firearms adept & have annual training. Should get yearly bonus." In addition, President Trump called for enhanced background checks prior to purchasing a gun and has said he supports consideration of raising the age to be eligible to buy an assault rifle to 21 years. The NRA opposes any raise of the age requirement from its current 18 years.

Another issue under debate concerns the type of guns available for sale. In the Florida school shooting an AR-15 rifle was used, a semi-automatic weapon with the power to penetrate a steel helmet from 500 yards. The AR-15 has been standard-issue to US military since Vietnam. The use of a bump stock essentially converts semi-automatic into automatic weapons, so that rather than fire just a single bullet after each trigger pull they fire repeatedly without continued pressure on the trigger. Automatic firearms such as machine guns, short-barrelled shotguns, and short-barrelled rifles are banned in the United States.

Will there be change or is the NRA successfully defending its corner? Well, time will tell but membership of gun rights organisations and shooting associations as well as the NRA have reported an upturn in new members, membership renewals, and financial donations. The message is that even when it is for the common good, be it smoking, excessive alcohol or weapons, it is hard to persuade the individual to surrender what they see as theirs by right.

Psychological models and evidence-based practice

The term "treatment" is frequently used in the context of working with offenders to reduce levels of crime. It is a term that attracts criticism for its medical overtones, implying that criminal behaviour is pathological and requires a cure. While some work with offenders may hold a pathological perspective, it is a minority view. The term treatment is used here in the broader sense of seeking to bring about positive change. Thus, teaching an offender to read or improve their problem-solving skills may precipitate a change that reduces offending, and while these interventions may be referred to as treatment, neither implies a pathology. The same point applies to punishment: to attempt to reduce offending through the imposition of penalties can be said to be treating the criminal in a particular way.

The goal of changing offenders through the application of psychological methods begins with the psychological model informing the process. In the following section two models of practice with offenders are contrasted: these are the Risk-Need-Responsivity (RNR) model and the Good Lives Model (GLM). The function of a model is to inform the content of treatment: an evidence-based model of practice holds that if proven procedures are followed then, on the basis of the supporting evidence, there is a strong likelihood of achieving a certain outcome. A model of practice is not the same as a theory, although a model may be informed by theory.

Risk-Need-Responsivity (RNR)

As described previously, the RNR model arose from the meta-analyses of treatment outcome studies (Andrews, 1995). Thus, the RNR model can claim to be evidence-based as it is formulated on the basis of empirical evidence. The key components of the model, *risk* and *need* (discussed in Chapter 6) continue to be subject to conceptual debate (Heffernan & Ward, 2017; Ward, Melser, & Yates, 2007) and empirical scrutiny (Basanta, Fariña, & Arce, 2018; Hamilton et al., 2017). There is a body of evaluative evidence of practice based on the RNR model which has informed and refined practice with different criminal populations on the basis of both success (Hollin & Palmer, 2009) and, importantly, failure (Prendergast et al., 2013).

The meta-analyses from which the RNR model grew highlighted the importance of cognitive-behavioural theory and practice. While cognitive-behavioural theory is important in understanding how offender treatment works, this does not preclude theoretical refinement. Andrews and Bonta (2003) developed the Psychology of Criminal Conduct which considers criminal behaviour in the context of "biological, personal, interpersonal, familial, and structural/cultural factors" (p. 11).

The critical point regarding evidence-based practice, as illustrated by the RNR model, is that the model is rooted in empirical evidence and its application is rigorously tested. This empirical focus does not mean that conceptual issues are neglected but that evidence is at the heart of the debate. These points are evident in considering another model, the Good Lives Model, which is also prevalent in offender treatment.

Good Lives Model (GLM)

The Good Lives Model (GLM) was developed by Ward and colleagues (Ward, 2002; Ward & Brown, 2004) and "represents a strengths-based rehabilitation theory that aims to equip clients with internal and external resources to live a good or better life – a life that is socially acceptable and personally meaningful" (Ward, Yates, & Willis, 2012; p. 95). The aim of treatment under the GLM rubric is to assist the offender to achieve his or her goals through legitimate means. In the same way as everyone else, the goals which offenders seek are primary human goods such as health, happiness, relationships, spirituality, and creativity (Harris, Pedneault, & Willis, in press; Ward & Gannon, 2006).

The GLM, originally formulated in the context of sexual offending (Ward & Marshall, 2004; Yates & Ward, 2008), has been applied to various offender groups including female delinquents (Van Damme et al., 2017), offenders with mental illness (Vandevelde et al., 2017), male perpetrators of domestic violence (Langlands, Ward, & Gilchrist, 2009), and young offenders (Fortune, 2018).

The GLM offers a way to conceptualise treatment rather than offering a set of techniques by which to treat offenders. Thus, Willis et al. (2012) state: "The GLM is an overarching rehabilitation framework and, as such, does not pre-scribe specific intervention content" (p. 133) and "The GLM is a rehabilitation framework that is intended to supply practitioners with a foundation from which specific, empirically supported interventions such as CBT are applied" (pp. 126–127). In the same vein, Whitehead, Ward, and Collie (2007) explain that: "The GLM can complement and embed traditional risk-management interventions within a meaningful framework" (p. 5).

Does the GLM complement the application of existing interventions? This question has sparked a lively conceptual debate between those who argue that the GLM adds little if anything to the RNR model (Andrews, Bonta, & Wormith, 2011; Bonta & Andrews, 2003; Looman & Abracen, 2013; Wormith, Gendreau, & Bonta, 2012) and those who argue in its favour (Ward & Stewart, 2003; Ward, Yates, & Willis, 2012). However, the bottom line, as Wormith, Gendreau, and Bonta (2012) state is: "Let's consider the evidence" (p. 111). Does adding the GLM to an extant treatment regime reduce recidivism?

Willis and Ward (2013) consider whether the GLM works and present the preliminary evidence. Given that the GLM has been around for a decade, *preliminary* evidence is not a strong basis for endorsing its use, although Willis and Ward make the argument that "The large body of empirical literature supporting the RNR also supports the main basis comprising the GLM" (p. 309). That aside, the evidence directly addressing the GLM is restricted to case studies and process recording; outcome evidence in the form of recidivism studies is awaited.

Finally, the GLM potentially faces a presentational problem. Interventions with offenders are never going to be vote winners for politicians, being tough on crime is a political mantra, and funding for treatment initiatives is never going to be high on the list of government spending priorities. The *realpolitik* is that it may be possible to persuade governments to use public funds for evidence-based programmes to reduce risk and ultimately save expenditure. It is a quite different proposition to coax government officials to spend public money to help offenders to lead a good life and attain their life goals with no indication of a reduction in crime.

While there are disagreements between proponents of the RNR and GLM models, both approaches are defensible in that they have their origins in robust empirical evidence or reputable psychological theory. A solid empirical or theoretical base is not always the case in correctional practice. Gendreau, Smith, and Thériault (2009) describe how too much practice with offenders relies on whimsy and rhetoric, encouraged by those in authority who lack the critical awareness to stand back from their favoured form of correctional quackery. The speed at which ideas are seized upon, applied, and then discarded before they have had the opportunity to be thoroughly evaluated is a feature of interventions with offenders. Pawson (2002) points to the time difference between the "policy cycle" and the "research cycle". In the former a large constraint is the political need to be seen to implement a policy; in the latter the main constraint is the time taken to conduct a robust evaluation. The net result of this disconnect is that contemporaneous empirical evaluations have little influence on policy making. In addition, there is pressure on politicians to shake off the old, regardless of the evidence, and come up with the next big idea – currently restorative justice (see Daly (2002) for a full and frank discussion of the origin of and the myths surrounding restorative justice) – that is going to solve all of life's problems.

Correctional quackery

What is correctional quackery? Gendreau, Smith, and Thériault (2009) state that:

> There are a multitude of other commonsense programs that have surfaced in the media that have escaped evaluation, such as acupuncture, the angel-in-you therapy, aura focus, diets, drama therapies, ecumenical Christianity, finger painting, healing lodges, heart mapping, horticulture, a variety of humiliation strategies (e.g., diaper baby treatment, dunce cap, cross dressing, John TV, sandwich board justice, Uncle Miltie treatment), no frills prisons, pet therapy, plastic surgery, and yoga ... [more instances] ... such as brain injury reality, cooking/baking, dog sledding, handwriting, interior dec-orating in prisons (e.g., pink and teddy bear décor), classical music, and ritualized tapping.
>
> (p. 386)

How can such spurious practice occur? Gendreau, Smith, and Thériault provide an illustration, referring to the evidence showing that bootcamps had little or no effect on reoffending:

> Reacting to the study (research on the lack of effectiveness of military boot camps), a spokesman for Governor Zell Miller said that "we don't care what the study thinks" – Georgia would continue to use its boot camps. Governor Miller is an ex-Marine, and says that the Marine boot camps he attended changed his life for the better: he believes that the boot camp experience can do the same for wayward Georgia youth .... "Georgia's Commissioner of Corrections" ... also

joined the chorus of condemnation, saying that academics were too quick to ignore the experiential knowledge of people "working in the system" and rely on research findings.

(quote cited from Vaughn, 1994, p. 2)

In the dubious exercise of "common sense" scientific evidence is dismissed in favour of anecdote and personal values and experience, solving highly complex issues with a magic bullet. As evaluative evidence is eschewed, the consequences of the imposition of many common-sense solutions are never known.

Gendreau, Smith, and Thériault apply the term *fartcatcher* – a disparaging term used to describe those obsequious servants who trail after their masters, acting with cloying humility, fawning and eager to please – to those administrators who condone poor practice. The use of evidence-free interventions in the criminal justice system raises two issues. First, it casts a shadow over the integrity of those charged with ensuring the highest possible standards: if medical services for people with physical ailments operated in such an *ad hoc* manner there would be a justifiable public outcry. Second, when in the fullness of time it becomes evident that the commonsense measure has no discernible effect on reoffending, the cry of "nothing works" is raised yet again.

Why do evidence-free interventions to reduce offending, including violent crime, continue to be promulgated? The absence of regulatory mechanisms is undoubtedly part of the problem but, leaving aside finger painting, heart mapping, humiliation strategies, and the like, there is perhaps a wider issue to consider. In some helping professions there is a culture of practitioner autonomy by which individual practitioners place greater weight on their unique knowledge and experience than on empirical evidence. It is not difficult to see how a belief in clinical artistry (Wilson, 1996) begins to over-ride the need for empirical evidence. An example of this is seen with use of the Family Group Conference (FGC), discussed in Chapter 4, where the use of FGCs continues despite the lack of supporting evidence. While it may be that practitioners and systems become wedded to their practice, there is also the inevitable delay in change as organisations absorb the messages from research and consider how to accommodate them in their systems.

The development and application of evidence-based practice relies on the gathering of robust, reputable evidence. How such evidence can be gathered is an issue that has generated much discussion among researchers. Before considering the questions raised by the design of evaluative studies, there is another topic to consider. While treatment has a focus on reducing crime through changing the offender, situational prevention shifts the emphasis to the environment.

Removing the person: situational prevention

As the polar opposite to treatment, situational prevention is concerned not with changing the individual but with modifying the environment. In practice two strategies may be applied to modify the environment with the aim of reducing interpersonal violence: first, reduce the opportunity for interpersonal violence to occur; second, increase the risk of detection to deter offenders.

At a broad level there are certain environments in which there is an increased likelihood of crime. As shown by Shaw and McKay (1942) there are certain city areas, which we might now call "hot spots", where crime is more likely to occur. The crime-prone parts of the city are typically characterised by social disorganisation, high levels of mobility, low quality housing, and so on. The people who become victims in such adverse environments may be those who fail to take care of their movements and so place themselves at risk or local residents moving around their own area. (See Chapter 5 for a discussion of personal strategies to reduce the likelihood of sexual assault.)

Alongside reducing opportunity, it is possible to deter the offender by increasing the chances of their being caught. The principal ways this aim can be achieved are through maintaining surveillance and improving the quality of the environment.

Reducing opportunity

Hardening the target

If a target for crime becomes physically "harder" to access it follows that the opportunity for that crime is reduced. Thus, potential victims can increase their personal security with alarms and locks, women may choose to carry a rape alarm, or to travel in pairs or in small groups. The provision of emergency contacts for a fast response to incidents of domestic violence can reduce assault and children can be taught about "stranger danger" and what to do should such an occasion arise.

Removing the target

As well as hardening the target, crime can be prevented by removing the target from the environment. Thus, potential targets may be removed from risky environments: the provision of transport for people who leave work at night, such as hospital staff, or for those socialising into the late hours places the target in a safe environment and reduces their vulnerability to attack. In the same way, a strategy to reduce interpersonal violence in universities (Regehr et al., 2017) is to provide transport from entertainment venues to halls of residence.

Increasing detection

Formal surveillance

The term *formal* indicates that the surveillance is being carried out by those with the authority to intervene if necessary. Thus, the police are often charged with the task of formal surveillance: we anticipate a large police presence where large crowds gather, particularly if there is likely to be trouble. As well as the police, a person in a position of authority may be involved in formal surveillance. A member of the railway police, a bus conductor, a car park attendant, a steward at sporting event, or a shop assistant may monitor people's actions and so reduce crime.

The speed of technological change enables surveillance to be carried out by means other than personal observation. The ubiquitous placement of cameras in public places has led to cameras that watch us drive on public roads, carry out our business in shops, petrol stations, and banks, travel on public transport, and even watch while we walk down the street. The use of closed circuit television (CCTV) has become so routine that we barely notice its presence, leading to the view that we increasingly live in a surveillance society (Gilliom & Monahan, 2013).

CCTV is put to two main uses to reduce crime: first, it allows formal surveillance of a specific location, say a district of a city, shops or residential premises; second, it acts as a crime prevention measure by increasing the risk of detection. While CCTV assists crime detection it is impossible to know how many crimes are solved because of CCTV: the police use many sources of evidence so that it is impossible to quantify the overall contribution of CCTV. However, with regard to the *preventative* effects of CCTV there is a body of empirical evidence to inform the debate.

Welsh and Farrington (2009) carried out a systematic review and meta-analysis of 44 studies of the effects of CCTV in preventing crime. They found that when comparing experimental areas with control areas, across a range of different settings, CCTV was associated with a significant

16 per cent reduction in crime. This overall reduction could mainly be accounted for by a 51 per cent decrease in crime in car parks, as opposed to town centres, public transport, and public housing.

Informal surveillance

The notion of *informal* surveillance refers to our natural willingness to monitor what happens in our own personal, or *defensible*, space, i.e., the geographical area which an individual takes as their territory and for which they are personally concerned (Newman, 1972).

One means of using informal surveillance is to organise people to take responsibility for looking out for themselves and their neighbours. *Neighbourhood Watch*, also variously known as *Home Watch, Block Watch, Community Alert*, and *Citizen Alert*, is a popular scheme that utilises public willingness to monitor and report crime. The idea informing *Neighbourhood Watch* is straightforward: by encouraging close relations between local residents and police, residents are on the alert for suspicious activity which, once detected, is promptly reported to the local police. An effective *Neighbourhood Watch* scheme can increase community cohesion and may reduce fear of crime, but can it reduce crime? Bennett, Holloway, and Farrington (2006) reported a meta-analysis of 18 evaluative studies of *Neighbourhood Watch*. They reported that the meta-analysis revealed that the scheme had the intended effect with a 16 per cent reduction in crime.

It is a fact that most forms of surveillance, human or camera, rely on light levels for vision to be effective. The strategic use of light to eliminate darkness can increase the risk of detection and counter the offender's feeling of anonymity which increases the chances of criminal behaviour (Zhong, Bohns, & Gino, 2010). Farrington and Welsh (2007b) reviewed the evidence concerning the effects of improved street lighting on crime prevention. They concluded that the weight of evidence was positive overall while, as well as reducing crime, street lighting is of general benefit to a neighbourhood, not just certain individuals, does not affect civil liberties, and generally increases public safety.

A question of design

The goal of evaluative research is to inform good practice. In order to do so, the research design must strive for maximum validity in the given circumstances. Cook and Campbell (1979) describe four types of validity: these are construct validity, external validity, internal validity and statistical conclusion validity. *Internal validity* refers to the degree of confidence that the findings are a true reflection of the experimental manipulation and not the consequence of some uncontrolled confounding variable. The greater the degree of experimental control over extraneous variables, the greater the confidence that the findings reflect a genuine cause and effect. For example, if an evaluation compared a treated group of adult men with an untreated control of young women there is an immediate confound on both age and gender (and much else besides). Such a study would have low internal validity and therefore we can have no confidence in the veracity of its findings. Sherman et al. (1997) formulated the Scientific Methods Scale (SMS) which ranks research designs through five levels on the basis of their internal validity; these designs range from a basic correlational design at one extreme to a fully randomised control trial at the other.

External validity speaks to the generalisability of the experiment: with what degree of confidence can the findings be generalised to other situations outside of the environment where they were originally gathered? In applied research there may be a trade-off between internal and external validity. The efforts to control confounding variables can produce conditions that are so far removed from the real world that the findings become artificial and have little generalisability. In the criminal justice system it can be difficult to ensure cooperation when institutions are unwilling to randomise participants, say to treatment or control, on ethical or legal grounds. External validity can be assessed by replication at different times and in different places, say as with offender treatment with different age groups and in different types of settings.

Randomisation

A randomised design has the highest internal validity because, given a sufficiently large sample size, the experimental and control conditions can be considered to be equivalent on all the measured and potentially confounding variables. Randomised designs were developed for drug trials where treatment and control conditions are easily separated (Everitt & Wessely, 2004). However, as Everitt and Wessely note, an absolute separation of treatment and control conditions is not so easily achieved when randomised studies are used to evaluate complex psychological interventions, including those with offenders (see Hollin, 2008). In particular they note the difficulties in achieving double blind conditions and of ensuring treatment fidelity. Shapiro et al. (1994) refer to the adoption of biomedical research designs to evaluate psychological interventions as a "drug metaphor". Finally, the design of a study does not preclude problems such as differential attrition from experimental and control conditions and *noncompliance* with the treatment regime (Brounstein et al., 1997; Farrington, 2003; Shadish & Cook, 2009).

In a randomised study the outcome for *all* participants is included in the analysis; this is known as *Intention to Treat* (ITT). As Gupta (2011) explains: "ITT analysis includes every subject who is randomized according to randomized treatment assignment. It ignores noncompliance, protocol deviations, withdrawal, and anything that happens after randomization" (p. 109). The advantages of ITT are that it maintains sample size and statistical power and gives an unbiased assessment of the magnitude of any treatment effect. The disadvantages are that if a participant did not receive treatment through noncompliance they are nevertheless counted as participating in treatment which dilutes the size of any treatment effect. High levels of noncompliance pose obvious difficulties for any evaluation. However, it is poor practice for applied research to dismiss or neglect the reasons why offenders fail to start or dropout of treatment not least because a perfectly sound intervention is judged to be ineffective and discontinued on the basis of flawed evidence.

If the group assigned to treatment is broken down into subgroups, say compliers and dropouts, the analysis then proceeds on the basis of *Treatment Received* (TR). The shortcoming of a TR analysis is that it negates the advantages of randomisation; the advantage is that it allows a close look at what happens in real life and potentially informs the improvement of treatment.

ITT analysis

In their discussion of the evaluation of community-based offending behaviour programmes Parker, Bush, and Harris (2014) state that "Evaluations should use an intention-to-treat (ITT) model" (p. 295). This view is not remarkable when evaluations used a randomised design but Parker, Bush, and Harris extend their argument in favour of an unconditional reliance on ITT analysis in quasi-experimental designs (i.e., non-randomised studies). Quasi-experimental designs are typically used in the majority of offender treatment outcome studies and, indeed, criminological research generally. They advocate ITT on the grounds that it maintains matching across conditions and avoids a selection effect.

Gross and Fogg (2004) state that: "Although the ITT principle has been controversial, it remains the standard guideline used for evaluating the credibility of findings based on RCTs" (p. 476). Thus, as noted, the position held by

Parker, Bush and Harris obviously holds when evaluations are based on randomisation to condition but does it apply equally well to quasi-experimental designs? The blunt answer is no: when there is no randomisation, as with quasi-experimental designs then, clearly, randomisation cannot be violated by looking inside the treatment condition to gain additional information.

Sherman (2003) notes that ITT and TR analyses actually address different questions: "The ITT principle holds that an RCT can test the effects of trying to get someone to take a treatment and, thus, provides a valid inference about the effect of the attempt, as distinct from the actual treatment received" (p. 12). Thus, as Sherman suggests, an ITT analysis considers what happens when something is offered; on the other hand, a TR analysis shows what happens when the offer is taken up.

The principal issue in treatment evaluation that impacts on outcome is noncompliance with the treatment regime through participant attrition. Attrition is particularly problematic when it is at a high level. Gross and Fogg (2004) expand on non-adherence to include:

> Participants who (a) never participated in any aspect of the intervention, (b) participated in some but not all aspects of the intervention, (c) were initially engaged in the intervention but abruptly terminated participation, or (d) attended intervention meetings but never engaged in the intervention in a meaningful or prescribed way.
>
> *(p. 484)*

Gross and Fogg state that understanding non-adherence may help with strategies to promote adherence thereby benefiting the future evaluations and participants:

> It is important to note that nonadherence to intervention protocols is relevant across many research paradigms. Although the proponents of ITT have mainly focused on randomized trials, the problems surrounding nonadherence generalize across experimental and quasi-experimental designs .... In cases where nonequivalent comparison groups are used one would still want to examine the level, sources, and effects of nonadherence.
>
> *(p. 487)*

In order to understand non-adherence, it is necessary to consider the characteristics and outcomes for the groups of offenders which naturally emerge after allocation to treatment. However, Parker, Bush, and Harris argue that attention to these various groups introduces a selection effect which, in turn, brings about a bias in favour of a positive outcome for those who complete treatment. This view is predicated on the view that offenders who complete treatment are different to non-completers and it is this difference, rather than the effects of the intervention, that accounts for any positive treatment effect.

Understanding attrition

In offender treatment four groups naturally form: (1) offenders not allocated to treatment; (2) offenders allocated to treatment but who fail to start; (3) offenders who start treatment but dropout; (4) offenders who complete treatment. The level of attrition from allocation to completion can be significant: for example, Hollin et al. (2008) reported that of 2,186 offenders allocated to treatment, only 616 actually completed, the remainder either failed to start (1,086 offenders) or started but later dropped out (509 offenders). Adherence to ITT analysis forecloses any understanding of why offenders fail to start and drop out in such numbers, making remedial action impossible.

The importance of understanding what happens to offenders allocated to treatment has been emphasised by the Home Office in their guidelines for the evaluation of treatment initiatives within the criminal justice system in England and Wales (Colledge, Collier, & Brand, 1999). The Home Office guidelines state that researchers should "Make sure that *selection effects* are accounted for by looking at outcomes for those not selected for the programme or who drop out as well as those who complete it" (p. 12, italics in original).

Several researchers have made the same point. Lösel (2001) emphasises the importance of understanding attrition:

> If data analysis allocates dropouts to the treated group, this often results in only low or no differences from untreated groups. However, such evaluations are unfair to program deliverers because non-completers have not been exposed to the whole program. In conclusion, the best way to perform a methodologically adequate data analysis is to present results separately for the different groups.
>
> *(p. 76)*

Similarly, MacKenzie (2002) states that: "Drop-outs from treatment present a major problem in terms of both evaluating the effectiveness of the programs and in determining how successful the program will be" (p. 376).

A body of research has accumulated looking at attrition and has identified both the organisational failures (e.g., Kemshall & Canton, 2002; Palmer et al., 2008, 2009; Stephens & Turner, 2004) and the offender characteristics (e.g., Olver, Stockdale, & Wormith, 2011) associated with attrition. These findings can be applied to reduce levels of noncompletion and their associated organisational costs in finance and a negative effect on staff morale and effectiveness (McMurran, Huband, & Overton, 2010; Sturgess, Woodhams, & Tonkin, 2016; Webb & McMurran, 2009) and maximise the treatment effect. Indeed, Nunes, Cortoni, and Serin (2010) have developed a scale for screening offenders for the likelihood of dropping out of treatment and so allowing remedial steps to be taken.

Research strategies to control the effect of attrition

Parker, Bush, and Harris (2014) argue for a reliance upon ITT analysis as (in a randomised design) it retains the equivalence of treatment and comparison groups, although this argument makes less sense in a quasi-experimental design. However, there are other sensitive methodologies to apply to quasi-experimental designs, such as statistical control and specific types of design and analysis, which can be used to counter any loss of equivalence. An example of statistical control is seen in a study of treatment attrition reported by Lockwood and Harris (2015) using cross-classified hierarchical generalised linear models to allow the effects of treatment attrition on juvenile recidivism to be estimated while controlling for various contextual factors. Propensity score matching (PSM; D'Agostino, 1998) is another statistical approach that can be used to counter the possibility of a selection effect in quasi-experimental designs (Holmes, 2014). PSM models propensity for dropout in the treatment group and then applies this model to the comparison group to estimate which of the comparison group would be more or less likely to drop out. This new variable of propensity to dropout can then be used as a control to moderate against selection effects and has been used in the evaluation of inter-partner violence programmes (Jones et al., 2004) and OBPs (McGuire et al., 2008).

What's to be gained?

This final section will consider what is to be gained by reducing interpersonal violence. As seen throughout the text, the consequences of violence are the victim's personal suffering and various financial costs. If it were possible to reduce crime, given that its elimination is highly improbable (read impossible!), personal and financial benefits would surely follow.

Personal costs

Surveys show that after the event many people do not report being a victim of crime, including violent and sexually violent crimes. It is therefore impossible to know the extent of the personal suffering caused by interpersonal violence in its various forms. It follows that there are many people whose lives are marred by a cluster of negative reactions to victimisation including diminished emotional well-being, self-blame, shame, fear, sleep disturbance, depression, anxiety, and fear of further victimisation. In some instances these sequelae to interpersonal violence may be of such intensity that the victim experiences posttraumatic stress disorder.

Financial costs

Society pays a heavy financial toll for interpersonal violence. There is the cost of the criminal justice system in financing the police, the courts, and the prison and probation services; there are costs to the health system in treating the physical and psychological consequences of victimisation; there are "hidden" costs such as rises in insurance premiums and retail prices in shops, and productivity costs for employees missing days.

The task of estimating those costs is not simple: even at a most basic economic level service costs do not remain constant but fluctuate with the cost of wages, materials, and so on. Nevertheless, the figures involved are astoundingly large: for example, the Prison Reform Trust (2011) collated information from a variety of government reports and statements for England and Wales and reported the following figures for 2011–12 for the supervision and detention of sentenced offenders (these costs will inevitably have risen since then): (i) the resource budget for the National Offender Management Service is £3.679 billion, which includes £1,870 million for prisons and a further £311 million for private prisons; (ii) the average annual cost of a prison place, not including expenditure by other government departments such as health and education, is £45,000; (iii) in 2007–08, the cost of reoffending by all recent ex-prisoners was between £9.5 billion and £13 billion. These figures do not include public spending on the police, courts and so on. The finances to maintain the criminal justice system, not including the additional costs for mentally disordered offenders, is billions and billions of pounds. Of course, not all expenditure is due to interpersonal violence but it is likely that it will account for a substantial proportion of the budget. If the many crime reduction strategies discussed in this text were successfully implemented, thereby reducing levels of interpersonal violence, financial benefits would undoubtedly accrue and public health would correspondingly improve.

REFERENCES

Abbey, A. (2002). Alcohol-related sexual assault: A common problem among college students. *Journal of Studies on Alcohol*, 14, 118–128.

Abracen, J., Looman, J., Ferguson, M., Harkins, L., & Mailloux, D. (2011). Recidivism among treated sexual offenders and comparison subjects: Recent outcome data from the Regional Treatment Centre (Ontario) high-intensity Sex Offender Treatment Programme. *Journal of Sexual Aggression*, 17, 142–152.

Afifi, T. O., Mota, N., MacMillan, H. L., & Sareen, J. (2013). Harsh physical punishment in childhood and adult physical health. *Pediatrics*, 132, 184–192.

Aichhorn, A. (1955). *Wayward youth* (Trans.) New York: Meridian Books. (Original work published 1925.)

Akoensi, T. D., Koehler, J. A., Lösel, F., & Humphreys, D. K. (2012). Domestic violence perpetrator programs in Europe, Part II: A systematic review of the state of evidence. *International Journal of Offender Therapy and Comparative Criminology*, 57, 1206–1225.

Allen, G., & Watson, C. (2017). *UK prison population statistics*. House of Commons Library, Briefing Paper Number SN/SG/04334. London: House of Commons Library.

Allen, J. J., Anderson, C. A., & Bushman, B. J. (2018). The General Aggression Model. *Current Opinion in Psychology*, 19, 75–80.

Allroggen, M., Rau, T., Ohlert, J., & Fegert, J. M. (2017). Lifetime prevalence and incidence of sexual victimization of adolescents in institutional care. *Child Abuse & Neglect*, 66, 23–30.

Altafim, E. R. P., & Martins, M. B. (2016). Universal violence and child maltreatment prevention programs for parents: A systematic review. *Psychosocial Intervention*, 25, 27–38.

Altman, R. L., Canter, J., Patrick, P. A., Daley, N., Butt, N. K., & Brand, D. A. (2011). Parent education by maternity nurses and prevention of abusive head trauma. *Pediatrics*, 128, 1164–1172.

Álvarez-García, D., García, T., & Núñez, J. C. (2015). Predictors of school bullying perpetration in adolescence: A systematic review. *Aggression and Violent Behavior*, 23, 126–136.

Amado, B. G., Arce, R., & Herraiz, A. (2015). Psychological injury in victims of child sexual abuse: A meta-analytic review. *Psychosocial Intervention*, 24, 49–62.

Amelung, T., Kuhle, L. F., Konrad, A., Pauls, A., & Beier, K. M. (2012). Androgen deprivation therapy of self-identifying, help-seeking pedophiles in the Dunkelfeld. *International Journal of Law and Psychiatry*, 35, 176–184.

American Psychiatric Association. (2013). *Diagnostic and statistical manual of mental disorders* (5th ed.). Washington, DC: APA.

An, S., Kim, I., Choi, Y. J., Platt, M., & Thomsen, D. (2017). The effectiveness of intervention for adolescents exposed to domestic violence. *Children and Youth Services Review*, 79, 132–138.

Andersen, S. N., & Telle, K. (2016). *Electronic monitoring and recidivism: Quasi-experimental evidence from Norway*. Discussion Papers No. 844. Oslo: Statistics Norway Research Department.

Andershed, A.-K., Gibson, C. L., & Andershed, H. (2016). The role of cumulative risk and protection for violent offending. *Journal of Criminal Justice*, 45, 78–84.

Anderson, C. A., & Bushman, B. J. (2002). Human aggression. *Annual Review of Psychology*, 53, 27–51.

Andrews, D. A. (1982). *The Level of Supervision Inventory (LSI): The first follow-up*. Toronto: Ontario Ministry of Correctional Services.

Andrews, D. A. (1995). The psychology of criminal conduct and effective treatment. In J. McGuire (Ed.), *What works: Reducing reoffending – guidelines for research and practice* (pp. 35–62). Chichester, West Sussex: John Wiley & Sons.

Andrews, D. A. (2011). The impact of nonprogrammatic factors on criminal-justice interventions. *Legal and Criminological Psychology*, 16, 1–23.

Andrews, D. A., & Bonta, J. (1995). *LSI-R: The Level of Service Inventory-Revised*. Toronto: Multi-Health Systems.

Andrews, D. A., & Bonta, J. (2003). *The psychology of criminal conduct* (3rd ed.). Cincinnati, OH: Anderson Publishing Co.

Andrews, D. A., & Bonta, J. (2010). Rehabilitating criminal justice policy and practice. *Psychology, Public Policy, and Law*, 16, 39–55.

Andrews, D. A., Bonta, J., & Wormith, J. S. (2006). The recent past and near future of risk and/or need assessment. *Crime & Delinquency*, 52, 7–27.

Andrews, D. A., Bonta, J., & Wormith, J. S. (2011). The risk-need-responsivity (RNR) model: Does adding the good lives model contribute to effective crime prevention? *Criminal Justice and Behavior*, 38, 735–755

Antonwicz, D. H. (2005). The Reasoning and Rehabilitation programme. In M. McMurran & J. McGuire (Eds.), *Social problem solving and offending: Evidence evaluation and evolution* (pp. 163–181). Chichester, West Sussex: John Wiley & Sons.

Arias, E., Arce, R., & Vilarino, M. (2013). Batterer intervention programmes: A meta-analytic review of effectiveness. *Psychosocial Intervention*, 22, 153–160.

Ascione, F. R., Thompson, T. M., & Black, T. (1997). Childhood cruelty to animals: Assessing cruelty dimensions and motivations. *Anthrozoos*, 10, 170–177.

Astbury, J. (2013). *Child sexual abuse in the general community and clergy-perpetrated child sexual abuse. A Review Paper prepared for the Australian Psychological Society to inform an APS Response to the Royal Commission into Institutional Responses to Child Sexual Abuse*. Victoria: Australian Psychological Society.

Austin, A. (2016). Is prior parental criminal justice involvement associated with child maltreatment? A systematic review. *Children and Youth Services Review*, 68, 146–153.

Auty, K. M., Cope, A., & Liebling, A. (2017). Psychoeducational programs for reducing prison violence: A systematic review. *Aggression and Violent Behavior*, 33, 126–143.

Averdijk, M., Zirk-Sadowski, J., Ribeaud, D., & Eisner, M. (2016). Long-term effects of two childhood psychosocial interventions on adolescent delinquency, substance use, and antisocial behavior: A cluster randomized controlled trial. *Journal of Experimental Criminology*, 12, 21–47.

Axford, N., Farrington, D. P., Clarkson, S., Bjornstad, G. J., Wrigley, Z., & Hutchings, J. (2015). Involving parents in school-based programmes to prevent and reduce bullying: What effect does it have? *Journal of Children's Services*, 10, 242–251.

Axlerod, S., & Apsche, J. (Eds). (1983). *The effects of punishment on human behavior*. New York: Academic Press.

Babcock, J., Armenti, N., Cannon, C., Lauve-Moon, K., Buttell, F., Ferreira, R., … Solano, I. (2016). Domestic violence perpetrator programs: A proposal for evidence-based standards in the United States. *Partner Abuse*, 7, 355–460.

Babcock, J. C., Green, C. E. & Robie, C. (2004). Does batterers' treatment work? A meta-analytic review of domestic violence treatment. *Clinical Psychology Review*, 23, 1023–1053.

Bailey, W. (1966). Correctional outcome: An evaluation of 100 reports. *Criminal Law, Criminology and Police Science*, 57, 153–160.

Baker, C. K., Billhardt, K. A., Warren, J., Rollins, C., & Glass, N. E. (2010). Domestic violence, housing instability, and homelessness: A review of housing policies and program practices for meeting the needs of survivors. *Aggression and Violent Behavior*, 15, 430–439.

Bakker, M. J., Greven, C. U., Buitelaar, J. K., & Glennon, J. C. (2017). Practitioner review: Psychological treatments for children and adolescents with conduct disorder problems – a systematic review and metaanalysis. *Journal of Child Psychology and Psychiatry*, 58, 4–18.

Baldry, A. C., & Farrington, D. P. (2004). Evaluation of an intervention program for the reduction of bullying and victimization in schools. *Aggressive Behavior*, 30, 1–15.

Baldry, A. C., Farrington, D. P., & Sorrentino, A. (2015). "Am I at risk of cyberbullying?" A narrative review and conceptual framework for research on risk of cyberbullying and cybervictimization: The risk and needs assessment approach. *Aggression and Violent Behavior*, 23, 36–51.

Baldry, A. C., Farrington, D. P., & Sorrentino, A. (2016). Cyberbullying in youth: A pattern of disruptive behaviour. *Psicología Educativa*, 22, 19–26.

Bandura, A. (1977). *Social learning theory*. Englewood Cliffs, NJ: Prentice Hall.

Bandura, A. (1978). Social learning theory of aggression. *Journal of Communication*, 28, 12–29.

Banyard, V. L., & Cross, C. (2008). Consequences of teen dating violence: Understanding intervening variables in ecological context. *Violence Against Women*, 14, 998–1013.

Barbero, J. A. J., Hernández, J. A. R., Esteban, B. L., & García, M. P. (2012). Effectiveness of antibullying school programmes: A systematic review by evidence levels. *Children and Youth Services Review*, 34, 1646–1658.

Barlow, J., Davis, H., McIntosh, E., Jarrett, P., Mockford, C., & Stewart-Brown, S. (2007). Role of home visiting in improving parenting and health in families at risk of abuse and neglect: Results of a multicentre randomised controlled trial and economic evaluation. *Archives of Disease in Childhood*, 92, 229–233.

Barnes, T. N., Smith, S. W., & Miller, M. D. (2014). School-based cognitive-behavioral interventions in the treatment of aggression in the United States: A meta-analysis. *Aggression and Violent Behavior*, 19, 311–321.

Barnett, G. D., Wakeling, H. C., & Howard, P. D. (2010). An examination of the predictive validity of the Risk Matrix 2000 in England and Wales. *Sexual Abuse: A Journal of Research and Treatment*, 22, 443–470.

Bartholow, B. D., Anderson, C. A., Carnagey, N. L., & Benjamin, A. J. (2005). Interactive effects of life experience and situational cues on aggression: The weapons priming effect in hunters and nonhunters. *Journal of Experimental Social Psychology*, 41, 48–60.

Bartlett, J. D., Kotake, C., Fauth, R., & Easterbrooks, M. A. (2017). Intergenerational transmission of child abuse and neglect: Do maltreatment type, perpetrator, and substantiation status matter? *Child Abuse & Neglect*, 63, 84–94.

Basanta, J. L., Fariña, F., & Arce, R. (2018). Risk-need-responsivity model: Contrasting criminogenic and noncriminogenic needs in high and low risk juvenile offenders. *Children and Youth Services Review*, 85, 137–142.

Bates, E. A., Graham-Kevan, N., Bolam, L. T., & Thornton, A. J. V. (2017). A review of domestic violence perpetrator programs in the United Kingdom. *Partner Abuse*, 8, 3–46.

Becker, F., & French, L. (2004). Making the link: Child abuse, animal cruelty and domestic violence. *Child Abuse Review*, 13, 399–414.

Beech, A. R., & Mann, R. (2002). Recent developments in the assessment and treatment of sexual offenders. In *Offender rehabilitation and treatment: Effective programmes and policies to reduce re-offending* (pp. 259–288). Chichester, West Sussex: John Wiley & Sons.

Beech, A., Erikson, M., Friendship, C., & Ditchfield, J. (2001). *A six-year follow-up of men going through probation-based sex offender treatment programmes*. Home Office Research Findings No. 144. London: Home Office.

Benda, B. B., Toombs, N. J., & Peacock, M. (2003). Discriminators of types of recidivism among boot camp graduates in a five-year follow-up study. *Journal of Criminal Justice*, 31, 539–551.

Benedini, K. M., Fagan, A. A., & Gibson, C. L. (2016). The cycle of victimization: The relationship between childhood maltreatment and adolescent peer victimization. *Child Abuse & Neglect*, 59, 111–121.

Benjamin, A. J. Jr., & Bushman, B. J. (2018). The weapons effect. *Current Opinion in Psychology*, 19, 93–97.

Benjet, C., & Kazdin, A. E. (2003). Spanking children: The controversies, findings, and new directions. *Clinical Psychology Review*, 23, 197–224.

Bennett, S. (2011). Female genital mutilation/cutting. In C. Jenny (Ed.), *Child abuse and neglect: Diagnosis, treatment, and evidence* (pp. 134–141). St Louis, MO: Saunders, Elsevier.

Bennett, T., Holloway, K., & Farrington, D. P. (2006). Does neighbourhood watch reduce crime? A systematic review and meta-analysis. *Journal of Experimental Criminology*, 2, 437–458.

Black, D. A. (1982). A 5-year follow-up study of male patients discharged from Broadmoor Hospital. In J. Gunn & D. P. Farrington (Eds.), *Abnormal offenders, delinquency, and the criminal justice system* (pp. 307–338). Chichester, West Sussex: John Wiley & Sons.

Black, M. M., & Oberlander, S. E. (2011). Psychological impact and treatment of neglect of children. In C. Jenny (Ed.), *Child abuse and neglect: Diagnosis, treatment, and evidence* (pp. 490–500). St Louis, MO: Saunders, Elsevier.

Bland, V. J., & Lambie, I. (2018). Does childhood neglect contribute to violent behavior in adulthood? A review of possible links. *Clinical Psychology Review*, 60, 126–135.

Blattner, R., & Dolan, M. (2009). Outcome of high security patients admitted to a medium secure unit: The Edenfield Centre study. *Medicine, Science, and the Law*, 49, 247–256.

Blomberg, T. G., Bales, W. D., Mann, K., Piquero, A. R., & Berk, R. A. (2011). Incarceration, education and transition from delinquency. *Journal of Criminal Justice*, 39, 355–365.

Bo, S., Abu-Akel, A., Kongerslev, M., Haahr, U. H., & Simonsen, E. (2011). Risk factors for violence among patients with schizophrenia. *Clinical Psychology Review*, 31, 711–726.

Boden, J. M., Fergusson, D. M., & Horwood, L. J. (2013). Alcohol misuse and criminal offending: Findings from a 30-year longitudinal study. *Drug and Alcohol Dependence*, 128, 30–36.

Boniface, S., Scannell, J. W., & Marlow, S. (2017). Evidence for the effectiveness of minimum pricing of alcohol: A systematic review and assessment using the Bradford Hill criteria for causality. *BMJ Open*, 7:e013497.

Bonta, J., & Andrews, D. A. (2003). A commentary on Ward and Stewarts's model of human needs. *Psychology, Crime & Law*, 9, 215–218.

Bonta, J., Blais, J., & Wilson, H. A. (2014). A theoretically informed meta-analysis of the risk for general and violent recidivism for mentally disordered offenders. *Aggression and Violent Behavior*, 19, 278–287.

Bonta, J., & Gendreau, P. (1990). Reexamining the cruel and unusual punishment of prison life. *Law and Human Behavior*, 14, 347–372.

Bonta, J., Law, M., & Hanson, R. K. (1998). Prediction of criminal and violent recidivism among mentally disordered offenders: A meta-analysis. *Psychological Bulletin*, 123, 123–142.

Bonta, J., Rugge, T., Scott, T.-L., Bourgon, G., & Yessine, A. K. (2008). Exploring the black box of community supervision. *Journal of Offender Rehabilitation*, 47, 248–270.

Boop, S., Axente, M., Weatherford, B., & Klimo, P. Jr. (2016). Abusive head trauma: An epidemiological and cost analysis. *Journal of Neurosurgery: Pediatrics*, 18, 542–549.

Booth, B. M., Curran, G. M., Han, X., & Edlund, M. J. (2013). Criminal justice and alcohol treatment: Results from a national sample. *Journal of Substance Abuse Treatment*, 44, 249–255.

Bourke, M. L., Prestridge, D., & Malterer, M. B. (2016). Interdiction for the protection of children: Preventing sexual exploitation one traffic stop at a time. *Aggression and Violent Behavior*, 30, 68–75.

Bowen, E. (2011). *The rehabilitation of partner-violent men*. Chichester, West Sussex: John Wiley & Sons.

Bowen, E., Gilchrist, E. A., & Beech, A. R. (2005). An examination of the impact of community-based rehabilitation on the offending behaviour of male domestic violence offenders and the characteristics associated with recidivism. *Legal and Criminological Psychology*, 10, 189–209.

Bowen, E., Gilchrist, E., & Beech, A. R. (2008). Change in treatment has no relationship with subsequent re-offending in UK domestic violence sample: A preliminary study. *International Journal of Offender Therapy and Comparative Criminology*, 52, 598–614.

Bowling, B., & Phillips, C. (2007). Disproportionate and discriminatory: Reviewing the evidence on police stop and search. *The Modern Law Review*, 70, 936–961.

Bradford, J. M. (2000). The treatment of sexual deviation using a pharmacological approach. *Journal of Sex Research*, 37, 248–257.

Braga, T., Gonçalves, L. C., Basto-Pereira, M., & Maia, Â. (2017). Unraveling the link between maltreatment and juvenile antisocial behavior: A meta-analysis of prospective longitudinal studies. *Aggression and Violent Behavior*, 33, 37–50.

Braham, L., Jones, D., & Hollin, C. R. (2008). The Violent Offender Treatment Program (VOTP): Development of a treatment programme for violent patients in a high security psychiatric hospital. *International Journal of Forensic Mental Health*, 7, 157–172.

Braham, L. G., Trower, P., & Birchwood, M. (2004). Acting on command hallucinations and dangerous behavior: A critique of the major findings in the last decade. *Clinical Psychology Review*, 24, 513–528.

Branas, C. C., Elliott, M. R., Richmond, T. S., Culhane, D., Ten Have, T. R., & Wiebe, D. (2009). Alcohol consumption, alcohol outlets, and the risk of being assaulted with a gun. *Alcoholism: Clinical and Experimental Research*, 11, 906–915.

Brandon, M., Belderson, P., Warren, C., Howe, D., Gardner, R., Dodsworth, J., & Black, J. (2008). *Analysing child deaths and serious injury through abuse and neglect:*

What can we learn? A biennial analysis of serious case reviews 2003–5. London: Department for Children, Schools and Families.

Brännström, L., Kaunitz, C., Andershed, A.-K., South, S., & Smedslund, G. (2016). Aggression replacement training (ART) for reducing antisocial behavior in adolescents and adults: A systematic review. *Aggression and Violent Behavior, 27,* 30–41.

Brennan, I. R., & Moore, S. C. (2009). Weapons and violence: A review of theory and research. *Aggression and Violent Behavior, 14,* 215–225.

Brody, S. (1976). *The effectiveness of sentencing: A review of the literature.* London: HMSO.

Broughton, D. D. (2011). Internet child sexual exploitation. In C. Jenny (Ed.), *Child abuse and neglect: Diagnosis, treatment, and evidence* (pp. 142–146). St Louis, MO: Saunders, Elsevier.

Brounstein, P. J., Emshoff, J. G., Hill, G. A., & Stoil, M. J. (1997). Assessment of methodological practices in the evaluation of alcohol and other drug (AOD) abuse prevention. *Journal of Health and Social Policy, 9,* 1–19.

Brown, A. S., Holden, G. W., & Ashraf, R. (2018). Spank, slap, or hit? How labels alter perceptions of child discipline. *Psychology of Violence, 8,* 1–9.

Bruce, R., & Hollin, C. R. (2009). Developing citizenship. *EuroVista: Probation and Community Justice, 1,* 24–31.

Bucci, S., Birchwood, M., Twist, L., Tarrier, N., Emsley, R., & Haddock, G. (2013). Predicting compliance with command hallucinations: Anger, impulsivity and appraisals of voices' power and intent. *Schizophrenia Research, 147,* 163–168.

Buchanan, A. (2013). Violence risk assessment in clinical settings: Being sure about being sure. *Behavioral Sciences and the Law, 31,* 74–80.

Buchanan, A., Taylor, P., & Gunn, J. (2004). Criminal conviction after discharge from special (high security) hospital: The circumstances of early conviction on a serious charge. *Psychology, Crime & Law, 10,* 5–19.

Bunting, L., Webb, M. A., & Healy, J. (2010). In two minds? Parental attitudes toward physical punishment in the UK. *Children and Society, 24,* 359–370.

Bussmann, K. D., Erthal, C., & Schroth, A. (2011). Effects of banning corporal punishment in Europe: A five-nation comparison. In J. E. Durrant & A. B. Smith (Eds.), *Global pathways to abolish physical punishment: Realizing children's rights* (pp. 299–322). New York: Routledge.

Caffaro, J. V., & Conn-Caffaro, A. (2005). Treating sibling abuse families. *Aggression and Violent Behavior, 10,* 604–623.

Caffey, J. (1972). On the theory and practice of shaking infants. Its potential residual effects of permanent brain damage and mental retardation. *American Journal of Diseases of Children, 124,* 161–169.

Caman, S., Kristiansson, M., Granath, S., & Sturup, J. (2017). Trends in rates and characteristics of intimate partner homicides between 1990 and 2013. *Journal of Criminal Justice, 49,* 14–21.

Campbell, M. A., French, S., & Gendreau, P. (2009). The prediction of violence in adult offenders: A meta-analytic comparison of instruments and methods of assessment. *Criminal Justice and Behavior, 36,* 567–590.

Cann, J., Friendship, C., & Gozna, L. (2007). Assessing crossover in a sample of sexual offenders with multiple victims. *Legal and Criminological Psychology*, 12, 149–163.

Cassidy, T., Bowman, B., McGrath, C., & Matzopoulos, R. (2016). Brief report on a systematic review of youth violence prevention through media campaigns: Does the limited yield of strong evidence imply methodological challenges or absence of effect? *Journal of Adolescence*, 52, 22–26.

Castellanos-Ryan, N., Séguin, J. R., Vitaro, F., Parent, S., & Tremblay, R. E. (2013). Impact of a 2-year multimodal intervention for disruptive 6-year-olds on substance use in adolescence: Randomised controlled trial. *British Journal of Psychiatry*, 203, 188–195.

Castillo, E. D., & Alarid, L. F. (2011). Factors associated with recidivism among offenders with mental illness. *International Journal of Offender Therapy and Comparative Criminology*, 55, 98–117.

Chalfin, A., & Deza, M. (in press). The intergenerational effects of education on delinquency. *Journal of Economic Behavior & Organization*.

Chalmers, J. (2014). Alcohol minimum unit pricing and socioeconomic status. *The Lancet*, 383(9929), 1616–1617.

Charyk Stewart, T., Polgar, D., Gilliland, J., Tanner, D. A., Girotti, M. J., Parry, N., & Fraser, D. D. (2011). Shaken Baby Syndrome and a triple-dose strategy for its prevention. *Journal of Trauma*, 71, 1801–1807.

Chen, C., Li, C., Wang, H., Ou, J.-J., Zhou, J.-S., & Wang, X.-P. (2014). Cognitive behavioral therapy to reduce overt aggression behavior in Chinese young male violent offenders. *Aggressive Behavior*, 40, 329–336.

Chen, M. K., & Shapiro, J. M. (2007). Do harsher prison conditions reduce recidivism? A discontinuity-based approach. *American Law and Economics Review*, 9, 1–29.

Chibnall, S., Wallace, M., Leicht, C., & Lunghofer, L. (2006). *I-safe evaluation. Final report*. Fairfax, VA: Caliber, an ICF Consulting Company.

Choi, K.-S., & Lee, J. R. (2017). Theoretical analysis of cyber-interpersonal violence victimization and offending using cyber-routine activities theory. *Computers in Human Behavior*, 73, 394–402.

Christenson, S. L., & Thurlow, M. L. (2004). School dropouts: Prevention considerations, interventions, and challenges. *Current Directions in Psychological Science*, 13, 36–39.

Citrome, L., & Volavka, J. (2011). Pharmacological management of acute and persistent aggression in forensic psychiatry settings. *CNS Drugs*, 25, 1009–1021.

Clarke, M., McCarthy, L., Huband, N., Davies, S., Hollin, C., & Duggan, C. (2016). The characteristics and course after discharge of mentally disordered homicide and non-homicide offenders. *Homicide Studies*, 20, 80–97.

Coccaro, E. F. (2000). Intermittent explosive disorder. *Current Psychiatry Reports*, 2, 67–71.

Cody, C. (2017). 'We have personal experience to share, it makes it real': Young people's views on their role in sexual violence prevention efforts. *Children and Youth Services Review*, 79, 221–227.

Cohen, J. R., Menon, S. V., Shorey, R. C., Le, V. D., & Temple, J. R. (2017). The distal consequences of physical and emotional neglect in emerging adults: A person-centered, multi-wave, longitudinal study. *Child Abuse & Neglect*, 63, 151–161.

Coid, J. W., Gonzalez, R., Igoumenou, A., Zhang, T., Yang, M., & Bebbington, P. (2017). Personality disorder and violence in the national household population of Britain. *Journal of Forensic Psychiatry and Psychology*, 28, 620–638.

Coid, J., Hickey, N., Kahtan, N., Zhang, T., & Yang, M. (2007). Patients discharged from medium secure forensic psychiatry services: Reconvictions and risk factors. *British Journal of Psychiatry*, 190, 223–229.

Colledge, M., Collier, P., & Brand, S. (1999). *Programmes for offenders: Guidance for evaluators*. Crime Reduction Programme – Guidance Note 2. London: Research, Development and Statistics Directorate, Home Office.

Colombino, N., Mercado, C. C., Levenson, J., & Jeglic, E. (2017). Preventing sexual violence: Can examination of offense location inform sex crime policy? *International Journal of Law and Psychiatry*, 34, 160–167.

Cook, A. N., & Roesch, R. (2012). "Tough on Crime" reforms: What psychology has to say about the recent and proposed justice policy in Canada. *Canadian Psychology*, 53, 217–255.

Cook, T. D., & Campbell, D. T. (1979). *Quasi-experimentation: Design and analysis issues for field settings*. Boston, MA: Houghton Mifflin Company.

Cooke, D. J. (2016). Violence risk: The actuarial illusion. In A. Kapardis & D. P. Farrington (Eds.), *The psychology of crime, policing and courts* (pp. 75–93). London: Routledge.

Cope, R., & Ward, M. (1993). What happens to Special Hospital patients admitted to medium security? *Journal of Forensic Psychiatry and Psychology*, 4, 14–24.

Cordilia, A. (1985). Alcohol and property crime: Exploring the causal nexus. *Journal of Studies on Alcohol and Drugs*, 46, 161–171.

Coster, D., Bryson, C., & Purdon, S. (2016). *Evaluation of Coping with Crying: Final report*. London: National Society for the Prevention of Cruelty to Children.

Coyle, A. (2008). The treatment of prisoners: International standards and case law. *Legal and Criminological Psychology*, 13, 219–230.

Craig, J. M., Piquero, A. R., Farrington, D. P., & Ttofi, M. M. (2017). A little early risk goes a long bad way: Adverse childhood experiences and life-course offending in the Cambridge study. *Journal of Criminal Justice*, 53, 34–45.

Criminal Justice Joint Inspection. (2009). *Report of a Joint Thematic Review of Victim and Witness Experiences in the Criminal Justice System*. London: HMCPSI Publications.

Crombie, G., & Trinneer, A. (2003). *Children and internet safety: An evaluation of the Missing Program*. A Report to the Research and Evaluation Section of the National Crime Prevention Centre of Justice Canada. Ottawa: University of Ottawa.

Cross, T. P., Mathews, B., Tonmyr, L., Scott, D., & Ouimet, C. (2012). Child welfare policy and practice on children's exposure to domestic violence. *Child Abuse & Neglect*, 36, 210–216.

Cross, T. P., & Whitcomb, D. (2017). The practice of prosecuting child maltreatment: Results of an online survey of prosecutors. *Child Abuse & Neglect*, 69, 20–28.

Crouch, J. L., Irwin, L. M., Milner, J. S., Skowronski, J. J., Rutledge, E., & Davila, A. L. (2017). Do hostile attributions and negative affect explain the association between authoritarian beliefs and harsh parenting? *Child Abuse & Neglect*, 67, 13–21.

Crozier, J. C., Van Voorhees, E. E., Hooper, S. R., & De Bellis, M. D. (2011). Effects of abuse and neglect on brain development. In C. Jenny (Ed.), *Child abuse and neglect: Diagnosis, treatment, and evidence* (pp. 516–525). St Louis, MO: Saunders, Elsevier.

Cukier, W., & Eagen, S. A. (2018). Gun violence. *Current Opinion in Psychology*, 19, 109–112.

Cullen, F. T., & Gilbert, K. E. (2013). *Reaffirming rehabilitation* (2nd ed.). Waltham, MA: Anderson Publishing.

Cusack, K. J., Morrissey, J. P., Cuddeback, G. S., Prins, A., & Williams, D. M. (2010). Criminal justice involvement, behavioral health service use, and costs of forensic assertive community treatment: A randomized trial. *Community Mental Health Journal*, 46, 356–363.

D'Agostino, R. B. (1998). Propensity score methods for bias reduction in the comparison of a treatment to a non-randomized control group. *Statistics in Medicine*, 17, 2265–2281.

Dadds, M. R., Turner, C. M., & McAloon, J. (2002). Developmental links between cruelty to animals and human violence. *Australian and New Zealand Journal of Criminology*, 35, 363–382.

Dadds, M. R., Whiting, C., Bunn, P., Fraser, J. A., Charlson, J. H., & Pinola-Merlo, A. (2004). Measurement of cruelty in children: The Cruelty to Animals Inventory. *Journal of Abnormal Child Psychology*, 32, 321–334.

Daffern, M., Jones, L., & Shine, J. (Eds.). (2010). *Offence paralleling behaviour: A case formulation approach to offender assessment and intervention.* Chichester, Sussex: John Wiley & Sons.

Daigneault, I., Vézina-Gagnon, P., Bourgeois, C., Esposito, T., & Hébert, M. (2017). Physical and mental health of children with substantiated sexual abuse: Gender comparisons from a matched-control cohort study. *Child Abuse & Neglect*, 66, 155–165.

Daly, K. (2002). Restorative justice: The real story. *Punishment and Society*, 4, 55–79.

Davies, S., Clarke, M., Hollin, C., & Duggan, C. (2007). Long-term outcomes after discharge from medium secure care: A cause for concern. *British Journal of Psychiatry*, 191, 70–74.

Davis, M. K., & Gidycz, C. A. (2017). Child sexual abuse prevention programs: A meta- analysis. *Journal of Clinical Child Psychology*, 29, 257–265.

Davis, R. C., & Auchter, B. (2010). National Institute of Justice funding of experimental studies of violence against women: A critical look at implementation issues and policy implications. *Journal of Experimental Criminology*, 6, 377–395.

Dawes, R. M., Faust, D., & Meehl, P. E. (1989). Clinical versus actuarial judgment. *Science*, 243(4899), 1668–1674.

de Jong, A., Alink, L., Bijleveld, C., Finkenauer, C., & Hendriks, J. (2015). Transition to adulthood of child sexual abuse victims. *Aggression and Violent Behavior*, 24, 175–187.

de Jong, R., & Dennison, S. (2017). Recorded offending among child sexual abuse victims: A 30-year follow-up. *Child Abuse & Neglect*, 72, 75–84.

De La Rue, L., Polanin, J. R., Espelage, D. L., & Pigott, T. D. (2017). A meta-analysis of school-based interventions aimed to prevent or reduce violence in teen dating relationships. *Review of Educational Research*, 87, 7–34.

de Vries Robbé, M., de Vogel, V., & de Spa, E. (2011). Protective factors for violence risk in forensic psychiatric patients: A retrospective validation study of the SAPROF. *International Journal of Forensic Mental Health*, 10, 178–186.

Deater-Deckard, K., Lansford, J. E., Dodge, K. A., Pettit, G. S., & Bates, J. E. (2003). The development of attitudes about physical punishment: An 8-year longitudinal study. *Journal of Family Psychology*, 17, 351–360.

Death, J. (2012). Lessons on sin and forgiveness: A crisis in the Roman Catholic Church. In A. Atta (Ed.), *Catholics and Catholicism in contemporary Australia: Challenges and achievements* (pp. 299–306). Melbourne, Australia: David Lovell Publishing.

Death, J. (2013). *"They did not believe me": Adult survivors' perspectives of child sexual abuse by personnel in Christian institutions*. Crime and Justice and Research Centre, Queensland University of Technology, Queensland, Australia.

Debowska, A., Willmott, D., Boduszek, D., & Jones, A. D. (2017). What do we know about child abuse and neglect patterns of co-occurrence? A systematic review of profiling studies and recommendations for future research. *Child Abuse & Neglect*, 70, 100–111.

DeGue, S., & DiLillo, D. (2009). Is animal cruelty a "red flag" for family violence? Investigating co-occurring violence toward children, partners, and pets. *Journal of Interpersonal Violence*, 24, 1036–1056.

DeGue, S., Valle, L. A., Holt, M. K., Massetti, G. M., Matjasko, J. L., & Tharp, A. T. (2014). A systematic review of primary prevention strategies for sexual violence perpetration. *Aggression and Violent Behavior*, 19, 346–362.

Deković, M., Slant, M. I., Asscher, J. J., Boendermaker, L., Eichelsheim, V. I., & Prinzie, P. (2011). Effects of early prevention programs on adult criminal offending: A meta-analysis. *Clinical Psychology Review*, 31, 532–544.

Della Cioppa, V., O'Neil, A., & Craig, W. (2015). Learning from traditional bullying interventions: A review of research on cyberbullying and best practice. *Aggression and Violent Behavior*, 23, 61–68.

Dennis, J. A., Khan, O., Ferriter, M., Huband, N., Powney, M. J., & Duggan, C. (2012). Psychological interventions for adults who have sexually offended or are at risk of offending. *Cochrane Database of Systematic Reviews*, Issue 12, Art. No.: CD007507.

Di Tella, R., & Schargrodsky, E. (2013). Criminal recidivism after prison and electronic monitoring. *Journal of Political Economy*, 121, 28–73.

Dias, M. S., Smith, K., Mazur, P., Li, V., & Shaffer, M. L. (2005). Preventing abusive head trauma among infants and young children: A hospital-based, parent education program. *Pediatrics*, 115, 470–477.

Dietz, T. L. (2000). Disciplining children: characteristics associated with the use of corporal punishment. *Child Abuse & Neglect*, 24, 1529–1542.

Dijkstra, S., Creemers, H. E., Asscher, J. J., Deković, M., & Stams, G. J. J. M. (2016). The effectiveness of family group conferencing in youth care: A meta-analysis. *Child Abuse & Neglect*, 62, 100–110.

Dobash, R. E., & Dobash, R. P. (2001). Evaluating criminal justice interventions for domestic violence. *Crime and Delinquency*, 46, 252–270.

Dobash, R. P., & Dobash, R. E. (2000). Criminal justice programmes for men who assault their partners. In C. R. Hollin (Ed.) *Handbook of offender assessment and treatment* (pp. 279–389). Chichester, West Sussex: John Wiley & Sons.

Doob, A. N., & Webster, C. M. (2003). Sentence severity and crime: Accepting the null hypothesis. *Crime and Justice*, 30, 143–195.

Dorsey, S., Kerns, S. E. U., Harrison, J. P., Lambert, H. K., Briggs, E. C., Cox, J. R., & Amaya-Jackson, L. (2017). Evidence base update for psychosocial treatments for children and adolescents exposed to traumatic events. *Journal of Clinical Child and Adolescent Psychology*, 46, 303–330.

Douglas, K. S., Guy, L. S., & Hart, S. D. (2009). Psychosis as a risk factor for violence to others: A meta-analysis. *Psychological Bulletin*, 135, 679–706.

Douglas, K. S., Hart, S. D., Webster, C. D., & Belfrage, H. (2013). *HCR-20 (Version 3): Assessing risk of violence – user guide*. Burnaby, BC: Mental Health, Law, and Policy Institute, Simon Fraser University.

Douglas, T., Bonte, P., Focquaert, F., Devolder, K., & Sterckx, S. (2013). Coercion, incarceration, and chemical castration: An argument from autonomy. *Bioethical Inquiry*, 10, 393–405.

Dowden, C., & Andrews, D. A. (2000). Effective correctional treatment and violent reoffending: A meta-analysis. *Canadian Journal of Criminology*, 42, 449–467.

Dowden, C., & Andrews, D. A. (2004). The importance of staff practice in delivering effective correctional treatment: A meta-analytic review of core correctional practice. *International Journal of Offender Therapy and Comparative Criminology*, 48, 203–214.

Dowdle, W. R. (1998). The principles of disease elimination and eradication. *Bulletin of the World Health Organization*, 76(Suppl. 2), 23–25.

Dubowitz, H. (2011). Epidemiology of child neglect. In C. Jenny (Ed.), *Child abuse and neglect: Diagnosis, treatment, and evidence* (pp. 28–34). St Louis, MO: Saunders, Elsevier.

Dubowitz, H. (2017). Child sexual abuse and exploitation: A global glimpse. *Child Abuse & Neglect*, 66, 2–8.

Duggan, C. F., Hollin, C. R., Huband, N., Clarke, M., McCarthy, L., & Davies, S. (2013). A comparison of mentally disordered male offenders with and without a sexual offence: Their characteristics and outcome. *Sexual Offender Treatment*, 8, 1–8.

Durrant, J. E., & Ensom, R. (2017). Twenty-five years of physical punishment research: What have we learned? *Korean Academy of Child and Adolescent Psychiatry*, 28, 20–24.

Durrant, J. E., Fallon, B., Lefebvre, R., & Allan, K. (2017). Defining reasonable force: Does it advance child protection? *Child Abuse & Neglect*, 71, 32–43.

Dymnicki, A. B., Weissberg, R. P., & Henry, D. B. (2011). Understanding how programs work to prevent overt aggressive behaviors: A meta-analysis of mediators of elementary school-based programs. *Journal of School Violence*, 10, 315–337.

Eades, C., Grimshaw, R., Silvestri, A., & Solomon, E. (2007). *'Knife Crime': A review of evidence and policy* (2nd ed.). London: Centre for Crime and Justice Studies, King's College London.

Eisenbraun, K. D. (2007). Violence in schools: Prevalence, prediction, and prevention. *Aggression and Violent Behavior*, 12, 459–469.

El Asam, A., & Samara, M. (2016). Cyberbullying and the law: A review of psychological and legal challenges. *Computers in Human Behavior*, 65, 127–141.

Elbogen, E. B., & Johnson, S. C. (2009). The intricate link between violence and mental disorder: Results from the National Epidemiologic Survey on Alcohol and Related Conditions. *Archives of General Psychiatry*, 66, 152–161.

Eldred, L. M., Gifford, E. J., McCutchan, S. A., & Sloan, F. A. (2016). Factors predicting prosecution of child maltreatment cases. *Children and Youth Services Review*, 70, 201–205.

Evans, G. (2012). Hold back the night: Nuit Blanche and all-night events in capital cities. *Current Issues in Tourism*, 15, 35–49.

Everitt, B. S., & Wessely, S. (2004). *Clinical trials in psychiatry*. Oxford: Oxford University Press.

Ezell, M. (1989). Juvenile arbitration: Net widening and other unintended consequences. *Journal of Research in Crime and Delinquency*, 26, 358–377.

Fahsl, A. J., & Luce, A. E. (2012). Improving interactions: The effects of implementing the Fight-Free Schools Violence Prevention Program. *Preventing School Failure: Alternative Education for Children and Youth*, 56, 214–218.

Falzer, P. R. (2013). Valuing structured professional judgment: Predictive validity, decision-making, and the clinical-actuarial conflict. *Behavioral Sciences and the Law*, 31, 40–54.

Farrell, D. P. (2009). Sexual abuse perpetrated by Roman Catholic priests and religious. *Mental Health, Religion & Culture*, 12, 39–53.

Farrington, D. P. (1996). Later life outcomes of truants in the Cambridge Study. In I. Berg & J. Nursten (Eds.), *Unwillingly to school* (4th ed., pp. 96–118). London: Gaskell.

Farrington, D. P. (2003). Methodological quality standards for evaluation research. *Annals of the American Academy of Political and Social Science*, 587, 49–68.

Farrington, D. P., Ditchfield, J., Hancock, G., Howard, P., Jolliffe, D., Livingston, M. S., & Painter, K. A. (2002). *Evaluation of two intensive regimes for young offenders*. Home Office Research Study 239. London: Home Office.

Farrington, D. P., Gaffney, H., Lösel, F., & Ttofi, M. M. (2017). Systematic reviews of explanatory risk factors for violence, offending, and delinquency. *Aggression and Violent Behavior*, 33, 91–106.

Farrington, D. P., Ttofi, M. M., & Lösel, F. A. (2016). Developmental and social prevention. In *What works in crime prevention and rehabilitation* (pp. 15–75). New York: Springer.

Farrington, D. P., & Welsh, B. C. (2007a). *Saving children from a life of crime: Early risk factors and effective interventions*. Oxford: Oxford University Press.

Farrington, D. P., & Welsh, B. C. (2007b). *Improved street lighting and crime prevention: A systematic review*. Stockholm: National Council for Crime Prevention.

Fazel, S., & Danesh, J. (2002). Serious mental disorder in 23,000 prisoners: A systematic review of 62 surveys. *Lancet*, 359, 545–550.

Fazel, S., Buxrud, P., Ruchkin, V., & Grann, M. (2010). Homicide in discharged patients with schizophrenia and other psychoses: A national case-control study. *Schizophrenia Research*, 123, 263–269.

Fazel, S., Gulati, G., Linsell, L., Geddes, J. R., & Grann, M. (2009). Schizophrenia and violence: Systematic review and meta-analysis. *PLoS Medicine*, 6(8), e1000120.

Fazel, S., & Yu, R. (2011). Psychotic disorders and repeat offending: Systematic review and meta-analysis. *Schizophrenia Bulletin*, 37, 800–810.

Feder, L., & Wilson, D. B. (2005). A meta-analytic review of court-mandated batterer intervention programs: Can courts affect abusers' behavior? *Journal of Experimental Criminology*, 1, 239–262.

Feder, L., Wilson, D. B., & Austin, S. (2008). Court-mandated interventions for individuals convicted of domestic violence. *Campbell Systematic Reviews* 12.

Fellmeth, G. L. T., Heffernan, C., Nurse, J., Habibula, S., & Sethi, D. (2013). Educational and skills-based interventions for preventing relationship and dating violence in adolescents and young adults. *Cochrane Database of Systematic Reviews*, Issue 6. Art. No.: CD004534.

Ferguson, C. J. (2013). Spanking, corporal punishment and negative long-term outcomes: A meta-analytic review of longitudinal studies. *Clinical Psychology Review*, 33, 196–208.

Fergusson, D. M., McLeod, G. F. H., & Horwood, L. J. (2013). Childhood sexual abuse and adult developmental outcomes: Findings from a 30-year longitudinal study in New Zealand. *Child Abuse & Neglect*, 37, 664–674.

Finkel, M. A., & Sapp, M. V. (2011). Adolescent sexual assault and statutory rape. In C. Jenny (Ed.), *Child abuse and neglect: Diagnosis, treatment, and evidence* (pp. 127–133). St Louis, MO: Saunders, Elsevier.

Finn, M. A., & Muirhead-Steves, S. (2002). The effectiveness of electronic monitoring with violent male parolees. *Justice Quarterly*, 19, 293–312.

Flacks, S. (in press). The stop and search of minors: A 'vital police tool'? *Criminology & Criminal Justice*.

Flam, H. (2015). Sexual abuse of children by the Catholic priests in the US: From a 'charismatic bureaucracy' to a governance regime. *Journal of Political Power*, 8, 385–410.

Fleegler, E. W., Lee, L. K., Monuteaux, M. C., Hemenway, D., & Mannix, R. (2013). Firearm legislation and firearm-related fatalities in the United States. *Journal of the American Medical Association: Internal Medicine*, 173, 732–740.

Flynn, C. P. (1999). Animal abuse in childhood and later support for interpersonal violence in families. *Society & Animals*, 7, 161–172.

Fontaine, N. M. G., Brendgen, M., Vitaro, F., & Tremblay, R. E. (2016). Compensatory and protective factors against violent delinquency in late adolescence: Results from the Montreal longitudinal and experimental study. *Journal of Criminal Justice*, 45, 54–62.

Foody, M., Samara, M., El Asama, A. Morsi, H., & Khattab, A. (2017). A review of cyberbullying legislation in Qatar: Considerations for policy makers and educators. *International Journal of Law and Psychiatry*, 50, 45–51.

Foran, H. M., & O'Leary, K. D. (2008). Alcohol and intimate partner violence: A meta-analytic review. *Clinical Psychology Review*, 28, 1222–1234.

Fortune, C.-A. (2018). The Good Lives Model: A strength-based approach for youth offenders. *Aggression and Violent Behavior*, 38, 21–30.

Foshee, V. A., Bauman, K. E., Ennett, S. T., Suchindran, C., Benefield, T., & Linder, G. F. (2005). Assessing the effects of the dating violence prevention program "Safe Dates" using random coefficient regression modeling. *Prevention Science*, 6, 245–258.

Foster, R. (2013). *Knife crime interventions: 'What works?' Report No. 04/2013.* Glasgow: The Scottish Centre for Crime and Justice Research.

Fowler, D. R., Cantos, A. L., & Miller, S. A. (2016). Exposure to violence, typology, and recidivism in a probation sample of domestic violence perpetrators. *Child Abuse & Neglect*, 59, 66–77.

Fox, B. (2017). It's nature and nurture: Integrating biology and genetics into the social learning theory of criminal behavior. *Journal of Criminal Justice*, 49, 22–31.

Fox, B. H., Farrington, D. P., & Ttofi, M. M. (2012). Successful bullying prevention programs: Influence of research design, implementation features, and program components. *International Journal of Conflict and Violence*, 6, 273–283.

Frazier, S. N., & Vela, J. (2014). Dialectical behavior therapy for the treatment of anger and aggressive behavior: A review. *Aggression and Violent Behavior*, 19, 156–163.

Fréchette, S., & Romano, E. (2017). How do parents label their physical disciplinary practices? A focus on the definition of corporal punishment. *Child Abuse & Neglect*, 71, 92–103.

Fried, C. S. (2001). Juvenile curfews: Are they an effective and constitutional means of combating juvenile violence? *Behavioral Sciences and the Law*, 19, 127–141.

Friendship, C., Mann, R. E., & Beech, A. R. (2003). Evaluation of a national prison-based treatment program for sexual offenders in England and Wales. *Journal of Interpersonal Violence*, 18, 744–759.

Friendship, C. & Thornton, D. (2001). Sexual reconviction for sexual offenders discharged from prison in England and Wales. Implications for evaluating treatment. *British Journal of Criminology*, 41, 285–292.

Friendship, C., Thornton, D., Erikson, M. & Beech, A. (2001). Reconviction: A critique and comparison of two main data sources in England and Wales. *Legal and Criminological Psychology*, 6, 121–129.

Frisén, A., Hasselblad, T., & Holmqvist, K. (2012). What actually makes bullying stop? Reports from former victims. *Journal of Adolescence*, 35, 981–990.

Fuller, J. M. (2009). The science and statistics behind spanking suggest that laws allowing corporal punishment are in the best interests of the child. *Akron Law Review*, 42, 257–262.

Fuller, J. (2011). Corporal punishment and child development. *Akron Law Review*, 44, 5–66.

Garcia, F. D., Delavenne, H. G., Assumpção, A. de F. A., & Thibaut, F. (2013). Pharmacologic treatment of sex offenders with paraphilic disorder. *Current Psychiatry Reports*, 15, 356.

Garrett, C. G. (1985). Effects of residential treatment on adjudicated delinquents: A meta-analysis. *Journal of Research in Crime and Delinquency*, 22, 287–308.

Gendreau, P. (1996). Offender rehabilitation: What we know and what needs to be done. *Criminal Justice and Behavior*, 23, 144–161.

Gendreau, P., Goggin, C., & Smith, P. (2001). Implementation guidelines for correctional programmes in the "real" world. In G. A. Bernfeld, A. W. Leschied, & D. P. Farrington (Eds.), *Offender rehabilitation in practice* (pp. 247–268). Chichester, West Sussex: John Wiley & Sons.

Gendreau, P., & Ross, R. R. (1979). Effective correctional treatment: Bibliotherapy for cynics. *Crime and Delinquency*, 25, 463–489.

Gendreau, P., & Ross, R. R. (1987). Revivification of rehabilitation: Evidence from the 1980s. *Justice Quarterly*, 4, 349–408.

Gendreau, P., Smith, P., & Thériault, Y. L. (2009). Chaos theory and correctional treatment: Common sense, correctional quackery, and the law of fartcatchers. *Journal of Contemporary Criminal Justice*, 25, 384–396.

Gershoff, E. T. (2002). Corporal punishment by parents and associated child behaviors and experiences: A meta-analytic and theoretical review. *Psychological Bulletin*, 128, 539–579.

Gershoff, E. T. (2010). More harm than good: A summary of scientific research on the intended and unintended effects of corporal punishment of children. *Law and Contemporary Problems*, 73, 31–56.

Gershoff, E. T., Grogan-Kaylor, A., Lansford, J. E., Chang, L., Zelli, A., Deater-Deckard, K., & Dodge, K. A. (2010). Parent discipline practices in an international sample: Associations with child behaviors and moderation by perceived normativeness. *Child Development*, 81, 487–502.

Gershoff, E. T. (2013). Spanking and child development: We know enough now to stop hitting our children. *Child Development Perspectives*, 7, 133–137.

Gershoff, E. T. (2017). School corporal punishment in global perspective: Prevalence, outcomes, and efforts at intervention. *Psychology, Health & Medicine*, 22(supp.1), 224–239.

Gershoff, E. T., & Bitensky, S. H. (2007). The case against corporal punishment of children: Converging evidence from social science research and international human rights law and implications for U.S. public policy. *Psychology, Public Policy, and Law*, 13, 231–272.

Gershoff, E. T., & Grogan-Kaylor, A. (2016). Spanking and child outcomes: Old controversies and new meta-analyses. *Journal of Family Psychology*, 30, 453–469.

Ghosh, A., & Pasupathi, M. (2016). Perceptions of students and parents on the use of corporal punishment at schools in India. *Rupkatha Journal on Interdisciplinary Studies in Humanities*, VIII, 270–280.

Gidycz, C. A., Lynn, S. J., Rich, C. L., Marioni, N. L., Loh, C., Blackwell, L. M., et al. (2001). The evaluation of sexual assault risk reduction program: A multisite investigation. *Journal of Consulting and Clinical Psychology*, 69, 1073–1078.

Gies, S., Gainey, R., & Healy, E. (2016). Monitoring high-risk sex offenders with GPS. *Criminal Justice Studies*, 29, 1–20.

Gilliom, J., & Monahan, T. (2013). *SuperVision: An introduction to the surveillance society*. Chicago, IL: The University of Chicago Press.

Glass, G. V., McGraw, B., & Smith, M. L. (1981). *Meta-analysis in social research*. Beverly Hills, CA: Sage.

Gleyzer, R., Felthous, A. R., & Holzer, C. E. (2002). Animal cruelty and psychiatric disorders. *Journal of the American Academy of Psychiatry and Law*, 30, 257–265.

Goldstein, A. P., & Glick, B. (2001). Aggression Replacement Training: Application and evaluation management. In G. A. Bernfield, D. P. Farrington, & A. W. Leschied (Eds.), *Offender rehabilitation in practice: Effective programs and policies to reduce re-offending* (pp. 122–148). Chichester, West Sussex: John Wiley & Sons.

Goldstein, A. P., Glick, B., & Gibbs, J. C. (1998). *Aggression Replacement Training* (2nd edition). Champaign, IL: Research Press.

Goldstein, A. P., Nensén, R., Daleflod, B., & KaltM. (Eds.). (2004). *New perspectives on Aggression Replacement Training: Practice, research and application*. Chichester, West Sussex: John Wiley & Sons.

Gondolf, E. W. (2004). Evaluating batterer counseling programs: A difficult task showing some effects and implications. *Aggression and Violent Behavior*, 9, 605–631.

Gordon Jr, R. S. (1983). An operational classification of disease prevention. *Public Health Reports*, 98, 107–109.

Grady, M. D., Edwards, D. E., & Pettus-Davis, C. (2017). A longitudinal outcome evaluation of a prison-based sex offender treatment program. *Sexual Abuse: A Journal of Research and Treatment*, 29, 239–266.

Graham, H., & McIvor, G. (2015). *Scottish and international review of the uses of electronic monitoring*. Stirling: Scottish Centre for Crime and Justice Research: University of Stirling.

Grant, E. (2016). Designing carceral environments for Indigenous prisoners: A comparison of approaches in Australia, Canada, Aotearoa New Zealand, the US and Greenland (Kalaallit Nunaat). *Advancing Corrections*, 1, 26–47.

Greco, A. M., Guilera, G., & Pereda, M. (2017). School staff members experience and knowledge in the reporting of potential child and youth victimization. *Child Abuse & Neglect*, 72, 22–31.

Greenland, C. (1969). The three Special Hospitals in England and Wales and patients with dangerous, violent or criminal propensities. *Medicine, Science and the Law*, 9, 253–264.

Grogan-Kaylor, A., Galano, M. M., Howell, K. H., Miller-Graff, L., & Graham-Bermann, S. A. (in press). Reductions in parental use of corporal punishment on pre-school children following participation in the Moms' Empowerment Program. *Journal of Interpersonal Violence.*

Grogan-Kaylor, A., Ma, J., & Graham-Bermann, S. A. (2018). The case against physical punishment. *Current Opinion in Psychology*, 19, 22–27.

Grønnerød, C., Grønnerød, J. S., & Grøndahl, P. (2015). Psychological treatment of sexual offenders against children: A meta-analytic review of treatment outcome studies. *Trauma, Violence, & Abuse*, 16, 280–290.

Gross, D., & Fogg, L. (2004). A critical analysis of the Intent-to-Treat principle in prevention research. *Journal of Primary Prevention*, 25, 475–489.

Guerzoni, M., & Graham, H. (2015). Catholic Church responses to clergy-child sexual abuse and mandatory reporting exemptions in Victoria, Australia: A discursive critique. *International Journal for Crime, Justice and Social Democracy*, 4, 58–75.

Gültekin, K., & Gültekin, S. (2012). Is juvenile boot camp policy effective? *International Journal of Human Sciences*, 9, 725–740.

Gumpert, C. H., Winerdal, U., Grundtman, M., Berman, A. H., Kristiansson, M., & Palmstierna, T. (2010). The relationship between substance abuse treatment and crime relapse among individuals with suspected mental disorder, substance abuse, and antisocial behavior: Findings from the MSAC Study. *International Journal of Forensic Mental Health*, 9, 82–92.

Gundersen, K., & Svartdal, F. (2006). Aggression replacement training in Norway: Outcome evaluation of 11 Norwegian student projects. *Scandinavian Journal of Educational Research*, 50, 63–81.

Gupta, S. K. (2011). Intention-to-treat concept: A review. *Perspectives in Clinical Research*, 2, 109–112.

Haden, S. C., & Scarpa, A. (2005). Childhood animal cruelty: A review of research, assessment, and therapeutic issues. *The Forensic Examiner*, 14, 23–32.

Haggård, U., Freij, I., Danielsson, M., Wenander, D., & Långström, N. (2017). Effectiveness of the IDAP treatment program for male perpetrators of intimate partner violence: A controlled study of criminal recidivism. *Journal of Interpersonal Violence*, 32, 1027–1043.

Hahn, R. A., Bilukha, O., Crosby, A., Fullilove, M. T., Liberman, A., Moscicki, E., … & Briss, P. A. (2005). Firearms laws and the reduction of violence: A systematic review. *American Journal of Preventive Medicine*, 28, 40–71.

Hamilton, L., Koehler, J. A., & Lösel, F. A. (2012). Domestic violence perpetrator programs in Europe, Part I: A survey of current practice. *International Journal of Offender Therapy and Comparative Criminology*, 57, 1189–1205.

Hamilton, Z., Campagna, M., Tollefsbol, E., Van Wormer, J., & Barnoski, R. (2017). A more consistent application of the RNR Model: The strong-R needs assessment. *Criminal Justice and Behavior*, 44, 261–292.

Hanson, R. K. (2014). Treating sexual offenders: How did we get here and where are we headed? *Journal of Sexual Aggression*, 20, 3–8.

Hanson, R. K., Bourgon, G., Helmus, L., & Hodgson, S. (2009). The principles of effective correctional treatment also apply to sexual offenders: A meta-analysis. *Criminal Justice and Behavior*, 36, 865–891.

Hanson, R. K., Gordon, A., Harris, A. J. R., Marques, J. K., Murphy, W., Quinsey, V. L. & Seto, M. C. (2002). First report of the collaborative outcome data project on the effectiveness of psychological treatment for sex offenders. *Sexual Abuse: A Journal of Research and Treatment*, 14, 169–194.

Hanson, R. K., & Yates, P. M. (2013). Psychological treatment of sex offenders. *Current Psychiatry Reports*, 15, 348.

Harris, D. A., Pedneault, A., & Willis, G. (in press). The pursuit of primary human goods in men desisting from sexual offending. *Sexual Abuse: A Journal of Research and Treatment*.

Hart, S. D., & Cooke, D. J. (2013). Another look at the (im-) precision of individual risk estimates made using actuarial risk assessment instruments. *Behavioral Sciences and the Law*, 31, 81–102.

Hartney, E., & Barnard, D. K. (2015). A framework for the prevention and mitigation of injury from family violence in children of parents with mental illness and substance use problems. *Aggression and Violent Behavior*, 25, 354–362.

Hasisi, B., Shoham, E., Weisburd, D., Haviv, N., & Zelig, A. (2016). The "care package," prison domestic violence programs and recidivism: A quasi-experimental study. *Journal of Experimental Criminology*, 12, 563–586.

Hatcher, R. M., Palmer, E. J., McGuire, J., Hounsome, J. C., Bilby, C. A. L., & Hollin, C. R. (2008). Aggression Replacement Training with adult male offenders within community settings: A reconviction analysis. *Journal of Forensic Psychiatry and Psychology*, 19, 517- 532.

Hawkins, B., & McCambridge, J. (2014). Industry actors, thinktanks, and alcohol policy in the United Kingdom. *American Journal of Public Health*, 104, 1363–1369.

Hawkins, J. D., Herrenkohl, T. I., Farrington, D. P., Brewer, D., Catalano, R. F., Harachi, T. W. & Cothern, L. (2000). *Predictors of youth violence*. Report Number NCJ-1790652000. Washington, D.C.: Juvenile Department of Justice, Office of Justice and Delinquency Prevention.

Heffernan, R., & Ward, T. (2017). A comprehensive theory of dynamic risk and protective factors. *Aggression and Violent Behavior*, 37, 129–141.

Heil, P., Ahlmeyer, S., & Simons, D. (2003). Crossover sexual offenses. *Sexual Abuse: A Journal of Research and Treatment*, 15, 221–236.

Heim, N. (1981). Sexual behavior of castrated sex offenders. *Archives of Sexual Behavior*, 10, 11–19.

Heim, N., & Hursch, C. J. (1979). Castration for sex offenders: Treatment or punishment? A review and critique of recent European literature. *Archives of Sexual Behavior*, 8, 281–304.

Hemphill, S. A., Heerde, J. A., & Scholes-Balog, K. E. (2016). Risk factors and risk-based protective factors for violent offending: A study of young Victorians. *Journal of Criminal Justice*, 45, 94–100.

Henderson, M., & Hollin, C. R. (1986). Social skills training and delinquency. In C. R. Hollin & P. Trower (Eds.), *Handbook of social skills training, Volume 1: Applications across the life span* (pp. 79–101). Oxford: Pergamon Press.

Hendricks, L., Lumadue, R., & Waller, L. R. (2012). The evolution of bullying to cyber bullying: An overview of the best methods for implementing a cyber bullying preventive program. *National Forum Journal of Counseling and Addiction*, 1, 1–9.

Henwood, K. S., Chou, S., & Browne, K. D. (2015). A systematic review and meta-analysis on the effectiveness of CBT informed anger management. *Aggression and Violent Behavior*, 25, 280–292.

Hepburn, L. M., & Hemenway, D. (2004). Firearm availability and homicide: A review of the literature. *Aggression and Violent Behavior*, 9, 417–440.

Herrenkohl, T. I., Maguin, E., Hill, K. G., Hawkins, J. D., Abbott, R. D., & Catalano, R. F. (2000). Developmental risk factors for youth violence. *Journal of Adolescent Health*, 26, 176–186.

Heydt, M. J., & O'Connell, W. P. (2012). The Hope and Healing Response Team Program Model: A social work intervention for clergy abuse. *Journal of Social Work Values & Ethics*, 9, 46–55.

Hibbett, A., & Fogelman, K. (1990). Future lives of truants: Family formation and health-related behaviour. *British Journal of Educational Psychology*, 60, 171–179.

Hickman, L. J., Setodji, C. M., Jaycox, L. H., Kofner, A., Schultz, D., Barnes-Proby, D., & Harris, R. (2013). Assessing programs designed to improve outcomes for children exposed to violence: Results from nine randomized controlled trials. *Journal of Experimental Criminology*, 9, 301–331.

HM Government. (2015). *Working together to safeguard children. A guide to inter-agency working to safeguard and promote the welfare of children*. London: HM Government.

HM Government. (2016). *Ending Violence against Women and Girls Strategy 2016–2020*. London: HM Government.

HM Inspectorate of Police. (2017). *PEEL: Police legitimacy 2016: A national overview*. London: HM Inspectorate of Police.

Hoare, J., & Jansson, K. (2007). Extent of intimate violence, nature of partner abuse and serious sexual assault, 2004/05, 2005/06, 2006/07 BCS. In D. Povey, K. Coleman, P. Kaiza, J. Hoare, & K. Jansson (Eds.), *Homicides, firearm offences and intimate violence 2006/07* (3rd ed.). Home Office Statistical Bulletin 03/08. London: Home Office.

Hoberman, H. M. (2016). Forensic psychotherapy for sexual offenders: Likely factors contributing to its apparent ineffectiveness. In A. Phenix and H. Hoberman (Eds.), *Sexual offending* (pp. 667–712). New York, NY: Springer.

Hodgins, S. (2008). Violent behaviour among people with schizophrenia: A framework for investigations of causes, and effective treatment, and prevention. *Philosophical Transactions of the Royal Society B*, 363, 2505–2518.

Hodgins, S., & Riaz, M. (2011). Violence and phases of illness: Differential risk and predictors. *European Psychiatry*, 26, 518–524.

Hoel, H., Glaso, L., Hetland, J., Cooper, C. L., & Einarsen, S. (2010). Leadership styles as predictors of self-reported and observed workplace bullying. *British Journal of Management*, 21, 453–468.

Hogh, A., & Viitasara, E. (2005). A systematic review of longitudinal studies of nonfatal workplace violence. *European Journal of Work and Organizational Psychology*, 14, 291–313.

Hohl, K., & Stanko, E. A. (2015). Complaints of rape and the criminal justice system: Fresh evidence on the attrition problem in England and Wales. *European Journal of Criminology*, 12, 324–341.

Holden, G. W. (2003). Children exposed to domestic violence and child abuse: Terminology and taxonomy. *Clinical Child and Family*, 6, 151–160.

Holland, G. W. O., & Holden, G. W. (2016). Changing orientations to corporal punishment: A randomized, control trial of the efficacy of a motivational approach to psycho-education. *Psychology of Violence*, 6, 233–242.

Hollin, C. R. (1990). *Cognitive-behavioural interventions with young offenders*. Oxford: Pergamon Press.

Hollin, C. R. (1999). Treatment programmes for offenders: Meta-analysis, "what works", and beyond. *International Journal of Law and Psychiatry*, 22, 361–372.

Hollin, C. R. (Ed). (2001a). *Handbook of offender assessment and treatment*. Chichester, West Sussex: John Wiley & Sons.

Hollin, C. R. (2001b). To treat or not to treat: An historical perspective. In C. R. Hollin (Ed.), *Handbook of offender assessment and treatment* (pp. 3–15). Chichester, West Sussex: John Wiley & Sons.

Hollin, C. R. (2003). Aggression Replacement Training: Putting theory and research to work. *Reclaiming Children and Youth: The Journal of Strength-Based Interventions*, 12, 132–135.

Hollin, C. R. (2008). Evaluating offending behaviour programmes: Does only randomisation glister? *Criminology & Criminal Justice*, 8, 89–106.

Hollin, C. R. (2012). A short history of corrections: The rise, fall, and resurrection of rehabilitation through treatment. In J. A. Dvoskin, J. L. Skeem, R. W. Novaco, & K. S. Douglas (Eds.), *Applying social science to reduce reoffending* (pp. 31–49). Oxford: Oxford University Press.

Hollin, C. R. (2016). *The psychology of interpersonal violence*. Chichester, West Sussex: Wiley Blackwell.

Hollin, C. R. (2018). Cognitive behavior therapy. In B. Puri & I. H. Treasaden (Eds.), *Forensic psychiatry: Fundamentals and clinical practice* (pp. 727–731). Boca Raton, FL: CRC Press.

Hollin, C. R., & Palmer, E. J. (2003). Level of Service Inventory-Revised profiles of violent and non-violent prisoners. *Journal of Interpersonal Violence*, 18, 1075–1086.

Hollin, C. R., & Palmer, E. J. (2006). Offending behaviour programmes: History and development. In C. R. Hollin & E. J. Palmer (Eds.), *Offending behaviour programmes: Development, application, and controversies* (pp. 1–32). Chichester, West Sussex: John Wiley & Sons.

Hollin, C. R., & Palmer, E. J. (2009). Cognitive skills programmes for offenders. *Psychology, Crime & Law*, 15, 147–164.

Hollin, C. R., McGuire, J., Hounsome, J. C., Hatcher, R. M., Bilby, C. A. L., & Palmer, E. J. (2008). Cognitive skills offending behavior programs in the community: A reconviction analysis. *Criminal Justice and Behavior*, 35, 269–283.

Hollin, C. R., Palmer, E. J., & Clark, D. (2003). The Level of Service Inventory-Revised profile of English prisoners: A needs analysis. *Criminal Justice and Behavior*, 30, 422–440.

Hollinshead, D. M., Corwin, T. W., Maher, E. J.Merkel-Holguin, L., Allan, H., & Fluke, J. D. (2017). Effectiveness of family group conferencing in preventing repeat referrals to child protective services and out-of-home placements. *Child Abuse & Neglect*, 69, 285–294.

Holmqvist, R., Hill, T., & Lang, A. (2009). Effects of aggression replacement training in young offender institutions. *International Journal of Offender Therapy and Comparative Criminology*, 53, 74–92.

Holmes, J., Meng, Y., Meier, P. S., Brennan, A., Angus, C., Campbell-Burton, A., ... & Purshouse, R. C. (2014). Effects of minimum unit pricing for alcohol on different income and socioeconomic groups: A modelling study. *The Lancet*, 383(9929), 1655–1664.

Holmes, W. M. (2014). *Using propensity scores in quasi-experimental designs*. Thousand Oaks, CA: Sage Publications.

Holoyda, B. J., & Newman, W. J. (2016). Childhood animal cruelty, bestiality, and the link to adult interpersonal violence. *International Journal of Law and Psychiatry*, 47, 129–135.

Home Office. (n.d.). *Domestic Violence Protection Orders (DVPO). One year on – Home Office assessment of national roll-out*. London: Home Office.

Home Office. (2002). *Criminal Statistics, England and Wales 2001*. Cm 5696. London: The Stationery Office.

Home Office. (2013). *Information for local areas on the change to the definition of domestic violence and abuse*. London: Home Office.

Homel, R. (2005). Developmental crime prevention. In N. Tilley (Ed.), *Handbook of crime prevention and community safety* (pp. 71–106). Cullumpton, Devon: Willan Publishing.

Hornsveld, R. H. J., Nijman, H. L. I., Hollin, C. R., & Kraaimaat, F. W. (2007). Development of the Observation Scale for Aggress Behav (OSAB) for Dutch forensic psychiatric inpatients with an antisocial behavior disorder. *International Journal of Law and Psychiatry*, 30, 15–27.

Hornsveld, R. H. J., Nijman, H. L. I., Hollin, C. R., & Kraaimaat, F. W. (2008). Aggression control therapy for violent forensic psychiatric patients: Method and clinical practice. *International Journal of Offender Therapy and Comparative Criminology*, 52, 206–221.

Horwath, J. (2007). *Child neglect: Identification and assessment*. London: Palgrave/Macmillan.

Houts, F. W., Taller, I., Tucker, D. E., & Berlin, F. S. (2011). Androgen deprivation treatment of sexual behavior. *Advances in Psychosomatic Medicine*, 31, 149–163.

Howell, K. H., Miller, L. E., Lilly, M. M., Burlaka, V., Grogan-Kaylor, A. C. & Graham-Bermann, S. A. (2015). Strengthening positive parenting through intervention: Evaluating the Moms' Empowerment Program for Women Experiencing Intimate Partner Violence. *Journal of Interpersonal Violence*, 30, 232–252.

Hudson, B. (1987). *Justice through punishment: A critique of the 'justice' model of corrections*. London: Macmillan.

Iguh, N. A., & Nosike, O. (2011). An examination of the child rights protection and corporal punishment in Nigeria. *Nnamdi Azikiwe University Journal of International Law and Jurisprudence*, 2, 97–111.

Institute of Alcohol Studies. (2010). *Alcohol & crime*. IAS Factsheet retrieved from http://www.ias.org.uk

Jack, A., & Wilcox, D. T. (2018). The psychological assessment of clerics. *Pastoral Psychology*, 67, 55–64.

James, D. V. (2010). Diversion of mentally disordered people from the criminal justice system in England and Wales: An overview. *International Journal of Law and Psychiatry*, 33, 241–248.

Jamieson, L., & Taylor, P. J. (2004). A re-conviction study of special (high security) hospital patients. *British Journal of Criminology*, 44, 783–802.

Jenaro, C., Flores, N., & Frías, C. P. (2018). Systematic review of empirical studies on cyberbullying in adults: What we know and what we should investigate. *Aggression and Violent Behavior, 38*, 113–122.

Jennings, J. L. (2009). Does Assertive Community Treatment work with forensic populations? Review and recommendations. *The Open Psychiatry Journal, 3*, 13–19.

Jennings, W. G., Okeem, C., Piquero, A. R., Sellers, C. S., Theobald, D., & Farrington, D. P. (2017). Dating and intimate partner violence among young persons ages 15–30: Evidence from a systematic review. *Aggression and Violent Behavior*, 33, 107–125.

Jeremiah, R. D., Quinn, C. R., & Alexis, J. M. (2017). Exposing the culture of silence: Inhibiting factors in the prevention, treatment, and mitigation of sexual abuse in the Eastern Caribbean. *Child Abuse & Neglect*, 66, 53–63.

Jewell, R. T., MotiA., & Coates, D. (2011). A brief history of violence and aggression in spectator sports. In R. T. Jewell (Ed.), *Violence and aggression in sporting contests, sports economics, management and policy* (pp. 11–26). New York: Springer.

Johnston, D. W., Shields, M. A., & Suziedelyte, A. (in press). Victimisation, well-being and compensation: Using panel data to estimate the costs of violent crime. *The Economic Journal*.

Jolliffe, D., Farrington, D. P., Piquero, A. R., Loeber, R., & Hill, K. G. (2017). Systematic review of early risk factors for life-course-persistent, adolescence-limited, and late-onset offenders in prospective longitudinal studies. *Aggression and Violent Behavior*, 33, 15–23.

Jolliffe, D., Farrington, D. P., & Howard, P. (2013). How long did it last? A 10-year reconviction follow-up study of high intensity training for young offenders. *Journal of Experimental Criminology*, 9, 515–531.

Jolliffe, D., Farrington, D. P., Loeber, R., & Pardini, D. (2016). Protective factors for violence: Results from the Pittsburgh Youth Study. *Journal of Criminal Justice*, 45, 32–40.

Jones, A. S., D'Agostino, R. B., Gondolf, E.W., & Heckert, A. (2004). Assessing the effect of batterer program completion on reassault using propensity scores. *Journal of Interpersonal Violence*, 19, 1002–1020.

Jones, A. S., & Logan-Greene, P. (2016). Understanding and responding to chronic neglect: A mixed methods case record examination. *Children and Youth Services Review*, 67, 212–219.

Jones, D., & Hollin, C. R. (2004). Managing problematic anger: The development of a treatment programme for personality disordered patients in high security. *International Journal of Forensic Mental Health*, 3, 197–210.

Jones, H., & Pells, K. (2016). *Undermining Learning: Multi-Country Longitudinal Evidence on Corporal Punishment in Schools. Innocenti Research Brief, 2016–01.* Florence, Italy: UNICEF Office of Research.

Kaseweter, K., Woodworth, M., Logan, M., & Freimuth, T. (2016). High-risk sexual offenders: Towards a new typology. *Journal of Criminal Justice*, 47, 123–132.

Katikireddi, S. V. & Hilton, S. (2015). How did policy actors use mass media to influence the Scottish alcohol minimum unit pricing debate? Comparative analysis of newspapers, evidence submissions and interviews. *Drugs: Education, Prevention and Policy*, 22, 125–134.

Kaukinen, C. (2014). Dating violence among college students: The risk and protective factors. *Trauma, Violence, & Abuse*, 15, 283–296.

Kazdin, A. E. (1987). Treatment of antisocial behaviour in children: Current status and future directions. *Psychological Bulletin*, 102, 187–203.

Kazdin, A. E. (2011). Conceptualizing the challenge of reducing interpersonal violence. *Psychology of Violence*, 1, 166–187.

Kelly, L., Adler, J. R., Horvath, M. A. H., Lovett, J., Coulson, M., Kernohan, D., … Nicholas, S. (2013). *Evaluation of the pilot of Domestic Violence Protection Orders.* Home Office Research Report 76. London: Home Office.

Kemp, A. M., Trefan, L. & Summers, A. (2015). *Traumatic head injury in children and young people: A national overview. A review of 6 months data from 2009–2010, collected from England, Wales, Northern Ireland, Channel Islands and the Isle of Man.* London: Healthcare Quality Improvement Partnership & Cardiff: Cardiff University.

Kemshall, H., & Canton, R. (2002). *The effective management of programme attrition: A report for the National Probation Service (Welsh Region).* Leicester: Community and Criminal Justice Unit, De Montfort University.

Kemshall, H., & Maguire, M. (2001). Public protection, partnership and risk penality: The multi-agency risk management of sexual and violent offenders. *Punishment & Society*, 3, 237–264.

Kennedy, D. M. (2009). *Deterrence and crime prevention: Reconsidering the prospect of sanction.* London: Routledge.

Kewley, S. (2017). Strength based approaches and protective factors from a criminological perspective. *Aggression and Violent Behavior*, 32, 11–18.

Khalifa, H. A. M. (2017). Physical punishment of children: Dimensions and predictors in Egypt. *International Journal of Psychology and Behavioral Sciences*, 7, 32–40.

Khan, O., Ferriter, M., Huband, N., Powney, M. J., Dennis, J. A., & Duggan, C. (2015). Pharmacological interventions for those who have sexually offended or are at risk of offending. *Cochrane Database of Systematic Reviews*, Issue 2. Art. No.: CD007989.

Khan, R., & Cooke, D. J. (2008). Risk factors for severe inter-sibling violence: A preliminary study of a youth forensic sample. *Journal of Interpersonal Violence*, 23, 1513–1530.

Khan, R., & Cooke, D. J. (2013). Measurement of sibling violence: A two-factor model of severity. *Criminal Justice and Behavior*, 40, 26–39.

Killias, G., Gilliéron, G., Kissling, I., & Villettaz, P. (2010). Community service versus electronic monitoring — What works better? Results of a randomized trial. *British Journal of Criminology*, 50, 1155–1170.

Kim, B., Benekos, P. J., & Merlo, A. V. (2016). Sex offender recidivism revisited: Review of recent meta-analyses on the effects of sex offender treatment. *Trauma, Violence, & Abuse*, 17, 105–117.

Kim, S., Noh, D., & Kim, H. (2016). A summary of selective experimental research on psychosocial interventions for sexually abused children. *Journal of Child Sexual Abuse*, 25, 597–617.

Kimber, M., Adham, S., Gill, S., McTavish, J., & MacMillan, H. L. (2018). The association between child exposure to intimate partner violence (IPV) and perpetration of IPV in adulthood – A systematic review. *Child Abuse & Neglect*, 76, 273–286.

Kirigin, K. A., Braukmann, C. J., Atwater, J. D., & Wolf, M. M. (1982). An evaluation of teaching family (Achievement Place) group homes for juvenile offenders. *Journal of Applied Behavior Analysis*, 15, 1–16.

Kitzmann, K. M., Gaylord, N. K., Holt, A. R., & Kenny, E. D. (2003). Child witnesses to domestic violence: A meta-analytic review. *Journal of Consulting and Clinical Psychology*, 71, 339–352.

Klepfisz, G., Daffern, M., & Day, A. (2017). Understanding protective factors for violent reoffending in adults. *Aggression and Violent Behavior*, 32, 80–87.

Knott, C. (1995). The STOP programme: Reasoning and Rehabilitation in a British setting. In J. McGuire (Ed.), *What works: Reducing reoffending* (pp. 115–126). Chichester, West Sussex: John Wiley & Sons.

Knox, M. (2010). On hitting children: A review of corporal punishment in the United States. *Journal of Pediatric Health Care*, 24, 103–107.

Knox, M., & Burkhart, K. (2014). A multi-site study of the ACT Raising Safe Kids program: Predictors of outcomes and attrition. *Children and Youth Services Review*, 39, 20–24.

Knox, M. S., Burkhart, K., & Hunter, K. E. (2011). ACT Against Violence Parents Raising Safe Kids Program: Effects on maltreatment-related parenting behaviors and beliefs. *Journal of Family Issues*, 32, 55–74.

Koehler, J. A., Lösel, F., Akoensi, T. D., & Humphreys, D. K. (2013). A systematic review and meta-analysis on the effects of young offender treatment programs in Europe. *Journal of Experimental Criminology*, 9, 19–43.

Kolko, D. J., & Kolko, R. P. (2011). Psychological impact and treatment of physical abuse of children. In C. Jenny (Ed.), *Child abuse and neglect: Diagnosis, treatment, and evidence* (pp. 477–489). St Louis, MO: Saunders, Elsevier.

Kolla, N., & Hodgins, S. (2013). Treatment of people with schizophrenia who behave violently towards others: A review of the empirical literature on treatment effectiveness. In L. A. Craig, L. Dixon and T. A. Gannon (Eds.), *What works in offender rehabilitation: An evidence-based approach to assessment and treatment* (pp. 321–339). Chichester, West Sussex: Wiley Blackwell.

Koper, C. S., & Mayo-Wilson, C. S. (2006). Police crackdowns on illegal gun carrying: a systematic review of their impact on gun crime. *Journal of Experimental Criminology*, 2, 227–261.

Koposov, R., Gundersen, K. K., & Svartdal, F. (2014). Efficacy of aggression replacement training among children from North-West Russia. *International Journal of Emotional Education*, 6, 14–24.

Kowalski, R. M., & Limber, S. P. (2013). Psychological, physical, and academic correlates of cyberbullying and traditional bullying. *Journal of Adolescent Health*, 53, S13-S20.

Krahé, B. (2013). *The social psychology of aggression* (2nd ed.). Hove, East Sussex: Psychology Press.

Krahé, B. (2018). Violence against women. *Current Opinion in Psychology*, 19, 6–10.

Kropp, P. R., & Hart, S. D. (2000). The Spousal Assault Risk Assessment (SARA) Guide: Reliability and validity in adult male offenders. *Law and Human Behavior*, 24, 101–118.

Krug, E. G., Dahlberg, L. L., Mercy, J. A., Zwi, A. B., & Lozano, R. (2002). *World report on violence and health*. Geneva, Switzerland: World Health Organization.

Kubak, A., Kayabas, P., & Vachal, K. (2016). *The effects of legislatively-mandated sobriety on first-time and repeat DUI offenders in North Dakota*. Department Publication No. 290. Upper Great Plains Transportation Institute, North Dakota University, Fargo, ND.

Kwan, G. C. E., & Skoric, M. M. (2013). Facebook bullying: An extension of battles in school. *Computers in Human Behavior*, 29, 16–25.

Kypri, K., Jones, C., McElduff, P., & Barker, D. (2011). Effects of restricting pub closing times on night-time assaults in an Australian city. *Addiction*, 106, 303–310.

Labella, M. H., & Masten, A. S. (2018). Family influences on the development of aggression and violence. *Current Opinion in Psychology*, 19, 11–16.

Labrum, T., & Solomon, P. L. (2016). Factors associated with family violence by persons with psychiatric disorders. *Psychiatric Research*, 244, 171–178.

Lalor, K., & McElvaney, R. (2010). Overview of the nature and extent of child sexual abuse in Europe. In *Protecting children from sexual violence: A comprehensive approach*. Strasbourg, France: Council of Europe.

Lamberti, J. S., Weisman, R. L., & Faden, D. I. (2004). Forensic assertive community treatment: Preventing incarceration of adults with severe mental illness. *Psychiatric Services*, 55, 1285–1293.

Lambie, I., & Randell, I. (2013). The impact of incarceration on juvenile offenders. *Clinical Psychology Review*, 33, 448–459.

Landers, A. L., McLuckie, A., Cann, R., Shapiro, V., Visintini, S., MacLaurin, B. … Carrey, N. J. (2018). A scoping review of evidence-based interventions available to parents of maltreated children ages 0–5 involved with child welfare services. *Child Abuse & Neglect*, 76, 546–560.

Langeveld, J., Bjørkly, S., Auestad, B., Barder, H., Evensen, J., ten Velden Hegelstad, W. … & Opjordsmoen, S. (2014). Treatment and violent behavior in persons with first episode psychosis during a 10-year prospective follow-up study. *Schizophrenia Research*, 156, 272–276.

Långström, N., Enebrink, P., Laurén, E. M., Lindblom, J., Werkö, S., & Hanson, R. K. (2013). Preventing sexual abusers of children from reoffending: Systematic review of medical and psychological interventions. *British Medical Journal*, 347, f4630.

Langlands, R. L., Ward, T., & Gilchrist, E. (2009). Applying the Good Lives Model to male perpetrators of domestic violence. *Behaviour Change*, 26, 113–129.

Lansford, J. E. (2010). The special problem of cultural differences in effects of corporal punishment. *Law and Contemporary Problems*, 73, 89–106.

Lansford, J. E., Cappa, C., Putnick, D. L., Bornstein, M. H., Deater-Deckard, K., & Bradley, R. H. (2017). Change over time in parents' beliefs about and reported use of corporal punishment in eight countries with and without legal bans. *Child Abuse & Neglect*, 71, 44–55

Larzelere, R. E., & Baumrind, D. (2010). Are spanking injunctions scientifically supported? *Law and Contemporary Problems*, 73, 57–87.

LeBlanc, S. A. (2003). *Constant battles: Why we fight.* New York: St. Martin's Griffin.

Lee, A. H., & DiGiuseppe, R. (2017). Anger and aggression treatments: A review of meta-analyses. *Current Opinion in Psychology*, 19, 65–74.

Lee, B. X. (2015). Causes and cures I: Toward a new definition. *Aggression and Violent Behavior*, 25, 199–203.

Lee, B. X. (2017a). Causes and cures XII: Public health approaches. *Aggression and Violent Behavior*, 33, 144–149.

Lee, B. X. (2017b). Causes and cures XIII: Global medicine approaches. *Aggression and Violent Behavior*, 33, 150–155.

Lee, S. J., Grogan-Kaylor, A., & Berger, L. M. (2014). Parental spanking of 1-year-old children and subsequent child protective services involvement. *Child Abuse & Neglect*, 38, 875–883.

Leen, E., Sorbring, E., Mawer, M., Holdsworth, E., Helsing, B., & Bowen, E. (2013). Prevalence, dynamic risk factors and the efficacy of primary interventions for adolescent dating violence: An international review. *Aggression and Violent Behavior*, 18, 159–174.

Leenarts, L. E., Diehle, J., Doreleijers, T. A., Jansma, E. P., & Lindauer, R. J. (2013). Evidence-based treatments for children with trauma-related psychopathology as a result of childhood maltreatment: A systematic review. *European Child & Adolescent Psychiatry*, 22, 269–283.

Lemerise, E. A., & Dodge, K. A. (2008). The development of anger and hostile interactions. In M. Lewis, J. M. Haviland-Jones & L. F. Barrett (Eds.), *Handbook of emotions* (3rd ed.) (pp. 730–741). New York: Guilford Press.

Lemos, G. (2004). *Fear and fashion. The use of knives and other weapons by young people.* London: Bridge House Trust, Lemon & Crane.

Lestico, A. R., Salekin, R. S., DeCoster, J., & Rogers, R. (2008). A large scale meta-analysis relating Hare measures of psychopathy to antisocial conduct. *Law and Human Behavior*, 32, 28–45.

Letourneau, E. J., Schaeffer, C. M., Bradshaw, C. P., & Feder, K. A. (2017). Preventing the onset of child sexual abuse by targeting young adolescents with universal prevention programming. *Child Maltreatment*, 22, 100–111.

Levey, E. J., Gelaye, B., Bain, P., Marta B. Rondone, M. B., Borba, C. P. C., Henderson, D. C., & Williams, M. A. (2017). A systematic review of randomized controlled trials of interventions designed to decrease child abuse in high-risk families. *Child Abuse & Neglect*, 65, 48–57.

Levitt, L., Hoffer, T. A., & Loper, A. B. (2016). Criminal histories of a subsample of animal cruelty offenders. *Aggression and Violent Behavior*, 30, 48–58.

Lewis, S. F., & Fremouw, W. (2001). Dating violence: A critical review of the literature. *Clinical Psychology Review*, 21, 105–127.

Li, F., Godinet, M. T., & Arnsberger, P. (2011). Protective factors among families with children at risk of maltreatment: Follow up to early school years. *Children and Youth Services Review*, 33, 139–148.

Lila, M., Oliver, A., Catalá-Miñana, A., & Conchell, R. (2014). Recidivism risk reduction assessment in batterer intervention programs: A key indicator for program efficacy evaluation. *Psychosocial Intervention*, 23, 217–223.

Lippel, K., Vézina, M., Bourbonnais, R., & Funes, A. (2016). Workplace psychological harassment: Gendered exposures and implications for policy. *International Journal of Law and Psychiatry*, 46, 74–87.

Lipsey, M. W. (1992). Juvenile delinquency treatment: A meta-analytic inquiry into the variability of effects. In T. Cook, D. Cooper, H. Corday, H. Hartman, L. Hedges, R. Light, T. Louis, & F. Mosteller (Eds.), *Meta-analysis for explanation: A casebook* (pp. 83–127). New York, NY: Russell Sage Foundation.

Lipton, D. S., Martinson, R., & Wilks, D. (1975). *The effectiveness of correctional treatment.* New York: Praeger.

Lipton, D. S., Thornton, D. M., McGuire, J., Porporino, F. J., & Hollin, C. R. (2000). Program accreditation and correctional treatment. *Substance Use and Misuse*, 35, 1705–1734.

Litzow, J. M., & Silverstein, M. (2008). Corporal punishment: A discussion of the debate. *Paediatrics and Child Health*, 18, 542–544.

Liu, J. (2011). Early health risk factors for violence: Conceptualization, evidence, and implications. *Aggression and Violent Behavior*, 16, 63–73.

Lloyd, M. H., & Kepple, N. J. (2017). Unpacking the parallel effects of parental alcohol misuse and low income on risk of supervisory neglect. *Child Abuse & Neglect*, 69, 72–84.

Lockwood, B., & Harris, P. W. (2015). Kicked out or dropped out? Disaggregating the effects of community-based treatment attrition on juvenile recidivism. *Justice Quarterly*, 32, 705–728.

Long, T., Murphy, M., Fallon, D., Livesley, J., Devitt, P., McLoughlin, M., & Cavanagh, A. (2014). Four-year longitudinal impact evaluation of the Action for Children UK Neglect Project: Outcomes for the children, families, Action for Children, and the UK. *Child Abuse & Neglect*, 38, 1358–1368.

Looman, J., & Abracen, J. (2013). The Risk Need Responsivity Model of offender rehabilitation: Is there really a need for a paradigm shift? *International Journal of Behavioral Consultation and Therapy*, 8, 30–36.

López-Ossorio, J. J., Álvarez, J. L. G., Pascuala, S. B., García, L. F., & Buela-Casal, G. (2017). Risk factors related to intimate partner violence police recidivism in Spain. *International Journal of Clinical and Health Psychology*, 17, 107–119.

Lorenz, K., & Ullman, S. E. (2016). Alcohol and sexual assault victimization: Research findings and future directions. *Aggression and Violent Behavior*, 31, 82–94.

Lösel, F. (1996). Working with young offenders: The impact of the meta-analyses. In C. R. Hollin & K. Howells (Eds.), *Clinical approaches to working with young offenders* (pp. 57–82). Chichester, Sussex: John Wiley & Sons.

Lösel, F. (2001). Evaluating the effectiveness of correctional programs: Bridging the gap between research and practice. In Bernfeld, G. A., Farrington, D. P., & Leschied, A. W. (Eds.), *Offender rehabilitation in practice: Implementing and evaluating effective programs* (pp. 67–92). Chichester, West Sussex: John Wiley & Sons.

Lösel, F., & Bender, D. (2012). Child social skills training in the prevention of antisocial development and crime. In B. C. Welsh & D. P. Farrington (Eds.), *The Oxford handbook of crime prevention* (pp. 102–129). Oxford: Oxford University Press.

Lösel, F., & Farrington, D. P. (2012). Direct protective and buffering protective factors in the development of youth violence. *American Journal of Preventive Medicine*, 43, S8–S23.

Lösel, F., & Schmucker, M. (2005). The effectiveness of treatment for sexual offenders: A comprehensive meta-analysis. *Journal of Experimental Criminology*, 1, 117–146.

Lösel, F., Stemmler, M., & Bender, D. (2013). Long-term evaluation of a bimodal universal prevention program: Effects on antisocial development from kindergarten to adolescence. *Journal of Experimental Criminology*, 9, 429–449.

Lovatt, A., & O'Connor, J. (1995). Cities and the night-time economy. *Planning Practice & Research*, 10, 127–134.

Luckenbill, D. F. (1977). Criminal homicide as a situated transaction. *Social Problems*, 25, 176–186.

Lund, E. M., Blake, J. J., Ewing, H. K., & Banks, C. S. (2012). School counselors' and school psychologists' bullying prevention and intervention strategies: A look into real-world practices. *Journal of School Violence*, 11, 246–265.

Liu, T., Ferris, J., Higginson, A., & Lynhame, A. (2016). Systematic review of Australian policing interventions to reduce alcohol-related violence – A maxillofacial perspective. *Addictive Behaviors Reports*, 4, 1–12.

Lunghofer, L., & Shapiro, K. (2014). The co-occurrence of human violence and animal abuse: Policy implications and interventions. *Psyke & Logos*, 35, 130–135.

Lussier, P., & Cale, J. (2016). Understanding the origins and the development of rape and sexual aggression against women: Four generations of research and theorizing. *Aggression and Violent Behavior*, 31, 66–81.

Lynas, J., & Hawkins, R. (2017). Fidelity in school-based child sexual abuse prevention programs: A systematic review. *Child Abuse & Neglect*, 72, 10–21.

Lynøe, N., Elinder, G., Hallberg, B., Rosén, M., Sundgren, P., & Eriksson, A. (2017). Insufficient evidence for 'shaken baby syndrome': A systematic review. *Acta Paediatrica*, 106, 1021–1027.

MacAskill, S., Parkes, T., Brooks, O., Graham, L., McAuley, A., & Brown, A. (2011). Assessment of alcohol problems using AUDIT in a prison setting: More than an 'aye or no' question. *BMC Public Health*, 11, 865–877.

Macdonald, G., Higgins, J. P. T., RamchandaniP., Valentine, J. C., Bronger, L. P., Klein, P., … Taylor, M. (2012). Cognitive-behavioural interventions for children who have been sexually abused. *Cochrane Database of Systematic Reviews*, Issue 5. Art. No.: CD001930.

MacKenzie, D. L. (2002). Reducing the criminal activities of known offenders and delinquents: Crime prevention in the courts and corrections. In L. W. Sherman, D. P. Farrington, B. C. Welsh & D. L. MacKenzie (Eds.), *Evidence-based crime prevention* (pp. 330–404). London: Routledge.

MacKenzie, D. L., Brame, R., McDowall, D., & Souryal, C. (1995). Boot camp prisons and recidivism in eight states. *Criminology*, 33, 327–357.

MacKenzie, M. J., Nicklas, E., Brooks-Gunn, J., & Waldfogel, J. (2015). Spanking and children's externalizing behavior across the first decade of life: Evidence for transactional processes. *Journal of Youth and Adolescence*, 44, 658–669.

MacMillan, H. L., & Mikton, C. R. (2017). Moving research beyond the spanking debate. *Child Abuse & Neglect*, 71, 5–8.

McCambridge, J., Hawkins, B., & Holden, C. (2013). Industry use of evidence to influence alcohol policy: A case study of submissions to the 2008 Scottish government consultation. *PLoS medicine*, 10, e1001431.

McCandless, R., Feist, A., Allan, J., & Morgan, N. (2016). *Do initiatives involving substantial increases in stop and search reduce crime? Assessing the impact of Operation BLUNT 2*. London: Home Office.

McCollister, K. E., French, M. T., & Fang, H. (2010). The cost of crime to society: New crime-specific estimates for policy and program evaluation. *Drug and Alcohol Dependence*, 108, 98–109.

McDowall, D., Loftin, C., & Wiersema, B. (2000). The impact of youth curfew laws on juvenile crime rates. *Crime and Delinquency*, 46, 76–91.

McGuire, J. (Ed.). (1995). *What works: Reducing reoffending*. Chichester, West Sussex: John Wiley & Sons.

McGuire, J. (2002). Integrating findings from research reviews. In J. McGuire (Ed.), *Offender rehabilitation and treatment: Effective programmes and policies to reduce reoffending* (pp. 3–38). Chichester, West Sussex: John Wiley & Sons.

McGuire, J. (2005). The Think First programme. In M. McMurran & J. McGuire (Eds.), *Social problem solving and offending: Evidence evaluation and evolution* (pp. 183–206). Chichester, West Sussex: John Wiley & Sons.

McGuire, J. (2008a). A review of effective interventions for reducing aggression and violence. *Philosophical Transactions of the Royal Society B*, 363, 2577–2597.

McGuire, J. (2008b). The impact of sentencing. In G. Davies, C. Hollin, & R. Bull (Eds), *Forensic psychology* (pp. 266–291). Chichester, West Sussex: John Wiley & Sons.

McGuire, J., Bilby, C. A. L., Hatcher, R. M., Hollin, C. R., Hounsome, J., & Palmer, E. J. (2008). Evaluation of structured cognitive-behavioural treatment programmes in reducing criminal recidivism. *Journal of Experimental Criminology*, 4, 21–40.

McLaughlin, M. (2017). Less money, more problems: How changes in disposable income affect child maltreatment. *Child Abuse & Neglect*, 67, 315–321.

McMurran, M. (2012). Individual-level interventions for alcohol-related violence: A rapid evidence assessment. *Criminal Behaviour and Mental Health*, 22, 14–28.

McMurran, M. (Ed.) (2013). *Alcohol-related violence: Prevention and treatment*. Chichester, West Sussex: John Wiley & Sons.

McMurran, M., Huband, N., & Overton, E. (2010). Non-completion of personality disorder treatments: A systematic review of correlates, consequences, and interventions. *Clinical Psychology Review*, 30, 277–287.

McMurran, M., & Priestley, P. (2004). Addressing substance-related offending. In B. Reading & M. Weegmann (Eds.), *Group psychotherapy and addiction* (pp. 194–210). London: Whurr Publishers.

McMurran, M., Riemsma, R., Manning, N., Misso, K., & Kleijnen, J. (2011). Interventions for alcohol-related offending by women: A systematic review. *Clinical Psychology Review*, 31, 909–922.

McPhedran, S. (2016). A systematic review of quantitative evidence about the impacts of Australian legislative reform on firearm homicide. *Aggression and Violent Behavior*, 28, 64–72.

Macklin, A., & Gilbert, R. (2011). *Working with Indigenous offenders to end violence. Brief 11*. New South Wales, Australia: Indigenous Justice Clearinghouse.

Maden, A., Rutter, S., McClintock, T., Friendship, C., & Gunn, J. (1999). Outcome of admission to a medium secure psychiatric unit. *British Journal of Psychiatry*, 175, 313–316.

Maden, A., Scott, F., Burnett, R., Lewis, G. H., & Skapinakis, P. (2004). Offending in psychiatric patients after discharge from medium secure units: Prospective national cohort study. *British Medical Journal*, 328, 1534.

Maguire, M., Grubin, D., Lösel, F., & Raynor, P. (2010). 'What Works' and the Correctional Services Accreditation Panel: Taking stock from an inside perspective. *Criminology and Criminal Justice*, 10, 37–58.

Maguire, M., & Nettleton, H. (2003). Reducing alcohol-related violence and disorder: An evaluation of the 'TASC' project. Home Office Research Study 265. London: Home Office.

Makarios, M. D., & Pratt, T. C. (2012). The effectiveness of policies and programs that attempt to reduce firearm violence: A meta-analysis. *Crime & Delinquency*, 58, 222–244.

Maldonado, M. (2004). Cultural issues in the corporal punishment of children. *Hispanic Journal of Behavioural Sciences*, 17, 275–304.

Mallory, A. B., Dharnidharka, P., Deitz, S. L., Barros-Gomes, P., Cafferky, B., Stith, S. M., & Van, K. (2016). A meta-analysis of cross cultural risk markers for intimate partner violence. *Aggression and Violent Behavior*, 31, 116–126.

Malvaso, C. G., Delfabbro, P. H., & Day, A. (2016). Risk factors that influence the maltreatment-offending association: A systematic review of prospective and longitudinal studies. *Aggression and Violent Behavior*, 31, 1–15.

Maneta, E. K., White, M., & Mezzacappa, E. (2017). Parent-child aggression, adult-partner violence, and child outcomes: A prospective, population-based study. *Child Abuse & Neglect*, 68, 1–10.

Mann, R. E., & Fernandez, Y. M. (2006). Sex offender programmes: Concept, theory, and practice. In C. R. Hollin & E. J. Palmer (Eds.), *Offending behaviour programmes: Development, application, and controversies* (pp. 155–177). Chichester, West Sussex: John Wiley & Sons.

Marques, J. K., Miederanders, M., Day, D. M., Nelson, C., & van Ommeren, A. (2005). Effects of a relapse prevention program on sexual recidivism: Final results from California's sex offender treatment evaluation project (SOTEP). *Sexual Abuse: A Journal of Research and Treatment*, 17, 79–107.

Marriage, N. D., Blackley, A. S., Panagiotaros, K., Seklaoui, S. A., van den Bergh, J., & Hawkins, R. (2017). Assessing parental understanding of sexualized behavior in children and adolescents. *Child Abuse & Neglect*, 72, 196–205.

Marsh, K., & Fox, C. (2008). The benefit and cost of prison in the UK. The results of a model of lifetime re-offending. *Journal of Experimental Criminology*, 4, 403–423.

Marshall, W. L., & Hollin, C. (2015). Historical developments in sex offender treatment. *Journal of Sexual Aggression*, 21, 125–135.

Marshall, W. L., & Marshall, L. E. (2007). The utility of the random controlled trial for evaluating sexual offender treatment: The gold standard or an inappropriate strategy? *Sexual Abuse: A Journal of Research and Treatment*, 19, 175–191.

Marshall, W. L., & McGuire, J. (2003). Effect sizes in the treatment of sexual offenders. *International Journal of Offender Therapy and Comparative Criminology*, 47, 653–663.

Martinson, R. (1974). What works? Questions and answers about prison reform. *The Public Interest*, 35, 22–54.

Martinson, R. (1979). New findings, new views: A note of caution regarding sentencing reform. *Hofstra Law Review*, 7, 243–258.

Matjasko, J. L., Vivolo-Kantor, A. M., Massetti, G. M., Holland, K. M., Holt, M. K., & Cruz, J. D. (2012). A systematic meta-review of evaluations of youth violence prevention programs: Common and divergent findings from 25 years of meta-analyses and systematic reviews. *Aggression and Violent Behavior*, 17, 540–552.

Mazzone, A., Nocentini, A., & Menesini, E. (2018). Bullying and peer violence among children and adolescents in residential care settings: A review of the literature. *Aggression and Violent Behavior*, 38, 101–112.

Meade, B., & Steiner, B. (2010). The total effects of boot camps that house juveniles: A systematic review of the evidence. *Journal of Criminal Justice*, 38, 841–853.

Mendelson, T., & Letourneau, E. J. (2015). Parent-focused prevention of child sexual abuse. *Prevention Science*, 16, 844–852.

Meehan, J., Flynn, S., Hunt, I. M., Robinson, J., Bickley, H., Parsons, R., … Shaw, J. (2006). Perpetrators of homicide with schizophrenia: A national clinical survey in England and Wales. *Psychiatric Services*, 57, 1648–1651.

Meehl, P. E. (1954). *Clinical versus statistical prediction: A theoretical analysis and a review of the evidence*. Minneapolis, MN: University of Minnesota Press.

Mews, A., Di Bella, L., & Purver, M. (2017). *Impact evaluation of the prison-based Core Sex Offender Treatment Programme*. Ministry of Justice Analytical Series. London: Ministry of Justice.

Meyer, W. J. III, & Cole, C. M. (1997). Physical and chemical castration of sex offenders: A review. *Journal of Offender Rehabilitation*, 25, 1–18.

Milan, M. A. (2001). Behavioral approaches to correctional management and rehabilitation. In C. R. Hollin (Ed.), *Handbook of offender assessment and treatment* (pp. 139–1154). Chichester, Sussex: John Wiley & Sons.

Miller, C. (2001). Childhood animal cruelty and interpersonal violence. *Clinical Psychology Review*, 25, 745–749.

Miller, T. Q., Smith, T. W., Turner, C. W., Guijarro, M. L., & Hallet, A. J. (1996). A meta-analytic review of research on hostility and physical health. *Psychological Bulletin*, 119, 322–348.

Miller-Perrin, C., & Perrin, R. (2017). Changing attitudes about spanking among conservative Christians using interventions that focus on empirical research evidence and progressive biblical interpretations. *Child Abuse & Neglect*, 71, 69–79.

Mills, L. G., Barocas, B., & Ariel, B. (2013). The next generation of court-mandated domestic violence treatment: A comparison study of batterer intervention and restorative justice programs. *Journal of Experimental Criminology*, 9, 65–90.

Ministry of Justice. (2016). *Multi-Agency Public Protection Arrangements Annual Report 2015/16*. Ministry of Justice Statistics Bulletin October 2016. London: Ministry of Justice.

Ministry of Justice, Home Office & the Office for National Statistics. (2013). *An overview of sexual offending in England and Wales*. *Statistics bulletin*. London: Ministry of Justice, Home Office and Office for National Statistics.

Ministry of Justice & the Youth Justice Board. (2015). *Youth Justice Statistics 2014/15 England and Wales*. *Statistics bulletin*. London: Ministry of Justice and the Youth Justice Board.

Mishna, F., Cook, C., Saini, M., Wu, M. J., & MacFadden, R. (2009). Interventions for children, youth, and parents to prevent and reduce cyber abuse. *Campbell Systematic Reviews* 2009:2.

Mitchell, K., Moynihan, M., Pitcher, C., Francis, A., English, A., & Saewyc, E. (2017). Rethinking research on sexual exploitation of boys: Methodological challenges and recommendations to optimize future knowledge generation. *Child Abuse & Neglect*, 66, 142–151.

Mncube, V., & Tshilidzi, N. (2014). Can violence reduce violence in schools? The case of corporal punishment. *Journal of Sociology and Social Anthropology*, 5, 1–9.

Monsalve, S., Ferreira, F., & Garcia, R. (2017). The connection between animal abuse and interpersonal violence: A review from the veterinary perspective. *Research in Veterinary Science*, 114, 18–26.

Moore, E., Farr, C., Tapp, J., & Hopkin, G. (2018). Reasoning and rehabilitation and enhanced thinking skills. In B. Puri & I. H. Treasaden (Eds.), *Forensic psychiatry: Fundamentals and clinical practice* (pp. 777–782). Boca Raton, FL: CRC Press.

Moore, S., Shepherd, J., Perham, N., & Cusens, B. (2007). The prevalence of alcohol intoxication in the night-time economy. *Alcohol & Alcoholism*, 42, 629–634.

Moyano, N., Monge, F. S., & Sierra, J. C. (2017). Predictors of sexual aggression in adolescents: Gender dominance vs. rape supportive attitudes. *The European Journal of Psychology Applied to Legal Context*, 9, 25–31.

Moynihan, M., Mitchell, M. K., Pitcher, C., Havaei, F., Ferguson, M., & Saewyc, E. (2018). A systematic review of the state of the literature on sexually exploited boys internationally. *Child Abuse & Neglect*, 76, 440–451.

Mpofu, E., Athanasou, J. A., Rafe, C., & Belshaw, S. H. (2018). Cognitive-behavioral therapy efficacy for reducing recidivism rates of moderate-and high-risk sexual offenders: A scoping systematic literature review. *International Journal of Offender Therapy and Comparative Criminology*, 62, 170–186.

Mrazek, P. J., & Haggerty, R. J. (1994). *Reducing risks for mental disorders: Frontiers for preventive intervention research*. Washington, DC: National Academy Press.

Muchhal, M. K., & Kumar, A. (2016). Attitude of parents, teachers and students towards corporal punishment. *International Journal of Indian Psychology*, 3, 125–130.

Muijs, D. (2017). Can schools reduce bullying? The relationship between school characteristics and the prevalence of bullying behaviours. *British Journal of Educational Psychology*, 87, 255–272.

Nagin, D. S., Cullen, F. T., & Jonson, C. L. (2009). Imprisonment and reoffending. In M. Tonry (Ed.) *Crime and justice: An Annual Review of Research*. Vol. 38 (pp. 115–200). Chicago, IL: University of Chicago Press.

National Police Chief Council. (2017). *National Strategy to address the issue of police officers and staff who abuse their position for a sexual purpose*. London: National Police Chief Council.

Nellis, M. (2000). Law and order: The electronic monitoring of offenders. In D. Dolowitz (Ed.) *Policy transfer and British social policy* (pp. 98–117). Buckingham: Open University Press.

Newberry, M. (2017). Pets in danger: Exploring the link between domestic violence and animal abuse. *Aggression and Violent Behavior*, 34, 273–281.

Newman, O. (1972). *Defensible space: Crime prevention through urban design*. New York: Macmillan.

Nicholaichuk, T. P., Gordon, A., Gu, D., & Wong, S. (2000). Outcome of an institutional sexual offender treatment program: A comparison between treated and matched untreated offenders. *Sexual Abuse: A Journal of Research and Treatment*, 12, 139–153.

Nielsen, M. B., Tangen, T., Idsoe, T., Berge, S. B., & Magerøy, N. (2015). Post-traumatic stress disorder as a consequence of bullying at work and at school. A literature review and meta-analysis. *Aggression and Violent Behavior*, 21, 17–24.

Nietzel, M. T., Hasemann, D. M., & Lynam, D. R. (1999). Behavioral perspective on violent behavior. In V. B. Van Hasselt & M. Hersen (Eds.), *Handbook of psychological approaches with violent offenders: Contemporary strategies and issues* (pp. 39–66). New York: Kluwer Academic/Plenum.

Nilsson, T., Wallinius, M., Gustavson, C., Anckarsäter, H., & Kerekes, N. (2011). Violent recidivism: A long-time follow-up study of mentally disordered offenders. *PLoS ONE* 6(10): e25768.

Nocentini, A., Zambuto, V., & Menesini, E. (2015). Anti-bullying programs and Information and Communication Technologies (ICTs): A systematic review. *Aggression and Violent Behavior*, 23, 52–60.

Noonan, R. K., & Charles, D. (2009). Developing teen dating violence prevention strategies. *Violence Against Women*, 15, 1087–1105.

Novaco, R. W. (1975). *Anger control: The development an evaluation of an experimental treatment*. Lexington, MA: D. C. Heath.

Novaco, R. W. (1997). Remediating anger and aggression with violent offenders. *Legal and Criminological Psychology*, 2, 77–88.

Novaco, R. W. (2007). Anger dysregulation: Its assessment and treatment. In T. A. Cavell & K. T. Malcolm (Eds.), *Anger, aggression and interventions for interpersonal violence* (pp. 3–54). Mahwah, NJ: Erlbaum.

Novaco, R. W. (2013). Reducing anger-related offending: What Works. In L. A. Craig, L. Dixon, & T. A. Gannon (Eds.), *What works in offender rehabilitation: An evidence-based approach to assessment and treatment* (pp. 211–236). Chichester, West Sussex: John Wiley & Sons.

Novaco, R. W., & Renwick, S. J. (1998). Anger predictors of the assaultiveness of forensic hospital patients. In E. Sanavio (Ed.), *Behavior and cognitive therapy today. Essays in honor of Hans J. Eysenck* (pp. 199–208). Oxford, UK: Elsevier Science.

Novaco, R. W., & Welsh, W. N. (1989). Anger disturbances: Cognitive mediation and clinical prescriptions. In K. Howells & C. R. Hollin (Eds.), *Clinical approaches to violence* (pp. 39–60). Chichester, West Sussex: John Wiley & Sons.

Nowrouzi, B., & Huynh, V. (2016). Citation analysis of workplace violence: A review of the top 50 annual and lifetime cited articles. *Aggression and Violent Behavior*, 28, 21–28.

Nunes, K. L., Cortoni, F., & Serin, R. C. (2010). Screening offenders for risk of drop-out and expulsion from correctional programmes. *Legal and Criminological Psychology*, 15, 341–356.

Nurse, A. M. (2017). Knowledge and behavioral impact of adult participation in child sexual abuse prevention: Evaluation of the Protecting God's Children Program. *Journal of Child Sexual Abuse*, 26, 608–624.

O'Brien, J. E., & Macy, R. J. (2016). Culturally specific interventions for female survivors of gender-based violence. *Aggression and Violent Behavior*, 31, 48–60.

O'May, F., Gill, J., Black, H., Rees, C., Chick, J., & McPake, B. (2016). Heavy drinkers' perspectives on minimum unit pricing for alcohol in Scotland: A qualitative interview study. *SAGE Open*, 6(3), 1–10.

O'Reilly, R., Beale, B., & Gillies, D. (2010). Screening and intervention for domestic violence during pregnancy care: A systematic review. *Trauma, Violence, & Abuse*, 11, 190–201.

Okuzono, S., Fujiwara, T., Kato, T., & Kawachi, I. (2017). Spanking and subsequent behavioral problems in toddlers: A propensity score-matched, prospective study in Japan. *Child Abuse & Neglect*, 69, 62–71.

Olver, M. E., Stockdale, K. C., & Wormith, J. S. (2011). A meta-analysis of predictors of offender treatment attrition and its relationship to recidivism. *Journal of Consulting and Clinical Psychology*, 79, 6–21.

Olver, M. E., Wong, S. C. P., & Nicholaichuk, T. P. (2009). Outcome evaluation of a high-intensity inpatient sex offender treatment program. *Journal of Interpersonal Violence*, 24, 522–536.

Omoyemiju, M. A., Ojo, O. O., & Olatomide, O. O. (2015). Parents and teachers' knowledge of violent disciplinary practices against secondary school students in Oyo State, Nigeria. *British Journal of Guidance & Counselling*, 43, 530–545.

Ornstein, A. E., Fitzpatrick, E., Hatchette, J., Woolcott, C. G., & Dodds, L. (2016). The impact of an educational intervention on knowledge about infant crying and abusive head trauma. *Paediatric Child Health*, 21, 74–78.

Oswald, Z. E. (2013). "Off with his __": Analyzing the ex disparity in chemical castration sentences. *Michigan Journal of Gender and Law*, 19, 471–503.

Padgett, K. G., Bales, W. D., & Blomberg, T. G. (2006). Under surveillance: An empirical test of the effectiveness and consequences of electronic monitoring. *Criminology & Public Policy*, 5, 61–92.

Palasinski, M., & Riggs, D. W. (2012). Young white British men and knife-carrying in public: Discourses of masculinity, protection and vulnerability. *Critical Criminology*, 20, 463–476.

Palmer, E. J., Hatcher, R. M., McGuire, J., Bilby, C. A. L., & Hollin, C. R. (2012). The effect on reconviction of an intervention for drink-driving offenders in the community. *International Journal of Offender Therapy and Comparative Criminology*, 56, 525–538.

Palmer, E. J., McGuire, J., Hatcher, R. M., Hounsome, J. C., Bilby, C. A. L., & Hollin, C. R. (2008). The importance of appropriate allocation to offending behavior programs. *International Journal of Offender Therapy and Comparative Criminology*, 52, 206–221.

Palmer, E. J., McGuire, J., Hatcher, R. M., Hounsome, J. C., Bilby, C. A. L., & Hollin, C. R. (2009). Allocation to offending behaviour programmes in the English and Welsh Probation Service. *Criminal Justice and Behavior*, 36, 909–922.

Palmer, E. J., McGuire, J., Hounsome, J. C., Hatcher, R. M., Bilby, C. A., & Hollin, C. R. (2007). Offending behaviour programmes in the community: The effects on reconviction of three programmes with adult male offenders. *Legal and Criminological Psychology*, 12, 251–264.

Papalia, N. L., Luebbers, S., Ogloff, J. R. P., Cutajar, M., Mullen, P. E., & Mann, E. (2017a). Further victimization of child sexual abuse victims: A latent class typology of re-victimization trajectories. *Child Abuse & Neglect*, 66, 112–129.

Papalia, N. L., Luebbers, S., Ogloff, J. R. P., Cutajar, M., & Mullen, P. E. (2017b). Exploring the longitudinal offending pathways of child sexual abuse victims: A preliminary analysis using latent variable modeling. *Child Abuse & Neglect*, 66, 84–100.

Parent, J., McKee, L. G., & Forehand, R. (2016). Seesaw discipline: The interactive effect of harsh and lax discipline on youth psychological adjustment. *Journal of Child and Family Studies*, 25, 396–406.

Parent, S., & Fortier, K. (2017). Prevalence of interpersonal violence against athletes in the sport context. *Current Opinion in Psychology*, 16, 165–169.

Parker, R., Bush, J., & Harris, D. (2014). Important methodological issues in evaluating community-based interventions. *Evaluation Review*, 38, 295–308.

Parkinson, P. N., Oates, R. K., & Jayakody, A. A. (2012). Child sexual abuse in the Anglican Church of Australia. *Journal of Child Sexual Abuse*, 21, 553–570.

Parratt, K. A., & Pina, A. (2017). From "real rape" to real justice: A systematic review of police officers' rape myth beliefs. *Aggression and Violent Behavior*, 34, 68–83.

Parrish, J. W., Schnitzer, P. G., Lanierd, P., Shanahan, M. E., Daniels, J. L., & Marshall, S. W. (2017). Classification of maltreatment-related mortality by Child Death Review teams: How reliable are they? *Child Abuse & Neglect*, 67, 362–370.

ParrottD. J., & Eckhardt, C. I. (2018). Effects of alcohol on human aggression. *Current Opinion in Psychology*, 19, 1–5.

Patno, K. M. (2011). Epidemiology of physical abuse. In C. Jenny (Ed.), *Child abuse and neglect: Diagnosis, treatment, and evidence* (pp. e8–e11). St Louis, MO: Saunders, Elsevier.

Patwardhan, I., Hurley, K. D., Thompson, R. W., Mason, W. A., & Ringle, J. L. (2017). Child maltreatment as a function of cumulative family risk: findings from the intensive family preservation program. *Child Abuse & Neglect*, 70, 92–99.

Pawson, R. (2002). Evidence-based policy: In search of a method. *Evaluation*, 8, 157–181.

Payne, B. K., & DeMichele, M. T. (2010). Electronic supervision for sex offenders: Implications for work load, supervision goals, versatility, and policymaking. *Journal of Criminal Justice*, 38, 276–281.

Peak, T., Ascione, F., & Doney, J. (2012). Adult Protective Services and animal welfare: Should animal abuse and neglect be assessed during Adult Protective Services screening? *Journal of Elder Abuse & Neglect*, 24, 37–49.

Pearson, D. A. S., McDougall, C., Kanaan, M., & Bowles, R. A., & Torgerson, D. J. (2011). Reducing criminal recidivism: Evaluation of Citizenship, an evidence-based probation supervision process. *Journal of Experimental Criminology*, 7, 73–102.

Peck, M. (2011). *Patterns of reconviction among offenders eligible for Multi-Agency Public Protection Arrangements (MAPPA)*. Ministry of Justice Research Series 6/11. London: Ministry of Justice.

Pence, E. (1983). The Duluth Domestic Abuse Intervention Project. *Hamline Law Review*, 6, 247–275.

Pence, E. I. & Paymar, M. (1993). *Education groups for men who batter: Lessons from Duluth and beyond*. Thousand Oaks, CA: Sage.

Pérez, D. M., & Jennings, W. G. (2012). Treatment behind bars: The effectiveness of prison-based therapy for sex offenders. *Journal of Crime and Justice*, 35, 435–450.

Peterson, C., Xu, L., Florence, C., Parks, S. E., Miller, T. R., Barr, R. G., Barr, M., & Steinbeigle, R. (2014). The medical cost of abusive head trauma in the United States. *Pediatrics*, 134, 91–99.

Peterson, M. L., & Farrington, D. P. (2007). Cruelty to animals and violence to people. *Victims and Offenders*, 2, 21–43.

Phillips, D. A., Bowie, B. H., Wan, D. C., & Yukevich, K. W. (in press). Sibling violence and children hospitalized for serious mental and behavioral health problems. *Journal of Interpersonal Violence*.

Pill, N., Day, A., Mildred, H. (2017). Trauma responses to intimate partner violence: A review of current knowledge. *Aggression and Violent Behavior*, 34, 178–184.

Piquero, A. R., Jennings, W. G., Diamond, B., Farrington, D. P., Tremblay, R. E., Welsh, B. C., & Reingle Gonzalez, J. M. (2016). A meta-analysis update on the effects of early family/parent training programs on antisocial behavior and delinquency. *Journal of Experimental Criminology*, 12, 229–248.

Piquero, A. R., Jennings, W. G., & Farrington, D. (2013). The monetary costs of crime to middle adulthood: Findings from the Cambridge Study in Delinquent Development. *Journal of Research in Crime and Delinquency*, 50, 53–74.

Plotnikoff, J., & Woolfson, R. (2007). *Evaluation of Young Witness Support: Examining the impact on witnesses and the criminal justice system*. http//www.lexiconlimited.co.uk.

Polaschek, D. L. L. (2011). High-intensity rehabilitation for violent offenders in New Zealand: Reconviction outcomes for high and medium-risk prisoners. *Journal of Interpersonal Violence*, 26, 664–682.

Polaschek, D. L. L., & Daly, T. E. (2013). Treatment and psychopathy in forensic settings. *Aggression and Violent Behavior*, 18, 592–603.

Polaschek, D. L. L., & Kilgour, T. G. (2013). New Zealand's special treatment units: The development and implementation of intensive treatment for high-risk male prisoners. *Psychology, Crime & Law*, 19, 511–526.

Polaschek, D. L. L., & Reynolds, N. (2011). Assessment and treatment: Violent offenders. In C. R. Hollin (Ed.), *Handbook of offender assessment and treatment* (pp. 415–431). Chichester, West Sussex: John Wiley & Sons.

Polaschek, D. L. L., Wilson, N. J., Townsend, M. R., & Daly, L. R. (2005). Cognitive-behavioral rehabilitation for high-risk violent offenders: An outcome evaluation of the Violence Prevention Unit. *Journal of Interpersonal Violence*, 20, 1611–1627.

Poole, M. K., Seal, D. W., & Taylor, C. A. (2014). A systematic review of universal campaigns targeting child physical abuse prevention. *Health Education Research*, 29, 388–432.

Popovici, I., Homer, J. F., Fang, H., & French, M. T. (2012). Alcohol use and crime: Findings from a longitudinal sample of U.S. adolescents and young adults. *Alcoholism: Clinical and Experimental Research*, 36, 532–543.

Pratt, D., Piper, M., Appleby, L., Webb, R., & Shaw, J. (2006). Suicide in recently released prisoners: A population-based cohort study. *Lancet*, 368, 119–123.

Prell, L., Vitacco, M. J., & Zavodny, D. (2016). Predicting violence and recidivism in a large sample of males on probation or parole. *International Journal of Law and Psychiatry*, 49, 107–113.

Prendergast, M. L., Pearson, F. S., Podus, D., Hamilton, Z. K., & Greenwell, L. (2013). The Andrews' principles of risk, needs, and responsivity as applied in drug treatment programs: Meta-analysis of crime and drug use outcomes. *Journal of Experimental Criminology*, 9, 275–300.

Prenzler, T., & Fardell, L. (2017). Situational prevention of domestic violence: A review of security-based programs. *Aggression and Violent Behavior*, 34, 51–58.

Prinz, R. J., Sanders, M. R., Shapiro, C. J., Whitaker, D. J., & Lutzker, J. R. (2009). Population-based prevention of child maltreatment: The US Triple P system population trial. *Prevention Science*, 10, 1–12.

Prison Reform Trust. (2011). *Bromley Briefings prison factfile*. London: Prison Reform Trust.

Quinn, P., & Ward, M. (2000). What happens to Special Hospital patients admitted to medium security? *Medicine, Science, and Law*, 40, 345–349.

Quinsey, V. L., Harris, G. T., Rice, M. E., & Cormier, C. A. (2006). *Violent offenders: Appraising and managing risk* (2nd ed). Washington DC: American Psychological Association.

Radford, L., Corral, S., Bradley, C., Fisher, H., Bassett, C., Howat, N. & Collishaw, S. (2016). *Child abuse and neglect in the UK today*. London: National Society for the Prevention of Cruelty to Children.

Randall, P., Carr, A., Dooley, B., & Rooney, B. (2011). Psychological characteristics of Irish clerical sexual offenders. *The Irish Journal of Psychology*, 32, 4–13.

Raskauskas, J., & Huynh, A. (2015). The process of coping with cyberbullying: A systematic review. *Aggression and Violent Behavior*, 23, 118–125.

Rassenhofer, M., Zimmer, A., Spröber, N., & Fegert, J. M. (2015). Child sexual abuse in the Roman Catholic Church in Germany: Comparison of victim-impact data collected through church-sponsored and government-sponsored programs. *Child Abuse & Neglect*, 40, 60–67.

Ratcliffe, J. H. (2012). The spatial extent of criminogenic places: A changepoint regression of violence around bars. *Geographical Analysis*, 44, 302–320.

Ratkoceri, V. (2017). Chemical castration of child molesters – Right or wrong?! *European Journal of Social Sciences Education and Research*, 11, 70–76.

Raynor, P., & Robinson, G. (2009). Why help offenders? Arguments for rehabilitation as a penal strategy. *European Journal of Probation*, 1, 3–20.

Raynor, P., & Vanstone, M. (1996). Reasoning and Rehabilitation in Britain: The results of the Straight Thinking on Probation (STOP) program. *International Journal of Offender Therapy and Comparative Criminology*, 40, 272–284.

Raynor, S., & Wylie, A. (2012). Presentation and management of school bullying and the impact of anti-bullying strategies for pupils: A self-report survey in London schools. *Public Health*, 126, 782–789.

Redondo, S., Sánchez-Meca, J., & Garrido, V. (2002). Crime treatment in Europe: A review of outcome studies. In J. McGuire (Ed.), *Offender rehabilitation and treatment: Effective programmes and policies to reduce re-offending* (pp. 113–141). Chichester, Sussex: John Wiley & Sons.

Reed, L. A., Tolman, R. M., & Ward, L. M. (2017). Gender matters: Experiences and consequences of digital dating abuse victimization in adolescent dating relationships. *Journal of Adolescence*, 59, 79–89.

Regehr, C., Glancy, G. D., Carter, A., & Ramshaw, L. (2017). A comprehensive approach to managing threats of violence on a university or college campus. *International Journal of Law and Psychiatry*, 54, 140–147.

Reid, W. J., & Donovan, T. (1990). Treating sibling violence. *Family Therapy*, 17, 49–59.

Reidy, D. E., Kearns, M. C., & DeGue, S. (2013). Reducing psychopathic violence: A review of the treatment literature. *Aggression and Violent Behavior*, 18, 527–538.

Renwick, S. J., Black, L., Ramm, M. & Novaco, R. W. (1997). Anger treatment with forensic hospital patients. *Legal and Criminological Psychology*, 2, 103–116.

Renzema, M., & Mayo-Wilson, E. (2005). Can electronic monitoring reduce crime for moderate to high-risk offenders? *Journal of Experimental Criminology*, 1, 215–237.

Rheingold, A. A., Zajac, K., Chapman, J. E., Patton, M., de Arellano, M., Saunders, B., & Kilpatrick, D. (2015). Child sexual abuse prevention training for childcare professionals: An independent multi-site randomized controlled trial of stewards of children. *Prevention Science*, 16, 374–385.

Rice, M. E., & Harris, G. T. (2011). Is androgen deprivation therapy effective in the treatment of sex offenders? *Psychology, Public Policy, and Law*, 17, 315–332.

Richards, T. N., Jennings, W. G., Tomsich, E. & Gover, A. (2014). A 10-year analysis of rearrests among a cohort of domestic violence offenders. *Violence and Victims*, 29, 887–906.

Risley-Curtiss, C., Rogge, M. E., & Kawam, E. (2013). Factors affecting social workers' inclusion of animals in practice. *Social Work*, 58, 153–161.

Risley-Curtiss, C., Zilney, L. A., & Hornung, R. (2010). Animal-human relationships in child protective services: Getting a baseline. *Child Welfare*, 89, 67–82.

Rivara, F. P., Shepherd, J. R., Farrington, D. E., Richmond, P. W., & Cannon, P. (1995). Victim as offender in youth violence. *Annals of Emergency Medicine*, 26, 609–614.

Roberts, A. D. L., & Coid, J. W. (2010). Personality disorder and offending behaviour: Findings from the national survey of male prisoners in England and Wales. *Journal of Forensic Psychiatry and Psychology*, 21, 221–237.

Robinson, E. (2013). *Parental involvement in preventing and responding to cyberbullying.* Family Matters, No. 92. Melbourne, Victoria: Australian Institute of Family Studies.

Rocque, M., Jennings, W. G., Piquero, A. R., Ozkan, T., & Farrington, D. P. (2017). The importance of school attendance: Findings from the Cambridge Study in Delinquent Development on the life-course effects of truancy. *Crime & Delinquency*, 63, 592–612.

Rosenfeld, R., & Fornango, R. (2014). The impact of police stops on precinct robbery and burglary rates in New York City, 2003–2010. *Justice Quarterly*, 31, 96–122.

Rösler, A., & Witztum, E. (2000). Pharmacotherapy of paraphilias in the next millennium. *Behavioral Sciences and the Law*, 18, 43–56.

Ross, J., Quayle, E., Newman, E., & Tansey, L. (2013). The impact of psychological therapies on violent behaviour in clinical and forensic settings: A systematic review. *Aggression and Violent Behavior*, 18, 761–773.

Ross, R. R., & Fabiano, E. A. (1985). *Time to think: A cognitive model of delinquency prevention and offender rehabilitation*. Johnson City, TN: Institute of Social Sciences and Arts.

Ross, R. R., Fabiano, E. A., & Ewles, C. D. (1988). Reasoning and rehabilitation. *International Journal of Offender Therapy and Comparative Criminology*, 32, 29–35.

Ross, R. R., Fabiano, E. A., & Ross, B. (1989). *Reasoning and Rehabilitation: A handbook for teaching cognitive skills*. Ottawa: The Cognitive Centre.

Rossow, I., & Norström, T. (2011). The impact of small changes in bar closing hours on violence. The Norwegian experience from 18 cities. *Addiction*, 107, 530–537.

Ruddle, A., Pina, A., & Vasquez, E. (2010). Domestic violence offending behaviors: A review of the literature examining childhood exposure, implicit theories, trait aggression and anger rumination as predictive factors. *Aggression and Violent Behavior*, 34, 154–165.

Rudolph, J., Zimmer-Gembeck, M. J., Shanley, D. C., & Hawkins, R. (2018). Child sexual abuse prevention opportunities: Parenting, programs, and the reduction of risk. *Child Maltreatment*, 23, 96–106.

Runyon, M. K., Deblinger, E., Ryan. E. E., Thakkar-Kolar, R. (2004). An overview of child physical abuse: Developing an integrated parent-child cognitive-behavioral treatment approach. *Trauma, Violence, & Abuse*, 5, 65–85.

Sabo, S., Shaw, S., Ingram, M., Teufel-Shone, N., Carvajal, S., de Zapien, J. G., ... Rubio-Goldsmith, R. (2014). Everyday violence, structural racism and mistreatment at the US-Mexico border. *Social Science & Medicine*, 109, 66–74.

Sadlier, G. (2010). *Evaluation of the impact of the HM Prison Service Enhanced Thinking Skills programme on reoffending outcomes of the Surveying Prisoner Crime Reduction (SPCR) sample*. Ministry of Justice Research Series 19/10. London: Ministry of Justice.

Salin, D. (2015). Risk factors of workplace bullying for men and women: The role of the psychosocial and physical work environment. *Scandinavian Journal of Psychology*, 56, 69–77.

Salvatore, A. (2006). *An anti-bullying strategy: Action research in a 5/6 intermediate school*. Dissertation Abstracts International Section A: Humanities and Social Sciences, 67 (3-A), 891.

Samnani, A-K., & Singh, P. (2012). 20 Years of workplace bullying research: A review of the antecedents and consequences of bullying in the workplace. *Aggression and Violent Behavior*, 17, 581–589.

San Kuay, H., Lee, S., Centifanti, L. C., Parnis, A. C., Mrozik, J. H., & Tiffin, P. A. (2016). Adolescents as perpetrators of aggression within the family. *International Journal of Law and Psychiatry*, 47, 60–67.

Sánchez-Meca, J., Rosa-Alcázar, A. I., & López-Soler, C. (2011). The psychological treatment of sexual abuse in children and adolescents: A meta-analysis. *International Journal of Clinical and Health Psychology*, 11, 67–93.

Santaella-Tenorio, J., Cerdá, M., Villaveces, A., & Galea, S. (2016). What do we know about the association between firearm legislation and firearm-related injuries? *Epidemiologic Reviews*, 38, 140–157.

Sartin, R. M., Hansen, D. J., & Huss, M. H. (2006). Domestic violence treatment response and recidivism: A review and implications for the study of family violence. *Aggression and Violent Behavior*, 11, 425–440.

Savell, E., Fooks, G., & Gilmore, A. B. (2016). How does the alcohol industry attempt to influence marketing regulations? A systematic review. *Addiction*, 111, 18–32.

Schindeler, E., & Reynald, D. M. (2017). What is the evidence? Preventing psychological violence in the workplace. *Aggression and Violent Behavior*, 36, 25–33.

Schmidtke, R. (2011). Workplace violence: Identification and prevention. *The Journal of Law Enforcement*, 1, 1–13.

Schreier, A., Pogue, J. K., & Hansen, D. J. (2017). Impact of child sexual abuse on non-abused siblings: A review with implications for research and practice. *Aggression and Violent Behavior*, 34, 254–262.

Schwalbe, C. S., Gearing, R. E., MacKenzie, M. J., Brewer, K. B., & Ibrahim, R. (2012). A meta-analysis of experimental studies of diversion programs for juvenile offenders. *Clinical Psychology Review*, 32, 26–33.

Schweinhart, L. J. (2013). Long-term follow-up of a preschool experiment. *Journal of Experimental Criminology*, 9, 389–409.

Scott, C. L., & Resnick, P. J. (2006). Violence risk assessment in persons with mental illness. *Aggression and Violent Behavior*, 11, 598–611.

Seewald, K., Rossegger, A., Gerth, J., Urbaniok, F., Phillips, G., & Endrass, J. (2018). Effectiveness of a risk–need–responsivity-based treatment program for violent and sexual offenders: Results of a retrospective, quasi-experimental study. *Legal and Criminological Psychology*, 23, 85–99.

Sentencing Guidelines Secretariat. (2007). *Sexual Offences Act 2003. Definitive guideline.* London: Sentencing Guidelines Secretariat.

Seto, M. C., Marques, J. K., Harris, G. T., Chaffin, M., Lalumière, M. L., Miner, M. H. … Quinsey, V. L. (2008). Good science and progress in sex offender treatment are intertwined: A response to Marshall and Marshall (2007). *Sexual Abuse: A Journal of Research and Treatment*, 20, 247–255.

Shadish, W. R., & Cook, T. D. (2009). The renaissance of field experimentation in evaluating interventions. *Annual Review of Psychology*, 60, 607–629.

Shanahan, M. E., Nocera, M., Zolotor, A. J., Sellers, C. J., Runyan, D. K. (2011). Education on abusive head trauma in North Carolina hospitals. *Child Abuse Review*, 20, 290–297.

Shapiro, D. A., Harper, H., Startup, M., Reynolds, S., Bird, D., & Suokas, A. (1994). The high water mark of the drug metaphor: A meta-analytic critique of process-outcome research. In R. L. Russell (Ed.) *Reassessing psychotherapy research* (pp. 1–35). New York: Guilford Press.

Shapiro, K., Randour, M. L., Krinsk, S., & Wolf, J. L. (Eds.). (2013). *The assessment and treatment of children who abuse animals: The AniCare Child Approach*. Cham, Switzerland: Springer International.

Shaw, C. R., & McKay, H. D. (1942). *Juvenile delinquency and urban areas*. Chicago: University of Chicago Press.

Sheehan, K. A., Thakor, S., & Stewart, D. E. (2012). Turning points for perpetrators of intimate partner violence. *Trauma, Violence, & Abuse*, 13, 30–40.

Sherman, L. W. (2003). Misleading evidence and evidence-led policy: Making social science more experimental. *Annals of the American Academy of Political and Social Science*, 589, 6–19.

Sherman, L. W., Gottfredson, D. C., MacKenzie, D. L., Eck, J. E., Reuter, P., & Bushway, S. D. (1997). *Preventing crime: What works, what doesn't, what's promising*. Washington, DC: Department of Justice, National Institute of Justice.

Shuker, R., & Sullivan, E. (2010). *Grendon and the emergence of forensic therapeutic communities: Developments in research and practice*. Chichester, Sussex: Wiley-Blackwell.

Sidebotham, P., Fox, J., Horwath, J., & Powell, C. (2011). Developing effective child death review: A study of 'early starter' child death overview panels in England. *Injury Prevention*, 17(Suppl I), i55–i63.

Silverstone, P. H., Greenspan, F., Silverstone, M., Sawa, H., & Linder, J. (2016). A complex multimodal 4-week residential treatment program significantly reduces PTSD symptoms in child sexual abuse victims: The Be Brave Ranch. *Journal of Child and Adolescent Behavior*, 4, 275–280.

Simon, J. D., & Brooks, D. (2017). Identifying families with complex needs after an initial child abuse investigation: A comparison of demographics and needs related to domestic violence, mental health, and substance use. *Child Abuse & Neglect*, 67, 294–304.

Singh, J. P., Fazel, S., Gueorguieva, R., & Buchanan, A. (2014). Rates of violence in patients classified as high risk by structured risk assessment instruments. *British Journal of Psychiatry*, 204, 180–187.

Singh, J. P., Grann, M., & Fazel, S. (2011). A comparative study of violence risk assessment tools: A systematic review and metaregression analysis of 68 studies involving 25,980 participants. *Clinical Psychology Review*, 31, 499–513.

Sjödin, A-K., Wallinius, M., Billstedt, E., Hofvander, B., & Nilsson, T. (2017). Dating violence compared to other types of violence: Similar offenders but different victims. *The European Journal of Psychology Applied to Legal Context*, 9, 83–91.

Slade, K., Samele, C., Valmaggia, L., & Forrester, A. (2016). Pathways through the criminal justice system for prisoners with acute and serious mental illness. *Forensic and Legal Medicine*, 44, 162–168.

Smith, P., Gendreau, P., & Swartz, K. (2009). Validating the principles of effective intervention: A systematic review of the contributions of meta-analysis in the field of corrections. *Victims and Offenders*, 4, 148–169.

Smith, R. (1984). Grendon, the Barlinnie Special Unit, and the Wormwood Scrubs Annexe: Experiments in penology. *British Medical Journal*, 288, 472–475.

Smith-Darden, J. P., Kernsmith, P. D., Victor, B. G., & Lathrop, R. A. (2017). Electronic displays of aggression in teen dating relationships: Does the social ecology matter? *Computers in Human Behavior*, 67, 33–40.

Smyth, P. (2011). Diverting young offenders from crime in Ireland: The need for more checks and balances on the exercise of police discretion. *Crime, Law and Social Change*, 55, 153–166.

Sorensen, J., & Davis, J. (2011). Violent criminals locked up: Examining the effect of incarceration on behavioral continuity. *Journal of Criminal Justice*, 39, 151–158.

Spraitz, J. D., & Bowen, K. N. (2016). Techniques of neutralization and persistent sexual abuse by clergy: A content analysis of priest personnel files from the Archdiocese of Milwaukee. *Journal of Interpersonal Violence*, 31, 2515–2538.

Steinert, T., & Whittington, R. (2013). A bio-psycho-social model of violence related to mental health problems. *International Journal of Law and Psychiatry*, 36, 168–175.

Stephens, K., & Turner, R. (2004). Barriers to programme start: Findings from an examination of case notes on a sample of offenders required to attend programmes. *VISTA*, 8, 18–25.

Stephens, S., Reale, K. S., Goodwill, A. M., & Beauregard, E. (2017). Examining the role of opportunity in the offense behavior of victim age polymorphic sex offenders. *Journal of Criminal Justice*, 52, 41–48.

Stinson, P. M., Liederbach, J., Brewer, S. L., & Mathna, B. E. (2015). Police sexual misconduct: A national scale study of arrested officers. *Criminal Justice Policy Review*, 26, 117–151.

Stinson, P. M., Liederbach, J., Freiburger, T. L. (2012). Off-duty and under arrest: A study of crimes perpetrated by off-duty police. *Criminal Justice Policy Review*, 23(2), 139–163.

Stith, S. M., Liu, T., Davies, L. C., Boykin, E. L., Alder, M. C., Harris, J. M., Som, A., McPherson, M., & Dees, J. E. M. E. G. (2009). Risk factors in child maltreatment: A meta-analytic review of the literature. *Aggression and Violent Behavior*, 14, 13–29.

Stockwell, T., Auld, M. C., Zhao, J., & Martin, G. (2012). Does minimum pricing reduce alcohol consumption? The experience of a Canadian province. *Addiction*, 107, 912–920.

Stoltenborgh, M., Bakermans-Kranenburg, M. J., & van Ijzendoorn, M. H. (2013). The neglect of child neglect: A meta-analytic review of the prevalence of neglect. *Social Psychiatry and Psychiatric Epidemiology*, 8, 345–355.

Stone, N. (2015). Eradicating 'This Dreadful Knife Problem': Legislative and judicial initiatives against knife possession. *Youth Justice*, 15, 182–194.

Straus, M. A. (2000). Corporal punishment and primary prevention of physical abuse. *Child Abuse & Neglect*, 24, 1009–1104.

Strickland, P., & Allen, G. (2017). *Domestic violence in England and Wales*. Briefing Paper Number 6337. London: House of Commons Library.

Sturgeon, M., Tyler, N., & Gannon, T. A. (2018). A systematic review of group work interventions in UK high secure hospitals. *Aggression and Violent Behavior*, 38, 53–75.

Sturgess, D., Woodhams, J., & Tonkin, M. (2016). Treatment engagement from the perspective of the offender: Reasons for non-completion and completion of treatment: A systematic review. *International Journal of Offender Therapy and Comparative Criminology*, 60, 1873–1896.

Stürup, G. K. (1972). Castration: The total treatment. In H. L. P. Resnik, & M. E. Wolfgang (Eds.), *Sexual behaviors. Social, clinical and legal aspects* (pp. 361–382). Boston, MA: Little, Brown and Company.

Sundell, K., & Vinnerljung, B. (2004). Outcomes of family group conferencing in Sweden: A 3-year follow-up. *Child Abuse & Neglect*, 28, 267–287.

Sutherland, A., & Jones, S. (2008). *MAPPA and youth justice: An exploration of youth offending team engagement with Multi-Agency Public Protection Arrangements*. Oxford: Centre for Criminology, University of Oxford.

Tan, S., & Haining, R. (2016). Crime victimization and the implications for individual health and wellbeing: A Sheffield case study. *Social Science & Medicine*, 167, 128–139.

Tang, J., Buzney, S. M., Lashkari, K., & Weiter, J. J. (2008). Shaken Baby Syndrome: A review and update on ophthalmologic manifestations. *International Ophthalmology Clinics*, 48, 237–246.

Taylor, B., & Li, J. (2015). Do fewer guns lead to less crime? Evidence from Australia. *International Review of Law and Economics*, 42, 72–78.

Taylor, B. G., Stein, N., & Burden, F. F. (2010). Exploring gender differences in dating violence/harassment prevention programming in middle schools: Results from a randomized experiment. *Journal of Experimental Criminology*, 6, 419–445.

Taylor, C. A., Al-Hiyari, R., Lee, S. J., Priebe, A., Guerrero, L. W., & Bales, A. (2016). Beliefs and ideologies linked with approval of corporal punishment: A content analysis of online comments. *Health Education Research*, 31, 563–575.

ter Beek, A., Kuiper, C. H. Z., van der Rijken, R. E. A., Spruit, A., Stams, G. J. J. M., & Hendriks, J. (2018). Treatment effect on psychosocial functioning of juveniles with harmful sexual behavior: A multilevel meta-analysis. *Aggression and Violent Behavior*, 39, 116–128.

Test, M. A., & Stein, L. I. (1976). Practical guidelines for the community treatment of markedly impaired patients. *Community Mental Health Journal*, 12, 72–82.

Thackeray, J. D., & Randell, K. A. (2011). Epidemiology of intimate partner violence. In C. Jenny (Ed.), *Child abuse and neglect: Diagnosis, treatment, and evidence* (pp. 23–27). St Louis, MO: Saunders, Elsevier.

Theobald, D., Farrington, D. P., Ttofi, M. M., & Crago, R. V. (2016). Risk factors for dating violence versus cohabiting violence: Results from the third generation of the Cambridge Study in Delinquent Development. *Criminal Behaviour and Mental Health*, 26, 229–239.

Thibaut, F., de la Barra, F., Gordon, H., Cosyns, P., Bradford, J. M. W., & the WFSBP Task Force on Sexual Disorders. (2010). The World Federation of Societies of Biol Psychiatry (WFSBP) Guidelines for the biological treatment of paraphilias. *World Journal of Biological Psychiatry*, 11, 604–655.

Thomas, S., Harty, M., Parrott, J., McCrone, P., Slade, M., & Thornicroft, G. (2003). *CANFOR: Camberwell Assessment of Need-Forensic version*. London: Royal College of Psychiatrists.

Thompson, E. H., & Trice-Black, S. (2012). School-based group interventions for children exposed to domestic violence. *Journal of Family Violence*, 27, 233–241.

Thompson, K. L., & Gullone, E. (2003). The children's treatment of animals questionnaire (CTAQ): A psychometric investigation. *Society & Animals*, 11, 1–15.

Thornberry, T. P., Knight, K. E., & Lovegrove, P. J. (2012). Does maltreatment beget maltreatment? A systemic review of the intergenerational literature. *Trauma, Violence, & Abuse*, 13, 135–152.

Thornton, D. M. (1987). Treatment effects on recidivism: A reappraisal of the 'nothing works' doctrine. In B. J. McGurk, D. M. Thornton, & M. Williams (Eds.), *Applying psychology to imprisonment: Theory and practice* (pp. 181–189). London: HMSO.

Thornton, D. (2013). Implications of our developing understanding of risk and protective factors in the treatment of adult male sexual offenders. *International Journal of Behavioral Consultation and Therapy*, 8, 62–65.

Thornton, D. M., Curran, L., Grayson, D., & Holloway, V. (1984). *Tougher regimes in detention centres: Report of an evaluation by the Young Offender Psychology Unit*. London: HMSO.

Thornton, D., Mann, R., Webster, S., Blud, L., Travers, R., Friendship, C., & Erikson, M. (2003). Distinguishing and combining risks for sexual and violent recidivism. *Annals of New York Academy of Sciences*, 989, 225–235.

Tiplady, C. M., Walsh, D. B., & Phillips, C. J. C. (2012). Intimate partner violence and companion animal welfare. *Australian Veterinary Journal*, 90, 48–53.

Tong, L. S. J., & Farrington, D. P. (2006). How effective is the "Reasoning and Rehabilitation" programme in reducing re-offending? A meta-analysis of evaluations in four countries. *Psychology, Crime and Law*, 12, 3–24.

Topping, K. J., & Barron, I. G. (2009). School-based child sexual abuse prevention programs: A review of effectiveness. *Review of Educational Research*, 79, 431–463.

Travers, R., Mann, R. E., & Hollin, C. R. (2014). Who benefits from cognitive skills programs? Differential impact by risk and offense type. *Criminal Justice and Behavior*, 41, 1103–1129.

Travers, R., Wakeling, H. C., Mann, R. E., & Hollin, C. R. (2011). Reconviction following a cognitive skills intervention: An alternative quasi-experimental methodology. *Legal and Criminological Psychology*, 18, 48–65.

Treasaden, I. H. (2018). Medium secure units. In B. Puri & I. H. Treasaden (Eds.), *Forensic psychiatry: Fundamentals and clinical practice* (pp. 667–672). Boca Raton, FL: CRC Press.

Ttofi, M. M., & Farrington, D. P. (2011). Effectiveness of school-based programs to reduce bullying: A systematic and meta-analytic review. *Journal of Experimental Criminology*, 7, 27–56.

Ttofi, M. M., & Farrington, D. P. (2012). Bullying prevention programs: the importance of peer intervention, disciplinary methods and age variations. *Journal of Experimental Criminology*, 8, 443–462.

Ttofi, M. M., Farrington, D. P., & Lösel, F. (2012). School bullying as a predictor of violence later in life: A systematic review and meta-analysis of prospective longitudinal studies. *Aggression and Violent Behavior*, 17, 405–418.

Ttofi, M. M., Farrington, D. P., Piquero, A. R., Lösel, F., DeLisi, M., & Murray, J. (2016). Intelligence as a protective factor against offending: A meta-analytic review of prospective longitudinal studies. *Journal of Criminal Justice*, 45, 4–18.

Turner, S., Taillieu, T., Cheung, K., & Afifi, T. O. (2017). The relationship between childhood sexual abuse and mental health outcomes among males: Results from a nationally representative United States sample. *Child Abuse & Neglect*, 66, 64–72.

Ullrich, S., & Coid, J. (2011). Protective factors for violence among released prisoners — effects over time and interactions with static risk. *Journal of Consulting and Clinical Psychology*, 79, 381–390.

Ulucanlar, S., Fooks, G. J., Hatchard, J. L., & Gilmore, A. B. (2014). Representation and misrepresentation of scientific evidence in contemporary tobacco regulation: A review of tobacco industry submissions to the UK Government consultation on standardised packaging. *PLoS Medicine*, 11(3), e1001629.

Valdebenito, S., Ttofi, M. M., Eisner, M., & Gaffney, H. (2017). Weapon carrying in and out of school among pure bullies, pure victims and bully-victims: A systematic review and meta-analysis of cross-sectional and longitudinal studies. *Aggression and Violent Behavior*, 33, 62–77.

van der Meer, T. (2014). Voluntary and therapeutic castration of sex offenders in The Netherlands (1938–1968). *International Journal of Law and Psychiatry*, 37, 50–56.

Van Damme, L., Fortune, C.-A., Vandevelde, S., & Vanderplasschen, W. (2017). The Good Lives Model among detained female adolescents. *Aggression and Violent Behavior*, 37, 179–189.

Van Horn, P., & Lieberman, A. F. (2011). Psychological impact on and treatment of children who witness domestic violence. In C. Jenny (Ed.), *Child abuse and neglect: Diagnosis, treatment, and evidence* (pp. 501–515). St Louis, MO: Saunders, Elsevier.

Van Wert, M., Mishna, F., Trocméa, N., & Fallon, B. (2017). Which maltreated children are at greatest risk of aggressive and criminal behavior? An examination of maltreatment dimensions and cumulative risk. *Child Abuse & Neglect*, 69, 49–61.

Vandevelde, S., Vander Laenen, F., Van Damme, L., Vanderplasschen, W., Audenaert, K., Broekaert, E., & Vander Beken, T. (2017). Dilemmas in applying strengths-based approaches in working with offenders with mental illness: A critical multidisciplinary review. *Aggression and Violent Behavior*, 32, 71–79.

Vanhaelemeesch, D., Vander Beken, T., & Vandevelde, S. (2014). Punishment at home: Offenders' experiences with electronic monitoring. *European Journal of Criminology*, 11, 273–287.

Vassallo, S., Edwards, B., & Forrest, W. (2016). Childhood behavior problems and fighting in early adulthood: What factors are protective? *Journal of Criminal Justice*, 45, 85–93.

Vertommen, T., Kampen, J., Schipper-van Veldhoven, N., Wouters, K., Uzieblo, K., Van Den Eede, F. (2017). Profiling perpetrators of interpersonal violence against children in sport based on a victim survey. *Child Abuse & Neglect*, 63, 172–182.

Vertommen, T., Kampen, J., Schipper-van Veldhoven, N., Wouters, K., Uzieblo, K., Van Den Eede, F. (2018). Severe interpersonal violence against children in sport: Associated mental health problems and quality of life in adulthood. *Child Abuse & Neglect*, 76, 459–468.

Vaughn, M. (1994). Boot camps. *The Grapevine*, 2, 2.

Vlahovicova, K., Melendez-Torres, G. J., Leijten, P., Knerr, W., & Gardner, F. (2017). Parenting programs for the prevention of child physical abuse recurrence: A systematic review and meta-analysis. *Clinical Child and Family Psychology Review*, 20, 351–365.

Volkow, N. D. (2009). Substance use disorders in schizophrenia – clinical implications of comorbidity. *Schizophrenia Bulletin*, 35, 469–472.

Walker, N. (1991). *Why punish?*Oxford: Oxford University Press.

Walsh, K., Zwi, K., Woolfenden, S., & Shlonsky, A. (2015). School-based education programmes for the prevention of child sexual abuse. *Cochrane Database of Systematic Reviews*, Issue 4. Art. No.: CD004380.

Walter, M., Wiesbeck, G. A., Dittmann, V., & Graf, M. (2010). Criminal recidivism in offenders with personality disorders and substance use disorders over 8 years of time at risk. *Psychiatry Research*, 186, 443–445.

Walters, G. D. (2013). Testing the specificity postulate of the violence graduation hypothesis: Meta-analyses of the animal cruelty-offending relationship. *Aggression and Violent Behavior*, 18, 797–802.

Walton, J. S., & Chou, S. (2015). The effectiveness of psychological treatment for reducing recidivism in child molesters: A systematic review of randomized and nonrandomized studies. *Trauma, Violence, & Abuse*, 16, 401–417.

Ward, T. (2002). Good lives and the rehabilitation of offenders: Promises and problems. *Aggression and Violent Behavior*, 7, 513–528.

Ward, T., & Brown, M. (2004). The Good Lives Model and conceptual issues in offender rehabilitation. *Psychology, Crime & Law*, 10, 243–257.

Ward, T., & Gannon, T. A. (2006). Rehabilitation, etiology, and self-regulation: The comprehensive good lives model of treatment for sexual offenders. *Aggression and Violent Behavior*, 11, 77–94.

Ward, T., & Marshall, W. L. (2004). Good Lives, etiology and the rehabilitation of sex offenders: A bridging theory. *Journal of Sexual Aggression*, 10, 153–169.

Ward, T., Melser, J., & Yates, P. M. (2007). Reconstructing the Risk–Need–Responsivity model: A theoretical elaboration and evaluation. *Aggression and Violent Behavior*, 12, 208–228.

Ward, T., & Stewart, C. (2003). Criminogenic needs and human needs: A theoretical model. *Psychology, Crime, & Law*, 9, 125–143.

Ward, T., Yates, P. M., & Willis, G. M. (2012). The Good Lives Model and the Risk Need Responsivity Model: A critical response to Andrews, Bonta, and Wormith (2011). *Criminal Justice and Behavior*, 39, 94–110.

Watt, K., Shepherd, J., & Newcombe, R. (2008). Drunk and dangerous: A randomised controlled trial of alcohol brief intervention for violent offenders. *Journal of Experimental Criminology*, 4, 1–19.

Webb, D., & McMurran, M. (2009). A comparison of women who continue and discontinue treatment for borderline personality disorder. *Personality and Mental Health*, 3, 142–149.

Webster, C. D., Douglas, K. S., Eaves, D., & Hart, S. D. (1997). *HCR-20: Assessing the risk for violence (Version 2)*. Vancouver: Mental Health, Law, and Policy Institute, Simon Fraser University.

Weinberger, L.E., Sreenivasan, S., Garrick, T., & Osran, H. (2005). The impact of surgical castration on sexual recidivism risk among sexually violent predatory offenders. *Journal of the American Academy of Psychiatry and Law*, 33, 16–36.

Welfare, H., & Hollin, C. R. (2012). Involvement in extreme violence and violence-related trauma: A review with relevance to young people in custody. *Legal and Criminological Psychology*, 12, 89–104.

Welfare, H. R., & Hollin, C. R. (2015). Childhood and offence-related trauma in young people imprisoned in England and Wales for murder and other acts of serious violence: A descriptive study. *Journal of Aggression, Maltreatment & Trauma*, 24, 955–969.

Welsh, B. C., & Farrington, D. P. (2009). Public area CCTV and crime prevention: An updated systematic review and meta-analysis. *Justice Quarterly*, 26, 716–745.

Welsh, B. C., & Farrington, D. P. (2011). The benefits and costs of early prevention compared with imprisonment: Toward evidence-based policy. *The Prison Journal, Supplement to* 91(3), 120–137.

Welsh, B. C., & Farrington, D. P. (2015). Monetary value of early developmental crime prevention and its policy significance. *Criminology & Public Policy*, 14, 673–680.

Welsh, B. C., Farrington, D. P., & Raffan Gowar, B. (2015). Benefit-cost analysis of crime prevention programs. *Crime and Justice*, 44, 447–516.

Wermink, H., Blokland, A., Nieuwbeerta, P., Nagin, D., & Tollenaar, N. (2010). Comparing the effects of community service and short-term imprisonment on recidivism: A matched samples approach. *Journal of Experimental Criminology*, 6, 325–349.

Whitaker, D. J., Lea, B., Hanson, R.K., Baker, C. K., McMahon, P. M., Ryan, G., Klein, A., Rice, D. D. (2008). Risk factors for the perpetration of child sexual abuse: A review and meta-analysis. *Child Abuse & Neglect*, 32, 529–548.

Whitehead, P. R., Ward, T., & Collie, R. M. (2007). Time for a change: Applying the Good Lives Model of rehabilitation to a high-risk violent offender. *International Journal of Offender Therapy and Comparative Criminology*, 51, 578–598.

Widom, C. S. (1989a). The cycle of violence. *Science*, 244, 160–166.

Widom, C. S. (1989b). Does violence beget violence? A critical examination of the literature. *Psychological Bulletin*, 106, 3–28.

Willis, G. M., & Ward, T. (2013). The Good Lives Model. Does it work? Preliminary evidence. In L. A. Craig, L. Dixon, & T. A. Gannon (Eds.), *What works in offender rehabilitation: An evidence-based approach to assessment and treatment* (pp. 305–317). Chichester, West Sussex: John Wiley & Sons.

Willis, G. M., Yates, P. M., Gannon, T. A., & Ward, T. (2012). How to integrate the Good Lives Model into treatment programs for sexual offending: An introduction and overview. *Sexual Abuse: A Journal of Research and Treatment*, 25, 123–142.

Wilson, D. B., Olaghere, A., & Gill, C. (2016). Juvenile curfew effects on criminal behavior and victimization: A Campbell Collaboration systematic review. *Journal of Experimental Criminology*, 12, 167–186.

Wilson, G. T. (1996). Manual-based treatments: The clinical application of research findings. *Behaviour Research and Therapy*, 34, 295–314.

Wilson, H. A., & Hoge, R. D. (2013). The effect of youth diversion programs on recidivism: A Meta-Analytic Review. *Criminal Justice and Behavior*, 40, 497–518.

Winokur, K. P., Smith, A., Bontrager, S. R., & Blakenship, J. L. (2008). Juvenile recidivism and length of stay. *Journal of Criminal Justice*, 36, 126–137.

Witt, A., Münzer, A., Ganser, H. G., Fegert, J. M., Goldbeck, L., & Plener, P. L. (2016). Experience by children and adolescents of more than one type of maltreatment: Association of different classes of maltreatment profiles with clinical outcome variables. *Child Abuse & Neglect*, 57, 1–11.

Witt, K., van Dorn, R., & Fazel, S. (2013). Risk factors for violence in psychosis: Systematic review and meta-regression analysis of 110 studies. *PLoS One*, 8(2), e55942.

Wolf, A., Fanshawe, T. R., Sariaslan, A., Cornish, R., LarssonH., & Fazel, S. (2018). Prediction of violent crime on discharge from secure psychiatric hospitals: A clinical prediction rule (FoVOx). *European Psychiatry*, 47, 88–93.

Wolfe, D., Crooks, C., Jaffe, P., Chiodo, D., Hughes, R., Ellis, W., et al. (2009). A school-based program to prevent adolescent dating violence: A cluster randomized trial. *Archives of Pediatrics & Adolescent Medicine*, 163, 692–699.

Wolitzky-Taylor, K. B., Ruggiero, K. J., Danielson, C. K., Resnick, H.S., Hanson, R. F., Smith, D. W., Saunders, B. E. & Kilpatrick, D. G. (2008). Prevalence and correlates of dating violence in a national sample of adolescents. *Journal of the American Academy of Child and Adolescent Psychiatry*, 47, 755–762.

Wong, J. S., & Balemba, S. (2016). Resisting during sexual assault: A meta-analysis of the effects on injury. *Aggression and Violent Behavior*, 28, 1–11.

Wood, J., Kemshall, H., Maguire, M., Hudson, K., & Mackenzie, G. (2007). *The operation and experience of Multi-Agency Public Protection Arrangements (MAPPA)*. Home Office Online Report 12/07. London: Home Office.

Woodhouse, J. (2018). *Alcohol: Minimum pricing*. Briefing Paper Number 5021. London: House of Commons Library.

World Health Organization. (2008). *Interpersonal violence and alcohol policy briefing*. Geneva: WHO.

World Health Organization. (2009). *Violence prevention: The evidence. Preventing violence by reducing the availability and harmful use of alcohol*. Geneva: WHO.

World Health Organization. (2014). *Global status report on violence prevention 2014*. Geneva: WHO.

Wormith, J. S., & Bonta, J. (2018). The Level of Service (LS) Instruments. In J. P. Singh, D. G. Kroner, J. S. Wormith, S. L. Desmarais, and Z. Hamilton (Eds.), *Handbook of recidivism risk/needs assessment tools* (pp. 117–145). Chichester, West Sussex: Wiley-Blackwell.

Wormith, J. S., Gendreau, P., & Bonta, J. (2012). Deferring to clarity, parsimony, and evidence in reply to Ward, Yates, and Willis. *Criminal Justice and Behavior, 39*, 111–120.

Wright, J., & Hensley, C. (2003). From animal cruelty to serial murder: Applying the graduation hypothesis. *International Journal of Offender Therapy and Comparative Criminology, 47*, 71–88.

Wurtle, S. K. (2012). *Best practices in safeguarding children: Report on Diocese of Wilmington's For the Sake of God's Children*. www.cdow.org/WurteleC DOWExecSummary-final.pdf

Yang, M., Wong, S. C. P., & Coid, J. (2010). The efficacy of violence prediction: A meta-analytic comparison of nine risk assessment tools. *Psychological Bulletin, 136*, 740–767.

Yates, P. M., & Ward, T. (2008). Good lives, self-regulation, and risk management: An integrated model of sexual offender assessment and treatment. *Sexual Abuse in Australia and New Zealand: An Interdisciplinary Journal, 1*, 3–20.

Yu, R., Geddes, J. R., & Fazel, S. (2012). Personality Disorders, violence, and antisocial behavior: A systematic review and meta-regression analysis. *Journal of Personality Disorders, 26*, 775–792.

Zhang, J., & Liu, N. (2015). Reliability and validity of the Chinese version of the LSI-R with probationers. *International Journal of Offender Therapy and Comparative Criminology, 59*, 1474–1486.

Zhong, C., Bohns, V. K., & Gino, F. (2010). Good lamps are the best police: Darkness increases dishonesty and self-interested behavior. *Psychological Science, 21*, 311–314.

Zhou, Y. Q., Gan, D. Z. Q., Hoo, E. C. C., Chong, D., & Chu, C. M. (2018). Evaluating the Violence Prevention Program: Group and individual changes in aggression, anger, self-control, and empathy. *The Journal of Forensic Psychiatry & Psychology, 29*, 265–287.

Zolotor, A. J., & Shanahan, M. (2011). Epidemiology of physical abuse. In C. Jenny (Ed.), *Child abuse and neglect: Diagnosis, treatment, and evidence* (pp. 10–14). St Louis, MO: Saunders, Elsevier.

Zolotor, A. J., Theodore, A. D., Chang, J. J., Berkoff, M. C., & Runyan, D. K. (2008). Speak softly – and forget the stick: Corporal punishment and child physical abuse. *American Journal of Preventative Medicine, 35*, 364–369.

Zweig, J. M., Dank, M., Yahner, J., & Lachman, P. (2013). The rate of cyber dating abuse among teens and how it relates to other forms of teen dating violence. *Journal of Youth and Adolescence*, 42, 1063–1077.

Zych, I., Ortega-Ruiz, R., & Del Rey, R. (2015). Systematic review of theoretical studies on bullying and cyberbullying: Facts, knowledge, prevention, and intervention. *Aggression and Violent Behavior*, 23, 1–21.

INDEX